Black Women Undergraduates, Cultural Capital, and College Success

Questions about the Purpose(s) of Colleges & Universities

Norm Denzin, Joe L. Kincheloe, Shirley R. Steinberg

General Editors

Vol. 20

PETER LANG
New York • Washington, D.C./Baltimore • Bern
Frankfurt am Main • Berlin • Brussels • Vienna • Oxford

Cerri A. Banks

Black Women Undergraduates, Cultural Capital, and College Success

PETER LANG
New York • Washington, D.C./Baltimore • Bern
Frankfurt am Main • Berlin • Brussels • Vienna • Oxford

Library of Congress Cataloging-in-Publication Data

Banks, Cerri A.
Black women undergraduates, cultural capital, and college success/
Cerri A. Banks.
p. cm. — (Higher ed, questions about the purposes
of colleges and universities; v. 20)
Includes bibliographical references and index.
1. African American women college students. 2. Academic achievement.
3. African American women college students—Social conditions. I. Title.
LC2781.B36   378.1'98296073—dc22   2009030270
ISBN 978-1-4331-0211-0
ISSN 1523-9551

Bibliographic information published by **Die Deutsche Nationalbibliothek**.
Die Deutsche Nationalbibliothek lists this publication in the "Deutsche
Nationalbibliografie"; detailed bibliographic data are available
on the Internet at http://dnb.d-nb.de/.

Cover photo by Kevin Colton

The paper in this book meets the guidelines for permanence and durability
of the Committee on Production Guidelines for Book Longevity
of the Council of Library Resources.

© 2009 Peter Lang Publishing, Inc., New York
29 Broadway, 18th floor, New York, NY 10006
www.peterlang.com

Printed in the United States of America

To

Loleta Banks, my mom,

Ethel Loveless, my grandma,

and

Dr. Ralphaline Banks, my aunt

who taught me the beauty, power, and value

of black women's experience and voice

and

to ALL undergraduates, from every race, class, and gender,

who take on the fight for educational equity.

Contents

CHAPTER ONE

The Complex Terrain of *Black* and *Woman* in Undergraduate Education

"That's some nappy headed hos there, I'm going to tell you that now man ..."
—Don Imus

On April 4, 2007, CBS and MSNBC shock radio personality Don Imus set off a firestorm in the world of talk radio and in the media at large. In an exchange with Bernard McGuirk, the executive producer of *Imus in the Morning*, Imus referred to the eight black undergraduate members of the Rutgers University women's basketball team, who had just lost the National Collegiate Athletic Association (NCAA) championship, as "nappy headed hos" and compared them to the women on the University of Tennessee team whom he described as "cute" (Boehler & Foser, 2007).

This verbal assault by Imus ignited a nationwide, media-fueled debate on the history of racism in the United States, historical and modern-day representations of black women, and the use of language. The question, "Who can say what?" drove much of the debate as the spotlight spread from Don Imus to include various hip-hop artists whose song lyrics commonly include terms such as *ho* (Kelefa, 2007). The "rappers are doing it" defense, while driving much of the debate, led some to respond that the act of one does not make any other less culpable (Harris, 2007). With the help of Al Sharpton and other black activists, racism took center stage during the discussion, prompting Imus to continually explain, "I am not a racist" (Robinson, 2007). The sexism his words represented was largely the talk of women in media and sports and feminist academic scholars (Rhoden, 2007).

Don Imus was eventually fired by CBS and MSNBC (Faber, 2007). Some argue the firing was less about the racism and sexism represented in Imus's comments and more about the loss of profits for the networks, since sponsors and scheduled guests (many of whom denounced Imus), pulled their support and cancelled their appearances. Whatever the reason for the firing, the debate this incident sparked pushed open a door of discussion on a largely ignored population, black women undergraduates.[1]

One of the ideas presented to reinforce the egregious nature of Imus's comments centered on *whom* Don Imus made these comments about. The argument was that *these particular* black women did not deserve this flagrant attack (Martin, 2007). Implicit in this argument is the faulty idea that there are some black women who deserve this type of degradation and some who do not. The eight black women undergraduates at Rutgers were getting a college education and had just played in a national basketball tournament, two traditional signifiers that *these* black women were "going somewhere" and that their lives had value. *These* black women undergraduates were not like the recently famous Miss New York from the popular reality show *Flavor of Love*[2] who was best known for cursing, scheming, fighting, and engaging in sexual antics while clawing her way through a group of women from multiple races and ethnicities all competing for the love of aging rapper Flavor Flav.[3] Nor were the black women from the Rutgers basketball team "Video Vixens," "Ride or Die Chicks," "Gold Diggers," or "Bitches" exposing their bodies on MTV, VH1, or BET.[4] They were not single mothers with too many children by too many fathers or "welfare queens" working the system or crack addicts wreaking havoc on their communities or any of the other least desirable reductionist stereotypes of black women most often portrayed, referenced, ridiculed, and denigrated. Yet even *these* black women undergraduates at Rutgers University, with all of their academic and social accomplishments, could not escape a racist and sexist attack by Don Imus.

Both the argument and its implications provide a glimpse into the intricacies of being *black* and *woman* in the United States. They give insight into the work that black women and, in this case, black women undergraduates must do to navigate the knotty terrain of who they are as they challenge the limited representations and stereotypes that render them socially undesirable. In the world of higher education, these same discourses mark them as underprepared academic and social liabilities. This book examines that complex terrain using the narrative tales of 19 black undergraduate women from one community college and three universities across the United States. These 19 participants are women who share at least race and gender with the black members of the Rutgers women's basketball team, and they represent the women who daily, in larger numbers than black men, face the consequences of inequities in higher education.[5]

A Book about Black Women Undergraduates

The purpose of this book is to invoke the narratives and perspectives of black undergraduate women about their processes of negotiation in higher education, particularly as related to social and academic success. This work explores their stories about education in their own words and from their own definitions and perspectives and presumes that most higher education systems in the United States are literal and figurative Eurocentric spaces, even when the majority of physical bodies in the literal space are not white and even though historically black colleges and universities work to minimize Eurocentrism in their institutions. I am not claiming that only white people create, own, and theorize knowledge and that nonwhites or, more specifically, black women undergraduates are deficient in these areas. Rather, I am claiming that these educational spaces are often constructed around whiteness. This social construction results in oppressive school settings for those not occupying this and other privileged social locations (Ferguson, 2000; Fordham, 1996; Tatum, 1997).[6] At the very least, this construction requires that attention is paid to the specialized work that black women undergraduates and others outside of these social locations do in their learning spaces.

Although this idea, that an individual is either privileged or not, sounds cut and dried, examining the complex lives of black women undergraduates reveals intricacies; multiple social locations bring with them both privilege and oppression concurrently and thus require multiple and simultaneous methods of negotiation. For instance, a black woman undergraduate who is wealthy and one who is poor may both experience racial- and gender-based oppression in school experiences. The black woman undergraduate who is wealthy may have had previous school experiences similar to those of her white, wealthy classmates; these experiences make her less vulnerable to oppressions stemming from social-class inequity. She may know from other middle- and upper-class interactions how to navigate administrative offices (Lareau, 2003, pp. 107–133). She may be able to avoid the stigma that comes with the receipt of grants and other special financial programs; she may not know the stigma of the inability to buy books that her counterpart who is poor and black experiences. Further, the wealthy black undergraduate woman could also participate in creating class-based oppressive environments for the black undergraduate woman who is poor.

The arguments in this book are framed by the historical prohibition on formal education for black men and women generated by enslavement and by the context of limited access to higher education for black women due to gender oppression (Brazzell, 1992; Ihle, 1992; Noble, 1956/1987; Terrell, 1901/1992). This book is also framed by contemporary discussions regarding inequalities that exist and the resulting consequences for nonwhites in current educational systems; topics for these discussions include the establishment of affirmative action and the recent attacks of the policy that claim it discriminates against white students (Willie, 2003, pp. 25–27). The necessity of specific policies in higher education aimed at the recruitment and retention of students who are not white reminds us of the impact of this historical context (Tinto, 1993, pp. 180–187). These policies divide bodies in higher education into categories. These categories include those claiming full membership and rightful positions in the education system and benefiting most from its practices and policies. These categories also include members who navigate the privileged educational norms and the resulting systems through both resistance and adaptation to obtain and retain even limited membership.

The ways the black women undergraduates who participated in this project discuss the contexts of higher education as they live them are dynamic and complex. As narrators, the women describe both the range of complexities involved in living their educational lives as well as how they live and learn among the complexities (Rosenwald & Ochberg, 1992; White, 1980). This book does not tell the story of every black undergraduate woman in higher education in the United States or even at the institutions represented. The findings here will not even tell the entire stories of the 19 participants. Rather the narratives of these women provide one window, with multiple panes, through which to examine phenomena in progress and challenge academic binaries that relegate black undergraduate women to educational victims or glorify them as educational survivors.

Wheri and Where I Enter

My curiosity about the schooling lives of black undergraduate women started long before the Don Imus controversy, and in many ways, this book is both personal and scholarly. In the tradition of feminist and qualitative researchers, I present this attempt to make visible my place in this project (Harding, 1987, p. 9). My interests in the self-described success of black women undergraduates in higher education has stemmed from my own social and academic experiences in this system. As an African American woman from a working-class family who returned to school after 10 years in the workforce, my educational experiences in a predominately white, private university differed from those of most of the young men and women with whom I sat in classes. I was black and most of them were white. Some of my classmates claimed a socioeconomic class that had visible perks (e.g., expensive sport utility vehicles (SUVs), exotic spring break locations, Tiffany jewelry) that were beyond my financial reach. I learned that some, due to middle- and upper-class backgrounds, had in the past and continued to have in college educational experiences and preparations for success in higher educational systems that I did not have. For example, I had never taken the Scholastic Assessment Test (SAT), since I started my schooling at a community college that did not require these exams for application. I also could not afford the Graduate Record Examination (GRE) test-taking workshops many students utilized during the last weeks of undergraduate years in preparation for graduate school. These differences were critical, and I soon began to realize that higher education (i.e., getting a college degree)—often peddled as the great social and economic equalizer—was not an equalizer. The educational process is filled with inequalities that make the journey more challenging for some than for others. As a black, working-class woman, I had obstacles and perspectives to overcome because of these particular identities that my white middle- and upper-class contemporaries did not.

When I entered graduate school, I began to understand that my education was teaching me to analyze worldviews and giving me a language to discuss situations or events that I had always thought of as *unfairness* or *injustice*. I also began to realize that education could simultaneously *fuel* inequity or injustice and offer ways to *combat* inequity or injustice. This knowledge helped me develop strategies for social and academic success as I began to understand that I was learning about oppression and at the same time experiencing it. From then on, whenever classmates challenged my sources of knowledge, belittled my experiences, or dismissed as extreme my resistance to their racist, classist, and sexist ideas, I had an intellectual foundation to draw upon that took away some of the sting. I realized that no one (including me) and no institution (including higher education) was immune from the lived consequences of racism, classism, and sexism. These consequences were manifest as privilege or oppression at varying degrees. All individuals in U.S. society collude in this systemic phenomenon; all operate as victims or as perpetrators, often simultaneously and even when that is not the intent.

The material consequences of racism, sexism, and classism are often made manifest in the academic curriculum. During my first semester of graduate school, I remember reading *Blacked Out* by Signithia Fordham (1996), who studied a predominately black high school in Washington, DC, she called Capital High. In the margins of certain pages of the book, I wrote over and over again, "What about black students like me?" or simply, "No!" I was angry—very angry—with Signithia Fordham! Later, I discovered that I agreed with a critique that put my anger into academic words. In a review symposium of *Blacked Out*, Coffey, Foley, and Mirza (1998) criticized Fordham for describing academic success and failure of black students as completely driven by whiteness and *their responses* to whiteness. Their review included the following analysis:

> The centrality of "acting white" in Fordham's theoretical logic highlights the problematic starting point of her analysis. In her powerful analysis of black negation and white dominance, Fordham ironically privileges the power of the white dominant "other" to reach in and shape every aspect of the black world. (p. 136)

In other words, Fordham (1996) claimed that when black students at Capital High, "the high achievers," performed well academically it was because they wanted to prove to white students that they could succeed. When black students at Capital High performed poorly, "the underachievers," it was because they did not want to be accused of "acting white," a derogatory label given to black students who were successful in school by black kids who disparaged academic success (pp. 235–281). I realized that this preoccupation with whiteness and the outcomes Fordham presented may have been the case for *some* black students. I also knew that many black students, myself included, viewed academic success as an important human accomplishment. I believed that education was just as important, if not more so, in the black community as in any other because of our collective history and our goals as a people determined to be educated even when learning could result in death. Intuitively, I recognized this analysis by Fordham as lacking, and Coffey, Foley and Mirza (1998) again filled the gap with language:

> Fordham's detailed ethnography reveals that the characteristics of the achievers were, for the boys, a celebration of their black masculinity, and for the girls, a celebration of their black religious community. This embedded sense of "blackness" did not seem to fit the description of "acting white" which was pivotal in Fordham's analysis. True, the young achievers articulated that they did not want to be like the collective, unidentified, mythical African American "others" who were messing things up for everyone else by failing. But then, neither did the underachievers want to be associated with failure, but Fordham does not suggest they are "acting white".... The actions of the students, parents, and teachers at Capital High seem comfortably, self-assuredly "black." They did not appear to be consumed by a constant conscious reference to the mainstream. (p. 136)

Equipped with this new analysis, I started to look for academic literature that supported intellectual success as a positive aspect of the black community and black culture, and later I decided I wanted to add to this body of literature with my own writing.

The material consequences of racism, sexism, and classism in higher education are also manifest in classroom interactions. I remember being accused by a black male professor (who was speaking in a sociology class) of "not wanting to air dirty laundry about black people" when I explained that negative, sweeping generalizations about "who we are" as black people contributed to stereotypes, bias, and oppression. On another occasion, a white female classmate who felt my experiences as a black woman were "not special" (her words) also challenged me. She felt that I deserved no additional consideration because she too grew up in a working-class environment, and her family had many struggles. She felt that I was "whining" (her word) when I shared my concerns and experiences regarding race, class, gender, and education. I left the classroom immediately after she made that comment because I felt her words and attitude became abusive and no one else in the classroom spoke up—not even the instructor. Later, I found out that the rumor circulating among students was that *I* made the other student cry. I do not know if she cried. I had left the room to avoid her continuing verbal assault. I could not understand how I was perceived as the perpetrator of an attack in this situation. Later, while conducting the interviews for this study, the women participants explained that this is an accusation commonly hurled at black women who speak out in their college classrooms—a matter this book will address in Chapter Four.

During this experience and others like it, my intellectual and academic understanding of the complexities of how the world works continued to grow. I remember learning about black feminist thought as a space or framework to talk about the marginalization of black women; I have used some components of black feminist thought to frame many of the discussions in this text. As I began to read the works of black feminists, I felt for the first time that scholarly language existed to discuss who I was as a black woman and my relationship to higher education. I began to understand how embedded societal stereotypes about my race and gender—such as the *angry black woman* who is overbearing and dominating—shaped the results of the confrontation with the white female student I mentioned earlier (Frazier, 1939/1947; see also U.S. Dept. of Labor, 1965). I discovered that qualitative research was a way to talk to people and hear their stories. This research method is a way to represent people defining themselves, making meaning of their perspectives, and creating knowledge. I was moved by the power of the resulting narratives and believed that social change can only come about if these stories are heard and if, in the pursuit of theoretical analysis, real lives are examined. I realized that qualitative research was a way black women could talk about their schooling lives in their own words and decided to practice this research strategy. While practicing, I gathered narratives of black women at various stages of their academic pursuits. Those narratives are the center of this book. My intellectual interests, academic growth, and experiences (those recounted here and many more) do not direct this work, but they do make up the lens through which I analyze and discuss the women's stories. It is "when and where I enter" (Giddings, 1984).

Studying Black Women Undergraduates

> Roe: I don't think there are as many African American [women], maybe, in comparison to white women that attend this campus. It can be difficult at times because you're in an environment where not a lot of your classmates that are... (pause) I don't know how to say it, just that there's not a lot of them going through the educational thing with you. You're just trying to find your way day by day in a society where you have to work like 10 times harder just to, you know, get the same piece of paper that the next woman, who may be white, can just say, "My parents signed the check." You know, I mean there's this privilege there, and you know it, so you have to work harder, you know, on this campus just being a black female. (Interview, summer 2004)

Roe, a nontraditional sophomore by age at the time of her interview and the mother of three, explained in the above quote that she feels black women undergraduates have workloads that are "harder" than other students' workloads, in this case, white women undergraduates who appear, in Roe's eyes, to have privileges that smooth their paths. Identifying the "harder" workload Roe mentioned, recognizing the causes of the "harder" workload, and examining how the "harder" workload is navigated in higher education systems are important reasons to study black undergraduate women. One premise for this study—the idea that the identity markers *black* and *women* are not homogenous descriptors or categories—reinforces the notion that the phenomenon of educational navigation, while having similar features for those involved (e.g., a desire to succeed), is in fact different for each individual.

Navigating Higher Education

Educational navigation is informed by the meanings that circulate in a society. These meanings are informed in part by history, media representations, political and social ideals, cultures, economic agendas, and institutions (e.g., religion, schooling) and are engulfed in power relations. Giroux and Searls Giroux (2004) clarified power relations and the production of social meaning as follows:

> In the last few decades, a number of critical and cultural studies…have provided valuable contributions to our understanding of how culture deploys power and is shaped and organized within diverse systems of representation, production, consumption, and distribution. Particularly important to such work is an ongoing critical analysis of how symbolic and institutional forms of culture and power are mutually entangled in constructing diverse identities, modes of political agency, and the social world itself. From this perspective, material relations of power and the production of social meaning do not cancel each other out but constitute the precondition for all meaningful practice. (p. 90)

These meanings, as discussed by Giroux and Searls Giroux, and the practices that result inform the collective interpretations members of a society make of their lives. The processes of living, navigating, and negotiating those interpretations, however, are specific and individual. These processes are influenced by the fluctuating nature of historical and current contexts, lived experiences, and social and political discourses. (Kellner, 1995, pp. 5–17). As a result, for black women undergraduates charting and navigating individual career trajectories and the outcomes of that navigation have both particularized and collective features.

The meanings that circulate in a society and inform the lived experiences of its members are not equal. That is, some meanings and their principles or standards are deemed superior to others. These meanings and standards might be related to ways to accumulate wealth, to what bodies are considered assets to society, to what languages or dialects are deemed proper, to who should be allowed to marry, to whose voices carry authority, and to which voices are deemed credible. Those members of society who hold social locations deemed superior enjoy a degree of power and privilege that makes their work of navigation and negotiation in society less encumbered than those closest to or at the bottom. Since this unearned privilege is often made invisible and not recognized as existing simultaneously with oppression, members of society who hold multiple dominant social locations are rarely called upon to engage in struggle against injustice and inequity (Wildman & Davis, 2002, pp. 92-94). For example, the societal ideologies and assumptions surrounding social-class status inform every institution in American society, including higher education. Americans, those with middle-class status and those who are wealthy, have access to higher education in ways that individuals with working-class status or who are poor often do not. For would-be students with low socioeconomic status, college preparation courses, admission and tuition fees, costs of books, and other hidden educational costs (e.g., bedding, toiletries, transportation) often make study at universities—touted as the highest level of educational excellence—unattainable for some and lifelong financial burdens for others who do manage to attend.

The Role of Social Locations

Schooling in the United States can be considered an institution charged with the work of creating responsible citizens, a necessity to claiming full membership in American society. Higher education is seen as "a vehicle for individual, familial, and collective progress" (Feagin, Vera, & Imani, 1996, p. 157). The democratic goals of schooling, particularly the ideals of citizenship and progress, are frequently thwarted because access to quality education is not equal among all members of U.S. society and is, in fact, tied to social location. Social locations in the United States are not equal, and this inequality impacts the process of schooling. No one ideology informs individual existence by itself; there are many ideologies that do so all at the same time. Therefore, social locations of privilege and power (e.g., whiteness, maleness, an able-bodied state, middle-class or wealthy status) can work simultaneously to make the specific educational work of those holding all or many of these locations fairly smooth. For many students, the complexities of social locations held—that may render one both privileged and not privileged or both empowered and powerless at the same time—often create a rocky educational path (Garrod et al., 1999; Jensen, 2002; Majors, 2001; Sleeter, 2000). For black undergraduate women, who often occupy the bottom rungs on ladders of privilege and power, navigating both literal and figurative college and university spaces is an ongoing, dynamic, and complex process.

The inequality of social locations (that is, the idea that some social locations wield more power and privilege than others) impacts the lives of each individual participating in the schooling process, and the effects are different for each one involved. For black women undergraduates, their status as *black* and *woman*, intersecting with their social classes and other social locations, makes their educational journeys specific. Since black women undergraduates are often deemed to be deficient and ill-equipped with traditional academic capital (e.g., skills, intellect, practice), there is a need to understand their particular strategies for academic success. This book is an analytical representation of the ways black women undergraduates talk about their educational journeys. It is a space where black women undergraduates discuss what they bring, use, and develop to navigate their paths in higher education and how they evaluate traditional school ideology, policy, and practice. This book thus broadens discussions of black women and college success and illuminates the impacts of race, class, and gender on their experiences.

Black Feminist Thought and Intersectionality

Components of black feminist thought heavily inform the lives of black undergraduate women. Studying black women's schooling lives requires an examination of this theoretical space and its practical implications. Black feminist theory and research methodology were born out of the historical exclusion that black women faced in the early feminist movement and in higher education. This exclusion forced black women scholars to adopt analytical tools, theories, and methods that put their complicated lives at the center of academic agendas (hooks, 1984, pp. 9, 10; see also Banks, 2004a, p. 177). There are several distinguishing features of black feminist thought that guide this work, including the centering of black women's voices, the acknowledgment that individual black women have not all "had the same experiences" nor do they all agree on the "significance of varying experiences" and the recognition of essential contributions made by black women intellectuals both inside and outside of the academy (Collins, 2000, pp. 20–43). Black women undergraduates are intellectual authorities on their diverse school experiences, and their input is necessary to combat the inequities faced in their college lives.

The concept of race, class, and gender intersectionality is a theoretical facet of black feminist thought. Brewer (1999) showed that intersectional analysis is a conceptual tool that links the experiences of women of color all over the world to discussions about "economic restructuring, capital mobility, racial formation and gender inequality" (p. 42). Race, class, and gender intersectionality engages identity. It is a framework for analyzing how all forms of identity impact social, economic, and political life. Intersectional analysis does not look at the various components of identity (i.e., race, class, gender, ability, sexuality, religion, ethnicity) as separate features of subjectivity but rather as "interlocking, overlapping, simultaneous spheres" that are always at work in the lives of men and women and evident in societal institutions such as family, government, schools, and the economy (Collins, 1995).

Intersectional analysis does not essentialize identity markers such as gender and race. It recognizes that these are socially constructed spaces with biological connections. An intersectional analysis also grants that there are lived consequences for those embodying the particular biological features. These consequences stem from the ways socially constructed standards are played out in daily interactions. Understanding *black* (i.e., race) and *woman* (i.e., gender) as socially constructed categories with changing contexts is a necessary intellectual and conceptual space to attend when discussing systemic dimensions of the lives of black women undergraduates. The way black undergraduate women *wear* evidence of their membership in these socially constructed spaces, in connection with society's understanding of these spaces, is a root of the oppression black women face and work to overcome. For example, the fact that the black women undergraduates at Rutgers University were in attendance at a college and playing a sport that was televised indicates that changes have occurred over time to the social locations of *woman* and *black* in higher education. Just as important is the recognition that the women were verbally attacked by Don Imus because of physical features he could *see* and what he believed about those physical features as compared to bodies he deemed most desirable. Don Imus drew upon the pervasiveness of racist and sexist discourses about the natural hair of black females as not beautiful and the sexual expression of black females as promiscuous and "for sale." He relied on these socially constructed dialogues to connect with what he deemed was a like-minded audience and appeared surprised at the vehement opposition to his slurs.

Brewer (1999) laid out five features of the concept of intersectionality. Discussing Brewer's tenets of intersectionality highlights how these features impact the lives of black women undergraduates.

1. "Critiquing dichotomous, oppositional thinking by employing *both/and* rather than *either/or* categorizations" (Brewer, 1999, p. 33)

Dichotomous thinking leads to conversations that are exclusive, not inclusive, of the characteristics or social locations that inform black women's lives (e.g., race, class, gender). Minh-ha (1989) found that in scholarly writing, thinking as *either/or* raises questions of loyalty to every aspect of self; she explained that women scholars are often put in positions of having to choose "from among three conflicting identities. Writer of color? Woman writer? or Woman of color?" (p. 6). The ideological, economic, political, and literally divided spaces that result are most often oppressive places. For black women, educational discourses that employ *either/or* theories cause marginalization in each discussion

(Crenshaw, 1995, p. 358). For instance, how do black women undergraduates respond when faced with issues of patriarchy from black men undergraduates in college classrooms? How do they show solidarity with black men around issues of racial oppression and academics yet not allow these same men to participate in gender oppression? Employing and theorizing the idea of *both/and* empowers disenfranchised groups, including black women undergraduates, because it includes all aspects of their lives rather than forcing them to choose.

2. "Allowing for the simultaneity of oppression and struggle" (Brewer, 1999, p. 33)

This allowance tells, among other things, that black women not only are victims of oppression but also are engaged in struggles against oppression. This struggle is often marked by resistance to institutions and societal norms that assign more value to some lives than to others. Participation in this struggle, at times, leads to more oppressive situations, and all of this occurs at the same time. This simultaneity opens up discussions to show that the struggles of black women undergraduates are not just about race and relationships with whites but also about class, gender, and relationships with other blacks; in institutions of higher learning, the obstacles to learning that occur as a result of these struggles must be addressed all at the same time. Resistance (i.e., the struggle) to biased curricula and testing practices, stereotyped ideas about learning, and exclusion due to racism and prejudice, often lead black women to further isolation (i.e., more oppression). For black women undergraduates, the simultaneity of oppression and struggle along with the energy drain that results can present challenges to success in education.

3. "Eschewing additive analysis: race+class+gender" (Brewer, 1999, p. 33)

Rockquemore (1999) asserted that when studying the lived experiences of black women "analyses which gaze through the lens of race[or any other single identity marker] alone, miss the complex reality of individual lives" and that "only when we accept the challenge of developing multifaceted theoretical frameworks can Black women's voices be located in all their various manifestations of self expression." (p. 71). This third feature of intersectionality identified by Brewer (1999) stressed that simply adding one category of identity to another is also not enough to capture the complexities of black women's lives. Rather, unearthing these complexities requires analysis that:

4. understands "the embeddedness and relationality of race, class, and gender and the multiplicative nature of these relationships: race × class × gender" (Brewer, 1999, p. 33)

Understanding the multiplicative nature of race, class, and gender infuses all discourse about any one of them with inclusive, political, and historical contexts and challenges traditional views and scholarship on racism, class inequality, sexism, homophobia, ableism and other identity concerns. This understanding challenges mentalities that have blamed individuals for the consequences of oppressions or have chastised marginalized groups to pull themselves up by their bootstraps. It does so by disclosing the systemic nature of the socially constructed forces acting upon lives and bodies. The multiplicative nature of the relationships across race, class, and gender explains how individual contexts can be different and can change. A white professional man or woman and a black professional man or woman do not have the same lives, and two black women undergraduates do not have the same lives; the differences exist across and within social locations and groups. Cole (1986) answered important questions regarding the relationships of women:

> Are U.S. women bound by our similarities or divided by our differences? The only viable answer is *both*.... Patriarchal oppression is not limited to women of one race or of one particular ethnic group, women in one class, women of one age group or sexual preference, women who live in one part of the country, women of any one religion, or women with certain physical abilities or disabilities. Yet, while oppression of women knows no such limitations, we cannot, therefore, conclude that the oppression of all women is identical. (p. 1)

Intersectionality at work does not mean that every black woman undergraduate will live an identical life. This is further evident by the fact that while the aspects of intersectionality are always at work simultaneously, at various times certain identity markers may be more easily identifiable or evident as the cause of oppression. For example, it may be evident to a black woman undergraduate who is a lesbian that her race and gender are the reasons a white male may lash out at her in a class on power and race. While homophobia may not be at the forefront of this particular oppressive attack since her sexuality may not be worn on the body in the same way her race and gender is, intersectional analysis teaches us that this facet of who she is will still inform the attack. She could feel compelled to hide this facet of her identity as she works to defend her raced and gendered being in that setting. The multiplicative and relational natures of race, class, and gender make black women undergraduates vulnerable to both similar and different oppressions, even if they appear to be part of the same group and share similar characteristics.

5. "Reconstructing the lived experiences, historical positioning, cultural perceptions, and social construction of black women who are enmeshed in and whose images emerge out of that experience" (Brewer, 1999, p. 33)

Zerai and Banks (2002) studied the lives and social demonization of mothers addicted to crack cocaine and use the concept of intersectionality to challenge traditional cultural perceptions of this group. The study pinpointed how intersecting spheres of oppression create images of black women that inform societal thinking and the healthcare and legal policies that impact these women's lives. This reconstruction is an example of how the concept of intersectionality expands discussions and provides alternate worldviews. For black women undergraduates, exploring their stories about education, both historical and contemporary, will help challenge societal perceptions and images that render them intellectually deficient.

Brewer's (1999) theorizing regarding intersectionality provides a basis for thinking about the lives of black women undergraduates in relation to the time and space in which they are living and participating in higher education, as well as the historical context of this phenomenon. She concluded that "theorizing about race, class, and gender is historicized and contextualized" (Brewer, 1999, p. 33). This history and context become important as we examine and learn about the lives of black women undergraduates *from* black women undergraduates. I used a black feminist, theoretical lens of intersectionality to collect and analyze data for this book. Intersectionality as a methodological tool for analysis can work to undo inequality, expose the social construction of features of identity, "disrupt our ideas about categories in the social world viewed as natural" and "provide an alternative vision of social reality" (Guillaumin, 1995, pp. 61–67). This book centers the schooling lives of black undergraduate women. Collins (1998) explained the importance of written works that highlight intersectionality:

> [These works] not only return subjectivity to black women by treating them as agents of knowledge, they simultaneously demonstrate that race, class, and gender intersectionality is not merely an approach one *should* adopt, but an approach having conceptual and methodological merit. (p. 117, emphasis hers)

It is my claim that focusing on the schooling lives and history of black women without this concept as an underpinning makes for a limited and inaccurate depiction. The educational history and modern-day educational experiences of black women are informed by the intersectional identity they embody.

Cultural Capital, Schooling, and Black Women Undergraduates

In a discussion about social class and culture, Bourdieu (1984) stated:

> The primary differences, those which distinguish the major classes of conditions of existence, derive from the overall volume of capital, understood as the set of actual usable resources and powers-economic capital, cultural capital, and also social capital. The distribution of the different classes (class fractions) thus runs from those who are best provided with both economic and cultural capital to those who are most deprived in both respects (p. 114).

Bourdieu (1984) purported that ideologies tied to power and privilege are tied up in the possession of resources, financial and intellectual, that are not equally distributed among all members of a society, but rather, are socially inherited. Individuals and families most endowed with cultural capital represent the most powerful societal classes.

Academic success is connected to cultural capital in that cultural capital operates in the same way as economic capital; both have "exchange value" (Perry, Steele, & Hilliard, 2003, p. 67). Perry (2003) further explained:

> Cultural capital is socially inherited cultural competence that facilitates achievement in school.... It is important to realize that for Bourdieu the mechanism for distributing economic opportunity resides in the academic culture.... Accordingly, schools transmit knowledge in cultural codes, which afford automatic advantages to those who already possess cultural and linguistic capital and disadvantages to those who possess little or no cultural capital. The existing educational system. given its interrelationship with the dominant culture and the close affinity between the dominant and the academic cultures has already picked the winners. (pp. 67, 68)

For black undergraduate women, the dominant view of cultural capital as a combination of educational resources, skills, intellect, and practice often highlights what black women are lacking in these areas. The portrayal of their race, gender, and sometimes class as less powerful or less desirable than those of the dominant culture *and* the fact that some of them are often underprepared (in the classic sense) for college, that is, for example, they have attended under-funded public schools with limited resources, or had parents or guardians who worked multiple jobs leaving little time for trips to a museum or library, makes them less likely to be, as Perry indicated, picked as academic winners.

The miscalculation of the ability of blacks to get educated is not new in the history of African Americans and education. Chapter Two will show that from slavery on, the dominant view of cultural capital as it relates to education underestimated and undervalued what blacks bring to negotiate their eventual educational success. Bourdieu (1984) certainly does not include these methods and tools of negotiation as cultural capital in his elitist discussion. Lareau (1987) critiqued Bourdieu's discussion of cultural capital and indicated that in his discussion "Bourdieu has focused almost exclusively on the social profits stemming from high culture" and that "his research on the cultural capital of elites may be construed as suggesting that the culture of elites is intrinsically more valuable than that of the working class" (p. 83). Since the elite are most often represented as white, able-bodied, and male and the working class or poor as black, brown, and disabled, this claim by Lareau needs intersectional attention since more than economic status is involved when societal value judgments are made. One of the dangers of Bourdieu's focus on high culture as most socially valuable is that the cultural capital that groups other than the privileged elite possess, share, and utilize goes unnoticed and unrecognized. For blacks in the United States, this occurred historically and still occurs today. In schooling this oversight leads to oppressive devaluation leaving some, like black undergraduate women, largely excluded from the discourse of academic success. Lareau (1987) described one solution to this dilemma when she suggested that academic research should analyze variations in definitions of cultural capital by examining historical studies of more social groups. She alleged that this research would show that throughout history the cultural capital of some groups held more value than that of others and that the result was oppression and inequity. Chapter Two further examines the issue of cultural capital and African American education from a historical viewpoint.

An additional goal of this text is to expand the idea of cultural capital as it relates to black women undergraduates as a social group in a particular social context, namely, higher education. Since many black undergraduate women have been academically successful, they can declare what currency aided their success and how it was informed by their race, class, and gender. This currency can be viewed as capital even if they do not speak of it with that vocabulary, much as dominant cultural capital often has many names. Scholars need to listen to black undergraduate women without placing judgment on the cultural capital they describe when recounting their experiences.

The Settings

Interviewing black undergraduate women in a variety of geographical locations and school cultures made visible both the similarities and differences in experiences connected to race, class, and gender. What follow are brief descriptions of the community college (1) and universities (3) the women attended. The four institutions are listed alphabetically and throughout this book are referred to using pseudonyms.[7]

Central University is a large, private 4-year institution located in the Northeast. The university is made up of eight professional colleges from which students earn undergraduate and graduate degrees. Central University has a student body of 15,500 (approximately 11,000 are undergraduates) that hail from over 100 countries. It would be considered a predominately white institution with 71.6% of the undergraduate population being white.

International Community College is a public institution located in the heart of metropolitan New York City and enrolls approximately 13,000 students. It is well known for its programs in English as a second language. This community college is primarily a commuter school yet attracts students from all over the world. At the time of my visits, it boasted a student body made up of representatives from 150 countries.

Sunshine State University is a 4-year public institution located in California that enrolls over 13,000 students and offers 46 bachelor and 29 masters programs. It is a commuter school, although a small population of students lives on campus. Ethnic minorities make up 63% of the student body at Sunshine State University.

The University of Borders and Crossings is a 4-year research institution that serves over 17,000 students, many of whom cross the international border from Mexico every day to attend school. The Mexican and Mexican American populations represent the university's racial and ethnic majority. The university offers 81 bachelor, 72 masters, and 11 doctoral programs.

The community college and each university discussed in this book has its own specific structure and focus in the larger social structure of higher education; the characteristics of each institution inform the lives of all its students. The black women undergraduates interviewed at these locations have traveled different paths to get to college; they have different academic backgrounds, different family situations, different socioeconomic statuses, different interests, and different professional goals. Their stories were similar at times and dissimilar at other times. What the black women undergraduates I interviewed shared was the work of navigating systems in their schools that did not value who they are as raced, classed, and gendered beings. They shared strategies that supported such navigation and that helped them negotiate obstacles. They also shared a desire to succeed in whatever school they attended. Therefore, it is also important to know who they are.

The Participants

Before I introduce the women, I will take a moment to thank each one of them again for their participation in this work; I was only able to complete this study because of the generosity they showed by candidly sharing their stories with me, whether their accounts were painful, joyous, funny, or sad. The reflective, analytical, and contemplative ways they thought and spoke reinforced the belief that they truly were active participants as knowledge holders, intellectuals and theorizers—experts of their own worlds (Collins, 2000, p. 34). What follow are brief profiles of the 19 participants;[8] see Appendix C for a summary table. The names of the participants used in this book are pseudonyms with one exception; one woman requested that I use part of her real name. It is my belief that this diverse group of women, who hailed from a variety of physical, spiritual, and intellectual places, provided a wide range of insight into the lives of black women undergraduates; this book is grounded in their lived experiences (Cuádraz & Uttal, 1999, p. 156).

Central University—12 Participants

Alana attended Central University as a junior working on double majors in history and African American studies with a minor in education. She explained: "ultimately I want to be a professor." Alana was raised by her mother and has one brother who is older by 14 years. Her mother, presently working for the federal government, completed a bachelor's degree at age 45. Her father graduated from a 4-year university. Alana described her family's socioeconomic status as "middle to upper class."

Blue was studying nursing at Central University to earn a second bachelor's degree. Her first degree, earned in 2002, is in social work. She decided to pursue the second degree since she did not want to "do bachelor's level social work, had not applied to graduate school, and always had an interest in nursing." Blue's parents are from the West Indies. Blue is the youngest child, she has one brother and two sisters. Blue's mother is a nursing aide, and her father works in construction. She described the family's socioeconomic status as "lower-middle class."

Cheryl was a senior at Central University pursuing a major in information management and technology with a minor in African American studies. Cheryl is the middle child in her family; she has a sister aged 32 and a sister aged 13. Her parents are divorced, and she lived with her mother who works for "cheap" for a local hotel that is part of a large chain. Cheryl described her socioeconomic status by saying, "I wouldn't say I'm just above the poverty level, but I definitely have a family that has had some troubles in terms of, you know, even the basic necessities." She later added, "I would say just about poor, but you know, we fake the funk."[9]

Kimberly was a senior political science and policy studies major at Central University. Kimberly's family is from Guyana; she explained that this background is the source of many of her cultural ideals including the importance of religion in her life. Kimberly's parents are married. Both her parents graduated from high school in Guyana; neither attended college. Kimberly's mother owns a beauty shop, and her father is also self-employed. She described her family's socioeconomic status as upper-middle class.

Leviticus was a junior at Central University who was working on dual majors in business (with a concentration in marketing) and African American studies. She described herself as "her mother's only child" since her parents are divorced and she lives with her mother. Leviticus' mother was working toward a bachelor's degree. She described her family's socioeconomic status in clear terms: "we're not poor and we're not rich." She later used the term *middle class.*

Malikah was a senior nursing major at Central University. She described herself as Caribbean American. Malikah described her family: "my father basically had nothing to do with us, so just my mother raised the three of us." She is the oldest child and has a brother who is taking college classes in the military and a sister who is also a college student. Malikah explained that her father is "education hungry" and has gone to college, but she has no idea of his educational level. Her mother started going to school for nursing but had to drop out because she was working two jobs to take care of the family. She described her personal socioeconomic status as "very bad" due to her credit card debt and her student loan debt. At the time of the interview, Malikah worked two jobs but said she only received "minimal" pay.

Nadia was a senior pursuing a major in psychology and a minor in African American studies at Central University. She is the younger of two girls in her family; her sister is older by 11 years. Nadia's parents are divorced, but she described a "tight-knit" family. Both Nadia's parents have advanced college degrees; her mother, a retired elementary school vice principal, has a master's degree, and her father, a college dean, has a Ph.D. Nadia described her current socioeconomic status as middle class: "When my father was living in the house, it was a little different, you know. (pause) Together, I might say middle to upper class but separately, definitely middle class."

Nicole was a junior pursuing double majors in education and sociology at Central University. Her parents are divorced. She is a middle child with one older brother, one older half brother, and one younger half sister. Nicole lived most of her childhood with her mother but now lives with her father. Neither of her parents went to a traditional 2- or 4-year college. Nicole's mother is unemployed, and her father does financial work for a church. Nicole explained that her father did "go through some kind of online 2-year program that allowed him a degree in finance." She described her mother as "poor, very poor," and her father as "well off, not rich, but doing well for himself."

RGB was a senior pursuing two majors at Central University, one in television, radio, and film and one in African American studies. She is the oldest of seven children, five of whom (according to RGB) "belong to her mom" and two to her biological father. RGB's parents are divorced, and she was raised by her mom and stepfather. She described her "home socioeconomic status as low income" because, "for the longest time, my mother was the only one in the house working." RGB's mother works as a teaching assistant in an elementary school, and her stepfather works in maintenance. RGB's father is an electrical technician but does not contribute to her mother's household income. RGB credited her mother's strict rules about completing her schoolwork as a major factor in her getting good grades in high school.

Roe was a 31-year-old, part-time student and mother of three. She was a sophomore at Central University majoring in child and family studies. Roe came from a single-parent home; her mother raised Roe and her four brothers, one of whom is her twin. She explained that while growing up, she always assumed that her family was middle class, but now, as an adult, she can remember her mother "working two or three jobs and going to school part time." This led Roe to believe that, while "basic needs were always met," the family may have been working class. Roe's mother eventually earned a masters degree in child and family studies at Central University. Roe first described her personal socioeconomic status at this point as "poor" but explained that she is uncomfortable with that term as a "part-time student at a private university who does have the things she needs, like a car." She finally settled on "middle/working class" as an accurate description.

Shonte was a senior education major who attended Central University. In her family, she is the oldest of four girls; she had one brother who is now deceased. Shonte's parents are divorced. Shonte's mother is a high school graduate who did not attend college, and her father, at the time of the interviews, was pursuing a master's degree in accounting. Shonte described her socioeconomic status and that of her mother as "very poor" and the status of her father as "working class." Because both her parents used drugs at some point, Shonte spent a number of years in foster care. She credited her high school principal and teacher with helping her attend college. Since the time of her interviews, Shonte has graduated and had begun teaching in New York City.

Teena was a senior working on double majors in broadcast journalism and African American studies at Central University. Teena explained why she decided to enter broadcast journalism: "since fourth grade, I have been winning oratory contests and have a love for public speaking." At the time of the interview, Teena said her immediate family was made up of her mother and her sister, who is older and married. She described her family in this way because her parents divorced when she was "very, very young" and her father had never been around. Teena knows that her mother attended a junior college in Belize, but she does not know anything about her father's educational background. Teena described her socioeconomic status as lower-middle class.

International Community College—3 Participants

Alex was a first year student at International Community College. At the time of the interview, she had not declared a major. She explained that, while growing up, she never wanted to go to college, and her high school grades reflected that inclination. She credited friends with changing her mind about school; she began to see college as a way to have a better future. Alex's parents are divorced. Her father was remarried and his new wife was pregnant. The new baby will be her third sibling. Alex and her older sister are the only members of the immediate family to attend college. Alex described her family's socioeconomic status as middle class.

Kayla was a first year student majoring in sociology at International Community College. Kayla wants to be a social worker for children and specialize in adoption cases. Kayla grew up in the "adoptive system" and has "five brothers, only one of which is blood related." Neither of her adoptive parents, whom she calls Mom and Dad, went to college, but she is proud of the fact that they "have been married for 35 years and know hard work." Kayla does not put a label on her socioeconomic status, but she readily described her parents: "Right now, my father is retired. He retired early due to a disability. He is a diabetic, and my mother stopped working a long time ago because she took in a lot of foster children. We were her main priority. So, I really don't know."

Lisa was a first year student at International Community College studying to be a veterinarian technician. She developed an interest in the field of veterinary medicine while attending a high school that had a specialty program in animal science. Her high school was also very diverse in that "80 countries and 50 languages were represented." Lisa has one brother who was in high school at the time of the interview. Both of Lisa's parents have bachelor's degrees. Lisa described her socioeconomic status as working class.

Sunshine State University—3 Participants

Amari was a first year student pursuing a major in child psychology with a minor in business at Sunshine State University. Amari's parents were never married to each other. Her mother, a cosmetologist, died a few years ago. At the time of the interview, Amari lived with her father, who is a minister, her stepmother, and her baby stepbrother. Amari has two older brothers and one older sister. She described her socioeconomic status as middle class.

Cherry was a first year student at Sunshine State University pursuing double majors in criminal justice and sociology. Cherry described herself as a "foster youth" and a "ward of the court." Her father died in 1994, and she does not know any of his family. Her mother has a bachelor's degree but also has "mental health problems" and was unable to take care of Cherry and her older sister. Cherry described her complex socioeconomic status by saying "I'm not poor, but because I don't really have income, I'm most likely called poor. I am a ward of the court, but I have money. Like, I can get by day to day; but poor, I guess, is when you don't have anything or very little. I think I'm just broke."

Jessica was a first year student at Sunshine State University who was hoping to transfer into a teaching program after completing her general education requirements. She has four siblings, two older and two younger; the two older are in college. Jessica's father is a pastor with an advanced degree. Her mother completed high school and some college. She described her socioeconomic status as middle class.

The University of Borders and Crossings—1 Participant

Jamie was a first year student majoring in physical therapy at the University of Borders and Crossings. She lived with her grandparents, who are black. Her mother, also black, lived with Jamie's younger brother in Georgia. Her father, who is white, was not part of Jamie's life; his level of education was unknown. Jamie's mother completed 2 years of college. Jamie's maternal grandfather completed a master's degree. She described her family's socioeconomic status as "upper-middle class" and explained that it was "never *if* I would go to college, but *when* I go to college." The undergraduate women I interviewed all self-identified as black, even though, for some participants, their race and ethnicities were layered by biracial and immigrant status. Later chapters will show that, in this book, the use of *black* by the participants was both an identity marker and a political stance. The women employed the word *black* to describe and explain their collective experiences with racism and classism in schooling systems in the United States. Their analyses were not always identical, but they consistently critiqued and examined race and power in American society and more specifically, higher education.

Outline of the Chapters and Appendices

Chapters

Chapter Two presents a synopsis of the historical contexts of black women in higher education in the United States and how they have informed contemporary discussions. It lays bare the scarcity of academic literature that centers the voices of black women in this discussion. This chapter also shows the ways race, class, and gender have historically informed the schooling lives of black women and the impact of cultural capital on this discussion.

   The next three chapters focus on the ways black women undergraduates discuss and describe the capital they see as crucial for college success. Chapter Three is conceptual. It lays out the argument that black women undergraduates utilize a specific historical, cultural, and social context to expand the traditional discourse about their schooling lives. Specifically, this chapter examines how black women undergraduates utilize their *sociological imaginations* to support college success (Mills, 1959, p.3). Here the women discuss what success in college means and the ways their biography, history, and place in U.S. society as black women inform their work in school. In this chapter, the black women undergraduates used intersectional talk to add complexity to academic discourses, like "acting white" aimed at simplifying their schooling success. Chapters Four and Five demonstrate some of the ways the reworking of discourse occurs in the women's lived reality. Chapter Four scrutinizes the cultural clashes that occur in the schooling lives of black undergraduate women and the strategies they employ to navigate them. This chapter explores the stereotype of the *angry black bitch* and the ways the women reject, own, and rename this stereotype. In this chapter, black women undergraduates critique systems of diversity and multiculturalism in the face of their dynamic and complex real-life experiences at their colleges and universities.

Chapter Five looks at the complex alliances black women undergraduates must negotiate for college success. Through their narratives, it becomes clear that the trajectories of these alliances in the lives of black women undergraduates are informed by the intersections of race, class, and gender. The women demonstrated the sophisticated ways they navigate these relationships as they decide and define those who are allies in the educational journey and those who are not.

Chapter Six discusses the implications of this theoretical discussion. This chapter presents suggestions for institutional and classroom policy and practice that foster the ideal of inclusive excellence and support the academic success of black women undergraduates and, I would argue, all students. Chapter Seven summarizes the argument that the knowledge and skills associated with the aforementioned processes are a form of cultural capital that black women undergraduates utilize for academic success. This chapter looks at the significance of the argument of broadening traditional discussions of cultural capital as it relates to black undergraduate women and schooling.

Appendices

Appendix A outlines the qualitative methods and methodologies utilized in the research design, interview process and data analysis of this text. It situates the text in phenomenology and grounded theory conceptual frameworks. This section also follows the feminist qualitative requirements of identifying my place as researcher in the study and centering my participants as knowledge makers and holders in the process.

Appendix B describes the Lumina Project. I served as a researcher in this multi-year national study on learning communities in higher education and conducted much of my research while simultaneously working on this grant. Appendix C provides a table with demographic information about each participant including their course of study at the time of the interview and their socio-economic statuses.

CHAPTER TWO

Historical and Modern-Day Contexts

Black Woman Undergraduates and the Discourse of Cultural Capital

The history of black people as an enslaved group has a direct impact on historical and modern discourses about black women undergraduates in higher education. Africans transported across the Atlantic Ocean and enslaved and most African Americans born into slavery were forbidden to participate in formal or informal education. The few black men and women afforded the opportunity were usually house servants who learned at the whim of an owner, whose goal was to make them better servants (Noble, 1956/1987, p. 17).

The description of blacks as sub-human and beast-like made it easy for slave owners to justify the prohibition of education (among other atrocities), since it was presumed and promoted that blacks were inferior to whites intellectually and were incapable of learning. Many Southern states [i.e., slave states] outlawed teaching slaves to read. Some states in the North purported that blacks should be taught to read (Noble,1956/1987, p. 17). From the time of slavery on, the dominant view of *cultural capital* (as related to education) underestimated what blacks brought with them to negotiate their eventual educational success. For example, Bourdieu (1984) did not include such methods and tools of negotiation in his elitist discussion of cultural capital.

For many enslaved blacks, the prohibition of education made learning seem even more valuable. They saw literacy as currency worth dying for, and many slaves risked physical abuse and death for daring to learn to read and write. Franklin (2002) explained that education, particularly "the desire for literacy and formal education became a *core value* in the African American cultural value system"; also, "for formerly enslaved African Americans and their descendents, literacy and formal schooling was closely associated with *freedom*, and they were willing to make great sacrifices to obtain them" (p. 176). For those who succeeded, their newfound knowledge served several purposes: it shed light on the conditions in which they lived; it gave them access to the political processes and climates that were the social, economic, and political ethos of the time; and it provided spaces and frameworks for resistance. Education provided intellectual information and skills. It also afforded ways to gain membership and citizenship and to solicit participation of like-minded allies in the work to end slavery and its leftover sequelae after Emancipation. Span (2002) wrote the following of blacks in Mississippi:

> In Reconstruction Mississippi, formerly enslaved African Americans regarded very highly the idea of being educated, and this sentiment served as an invaluable resource in their earliest educational initiatives. Between 1862 and 1869, this collective group consciousness served as the resource or *cultural capital* needed to begin and sustain their grassroots educational enterprises. Education—or at least some degree of literacy—was a paramount and invaluable acquisition for Mississippi's black masses. Whereas poor whites, according to W. E. B. Du Bois, viewed "formal schooling" as a "luxury connected to wealth" and did not demand an opportunity to acquire it, African Americans in Mississippi, both during and after slavery, demanded schooling, connecting it with freedom, autonomy, and self-determination. (p. 198)

Franklin (2002) delineated how poor African Americans, no longer enslaved, utilized their collective *cultural capital*—that is, their collective financial, physical, and human resources as well as a "sense of group consciousness and collective identity"—to advance the education of the entire group (p. 179; see also Span, 2002). This utilization resulted in the funding of colleges and universities, including all-black schools designed to educate black youth and combat the racist " educational *Black Laws*" that excluded them from public schools in states such as Ohio (Randolph, 2002). This use of cultural capital spurred not only the preparation of black teachers who accepted personal responsibility for the academic success of their students but also a community-based effort to combat white supremacy in education (Franklin, 2002); these efforts continue to be necessary to the present day. Collectively, formerly enslaved blacks and their descendents used their communal skills (i.e., their cultural capital) to overcome the material consequences of slavery, segregation, and other prohibitions to learning.

Viewed in this historical context, attention is drawn to the definition of cultural capital as a sense of group consciousness that can be used as a resource to develop collective economic enterprises (Span, 2002). I contend that for black women undergraduates, their education is, in part, an economic enterprise, and they understand this as a group and as individuals (see Chapter Three). The resources they create, including social networks, families, and cultural institutions (i.e., their *social capital*), and the ways in which they negotiate these resources— all of which make up *cultural capital*—are influenced by the intersection of race, class, and gender; historically, this cultural capital has been overlooked for black women, even though they have been at the center of debates about higher education and race and class (Span, 2002, p.197).

Educating Black Women Undergraduates in Historical Contexts

In times past, women, as a collective, have had to fight for access to education. For black women undergraduates, their overlapping and simultaneous racial and gender identities made the rules and outcomes of that engagement quite different in many ways from those of their white counterparts. When many white women began to be afforded the formerly only patriarchal privilege of being taught (in order to benefit society by functioning as better homemakers), most black women were still viewed in matriarchal ways—heads of "disorganized families, equal to enslaved men but inferior to white women" (Noble, 1956/1987, p. 16). Terrell (1901/1992) outlined a dominant societal force regarding education of black girls and women in a response to W. H. Thomas (1843–1935), the author of *The American Negro* (1901). Terrell's response included the following passage:

> In order to prove the utter worthlessness and total depravity of colored girls, it is boldly asserted by the author of *The American Negro* that under the best educational influences they are not susceptible to improvement. Educate a colored and a white girl together, he says, and when they are twenty years old, the colored girl will be either a physical wreck or a giggling idiot, while her white companion will have become an intelligent, cultured, chaste young woman. (p. 81)

Terrell (1901/1992) challenged the accuracy of Thomas's assertion with comments about her own educational experiences and those of "colored women" whom she described as "useful member[s] of society, either pursuing their chosen vocations or presiding over their homes" as "useful, cultured women who would be a blessing and a credit to any race" (p. 81). The original assertion by Thomas as well as Terrell's response illustrate the challenges black women have faced historically in obtaining an education and point out the specific educational journey they must navigate. As black women become students, they remain raced, classed, and gendered beings.

Gender, Race, Class, and College in Historical Representations

Historically, black women faced the obstacle of race and gender discrimination while trying to become educated. In her discussion of black women college students, Ihle (1992) wrote, "Black women who pursued college work [in the late 1800s and early 1900s] were truly pioneers" (p. xiv). Noble (1956/1987) wrote that these women "were venturesome, considering the fact that their people were still enslaved and had no assurance about the future" (p. 20). During that time, black women college students faced the societal norm that formal education for women, in general, was taboo. In 1891, Anna Julia Cooper (1858–1964) wrote, "the atmosphere and the standards of the world do not afford any special stimulus to the development of women" (Ihle, 1992, p. 58). Overcoming these restrictive ideas and discriminations required courage to even apply to school and to continue studying despite patriarchal and racist pressures to stop.

Oberlin College (Oberlin, OH) played a significant role in the educational progress of black women. The college was the first to admit an African American woman, Mary Jane Paterson (1840-1894), who became a teacher and principal (Ihle, 1992, p. xv). The black women who attended Oberlin were not a homogenous group. Some, like Fanny Jackson Coppin (1837–1913), were poor and faced financial struggles in attempts to get their degree; others, like Mary Church Terrell (1863–1954),[1] escaped pecuniary challenges. Even so, black women who attended Oberlin College and, eventually, other institutions showed "persistent determination in the face of many obstacles, to gain knowledge and empowerment through formal education at colleges and universities" (Ihle, 1992, p. xiv). In time and after much struggle against oppression, black women were in attendance at many institutions of higher education including, University of California-Berkeley, Wellesley College, and Atlanta University (now Clark Atlanta University). Institutions specifically for black women, like Bennett College (Greensboro, NC; founded in 1873) and Spelman College (Atlanta, GA; founded in 1881), were also established (Marteena, 1938/1992; Read, 1937/1992).

Questions regarding what subjects black women should be taught were of great debate. According to Lawson and Merrill (1984), many of the colleges that were admitting black women in the nineteenth century were closely aligned with religious organizations and were founded to train ministers and teachers. These interests were shared by many of the students; consider, for example, "the three Sarahs"—Sarah Kinson, Sara Woodward, and Sarah Woodson—all of whom attended Oberlin College and were teachers and missionaries that claimed a commitment to Christianity and Protestant values (pp. xvii–xix).

After Emancipation, blacks, as a collective group, increased their efforts to gain access to equitable education, and the debate over classical versus technical or practical training for black women became intense. The debate was raced, classed, and gendered. Women's colleges in general were being criticized for teaching curricula and methods in philosophy and other liberal arts studies (Noble, 1956/1987, p. 21). Many people, both black and white, felt those courses should be reserved for men (Brazzell, 1992, p. 35). Black women were plagued by theories that their gender (woman) and race (black) rendered them mentally inferior. This made their fight for arts education both political and cultural in the North (Brazzell, 1992, p. 40). In the South, at historically black colleges for women like Spelman College, the purpose of practical and religious courses was to train black women for work in the home and the workplace. Black women "depraved by slavery" and work in the fields of slave owners had to be "purified and changed" in order to claim femininity, work in the home, "uplift the masses" of their race and lead the black community to "respectability" (Brazzell, 1992, p.36). This raced, classed, and gendered aim was based on the social and stereotypical reputation—held in particular by white, religious benefactors of black colleges—of the black slave woman as sexually immoral and in need of lessons regarding cleanliness (sexually, physically, and in the home) (Noble, 1956/1987. pp. 22–24). This shift in roles, from slaves in the field to homemakers with ascribed moral responsibility for their race, created a "dual status" for black women since as Brazzell (1992) wrote:

> In pursuit of the most "efficient" use of labor, slave owners recognized no gender differences when assigning field work. Black women were expected to plow, hoe, pick cotton and perform all other tasks as men did. However, once the slaves left the field gender differences came into play. Black women were expected to be responsible for all the tasks thought to be within the purview of women. They were responsible for cooking, housecleaning, sewing and washing clothes. (p. 36)

In this domain, black women were also wage earners. Brazzell (1992) explained that black women had to "earn their bread and make it too" as "full participants in the material world dominated by men. (p. 36). While Brazzell described the roles of black women at this time as dual, it is evident that the race, class, and gender of these women came into play simultaneously in this discussion. As a result, the roles Brazzell outlined are better described as multiple and intersectional.

Education for self-fulfillment or job training was, for the most part, excluded from nineteenth-century debates about what to teach black women. Instead, the educational focus for black women was on learning, accepting, and teaching white culture and morals (i.e., race); remaining in their place in the home while being subservient to men, whose domain was the workplace (i.e., gender); and earning limited wages, when possible, to supplement the family income (i.e., class).

The idea of education for self-fulfillment, along with the discourse regarding the motivations of black women students, began to be considered in the late nineteenth century and early twentieth century. During this time, black women united in organizations, such as the National Federation of Afro-American Women and worked toward the "suffrage of women" and the justification of the "dignity" of Negro women (Noble, 1956/1987, p. 26). This work involved examination (through research) of the status of higher education for the black woman. Cuthbert's (1942) text, *Education and Marginality: A Study of the Negro Woman College Graduate*, was a sociological attempt to represent the specific experiences of black women who pursued higher education. Cuthbert (1942) surveyed 44 black women college graduates. What stands out in Cuthbert's work is the presentation of the strengths of black women rather than focusing on their real and perceived deficits. Cuthbert (1942) looked at systemic causes for the obstacles these black women faced such as "severe criticism" and "limitations in work opportunities due to racial and sexual prejudice" (pp. 117, 118). Her findings included the idea that for black women, race, class, and gender are overlapping structures of oppression—though not named as such—and are always at work. For example, the study revealed that the majority of black women interviewed believed higher education was a path to improve their grave personal and familial economic situations. Their goal was to become financially self-supporting. Cuthbert (1942) identified the idea of being self-supporting as part of a discourse on race and class; the women wanted to be eligible for work opportunities but realized their options would be limited to those "the best work opportunities open to Negroes". Such limitations regulated the level of economic success a black woman could achieve even with a college education (p. 28).

Integration and the Law

The period of integration, particularly the 1950s and 1960s, saw a "shifting racial climate in the United States" and "the lifting of some racial barriers," particularly in education (Higginbotham, 2001, p. 1). This climate and shift in educational practice and policy was facilitated by the work of groups like the National Association for the Advancement of Colored People (NAACP), who were actively exposing the legal issues of access and equity. There were protests organized, in part, to challenge law-codified educational concepts such as the "separate but equal" practice that was protected by the U.S. Supreme Court in *Plessy v. Ferguson* (1896) and *Berea College v. Commonwealth of Kentucky* (1908). These protests intensified during the 1950s and 1960s, leading to major shifts in educational policy (Berry and Asamen, 2001; Higginbotham, 2001; Willie, 2003).

Brown v. Board of Education of Topeka (1954) and subsequent cases (e.g., *Brown II*, 1955; *Brown III*, 1978) became landmark decisions in the field of education law. As a result of such legal work, the U.S. Supreme Court's decision was that "separate schools, like other facilities, were inherently unequal" (Higginbotham, 2001, p. 92) and that segregated schools were unconstitutional (Willie, 2003, p. 17; see also White, 2002, p. 271).[2] An outcome of these rulings was a mandate that schools become spaces where both blacks and whites attend; that together, they make up one student body. Further impacting this social change was the Higher Education Act of 1965. This act made financial grants available to "disadvantaged students, which greatly increased minority enrollment" (Roebuck and Murty, 1993, p. 39).

Integration in *theory* meant that black and white students would have equal access and equal education. This theory was not without obstacles in *practice*. For example, integration practices initially supported placing black students at schools that had previously enrolled predominately white students. During this period, the criterion for entrance into colleges and universities was still "based on solid secondary educational preparation" and "the regular requirements for admission" (Higginbotham, 2001, p.7). No accounting was made for institutional racism or gender and class bias, resulting in barriers, inequities, and curricular limitations that rendered many students of color less prepared for college classes (Higginbotham, 2001, p. 5–7).

Higginbotham (2001) interviewed "fifty-six black women who graduated from predominately white colleges [and universities] in the late 1960s" (p. x). Her goals were to "examine the race, social class, and gender constraints" (p. x) the women faced as undergraduates and pioneers in integration and to understand the strategies they used to overcome these constraints (pp. x–4). Higginbotham (2001) found that as a result of "no public acknowledgement of the differential needs" (p. 169) of black women college students integrated into white schools, the black women in her study reported the need to immerse themselves in African American culture, develop predominantly black peer groups, and create safe spaces to combat the impact of racism on their predominately white campuses (pp. 188–190). The black women undergraduates in Higginbotham's study, like the black women at Oberlin College, were individuals; that is, they were not all the same. Their differences (e.g., educational level, socioeconomic class) were not just differences in relation to white students; there were also intra-group differences. Higginbotham (2001) elucidated the complexities of this group as she explained:

> There were black women from the South who graduated from segregated high schools as well as women who grew up in the North in overwhelmingly white, suburban communities. There were women from working-class communities who struggled in comprehensive high schools where their talents were unrewarded and who then found more support and encouragement in colleges, and there were others who found college to offer experiences similar to their previous schooling. There were middle-class women from highly ranked high schools where they were encouraged to attend college, but not prestigious ones. The nuances in the interactions these women had in educational settings structured the varied paths and patterns of their lives. (p. xi)

> This group of women was not homogeneous; some were raised working class and some middle class. In the black experience, social class is related to power in occupational settings, economic resources, information, expectations, and the strategies employed to overcome obstacles. (p. 3)

Some black women college students were able to become upwardly mobile while others reproduced their parents' middle-class positions (Higginbotham, 2001, p. 184). As a result of these distinctions, some middle-class black women students may have found academic similarities in their college experiences and their high school experiences that made both academic and social transitions less cumbersome. Still, women from all socioeconomic levels displayed a desire to succeed in college. Higginbotham did not assign a scale to their desire; that is, she did not claim that one group had more desire than another, Rather, Higginbotham explained how the individual facets of their identities informed their collective educational lives.[3]

All of the women in Higginbotham's study (2001), both working and middle class, spoke of seeking refuge and developing strategies for survival with other black women who understood struggles with race and who were committed to improving the economic status of the black community and of black women. Willie and McCord (1972) identified this phenomenon, often labeled as *black separatism*, as really the impact of white racism on campuses where black students struggle to find cultural experiences and social connections and where they seek refuge from "racism, rejection, ridicule and arbitrary behavior" (p. 10). The survival strategies the women identified were necessary tactics for black women as raced, classed, and gendered students on campuses that offered little or no institutional support.

Even when reaching across racial lines, women talked of bicultural experiences. They explained that their roommates and social acquaintances may have been white, but their friends and support systems were women like themselves (Higginbotham, 2001). Traversing these contexts called for a fracturing of the self and a development of scripts to be used during interactions and altered depending on the educational or social settings. Higginbotham (2001) showed that learning to adjust and incorporating this raced and classed adaptation in their academic life was *cultural capital* that black women used to be successful in college. These types of negotiations and adaptations related to race, class, and gender are also evident in contemporary scholarship about black women in higher education.

Black Women Students in Contemporary Contexts

Negotiating Race, Class, and Gender in High School

Black women begin school negotiations related to their race, class, and gender before they enroll in college. There are many documented accounts that address race, class, and gender oppressions in the K–12 school system in the United States (Anyon, 1997; Fox, 2001; Ladson-Billings, 1994; Leadbeater & Way, 1996; Fordham, 1991).

In their study of "African American, Asian American, and Latino" students at an urban high school, Rosenbloom and Way (2004) outlined some of the ways discrimination makes navigation around obstacles necessary (pp. 420-427). Their research revealed that African American and Latino students experience discrimination from persons in positions of authority (including teachers and police who patrolled their schools and neighborhoods) and from Asian American peers, who experienced their own discrimination, and who were leery of associating with their African American and Latino classmates (pp. 434, 443). Rosenbloom and Way (2004) attributed this doubtfulness on the part of Asian American students to harassment by Black and Latino students regarding the assumed academic superiority of Asian American students and to the negative stereotypes Asian American students held about their Black and Latino schoolmates (p. 443). According to Black and Latino students in this study, teachers frequently sent messages of distrust, made remarks that were culturally insensitive, and had low academic expectations (pp. 436, 437). Rosenbloom and Way (2004) concluded that the multiple patterns of discrimination, harassment, and stereotypes that high school students of color in the study faced caused them to struggle with the "contradictions of American egalitarianism" and their lived experiences (p. 447). Students' negotiation of these discrepancies included defining "themselves in opposition to particular stereotypes about their own groups" (Rosenbloom & Way, 2004, p. 446).

Alexander-Snow (1999) connected the high school experience with the transition to college in her study examining the social integration of two African American women (who had attended historically white boarding schools) at a predominately white university (p. 106). Alexander-Snow (1999) argued that despite the reputation of Black independent boarding schools as institutions that promote culturally relevant teaching and self-esteem among black students, most black parents who send their children to boarding schools send them to schools that are predominately white and Eurocentric because these schools have better resources, a wider range of programs, and nicer facilities (p. 107). Alexander-Snow claimed that this earlier experience informs the social and cultural transitions of black women from high school to college. She explained that the saturation of Eurocentric culture and practice in their predominately white boarding schools helped the Black women in her study to be successful academically and made it necessary for them to negotiate their identities at their predominately white college campuses (Alexander-Snow, 1999, p. 115). This need for negotiation stemmed from what Alexander-Snow (1999) called, being "caught between two worlds," where they were not black enough and not white (p. 113). The navigation included the following: managing interactions with white students and teachers who asked stereotyped questions about culture and [dealing with] their stereotyped ideas, informed by class privilege, about black students who were not as academically successful (pp. 113–115). Alexander-Snow (1999) concluded that for the black women undergraduates in her study, strong academic preparation was not enough to undo challenges they faced due to race, class, and gender (p. 117).

While the academic discussion of race, class, and gender oppression in the K-12 school system in the United States is not new, each of the studies presented here has outlined a particular type of high school experience. What becomes evident is that whether a black woman undergraduate comes from an urban, multicultural, high school setting or from a suburban, predominately white, high school setting, there is a process of negotiation that adds an additional layer of work to her college life. While it can be argued that this is the case for most students, these investigations showed that the work required of black women is directly connected to their race, class, and gender (Alexander-Snow, 1999; Rosenbloom and Way, 2004).

Black Undergraduates in Colleges and Universities

The presence of black women at colleges and universities in the United States has led to a barrage of contemporary scholarship related to their experiences as various academics and others attempt to understand ways this population can be better served by their institutions. The literature covers a range of topics including the following: participation in study abroad programs, sexual behaviors in college, body image, representations in specific fields of study (e.g., math, science, foreign languages), being adult learners, college choice practices, impacts of affirmative action, presence in predominately white or predominately black college and universities, and life as graduate students (Butner et al., 2001; Coker, 2003; Dahl, 2000; Falconer & Neville, 2000; Foreman, 2003; McCombs, 1989; Morgan, Mwegelo, and Turner, 2002; Mullen, 2001; Schwartz & Bower, 1997; Schwartz et al., 2003; Thomas, 2001). Additionally, contemporary academic literature outlines specific needs and supports for black undergraduate women including the following: need for mentors, building positive academic self-concept, inclusion of their voices in academic discourses, role models of the same race or ethnicity or both, college preparatory programs that reinforce the idea that women can be successful in college, and recognition by educational institutions that cultural traditions in familial and community relationships can support school success (Beoku-Betts, 2000; Howard-Vital & Morgan, 1993; Matthews-Armstead, 2002; Schwartz & Washington, 1999; Stewart, 2002).

In discussions about black college students, issues of identity are plentiful (Gurin & Epps, 1975; Jackson & Solís Jordán, 1999; Shorter-Gooden & Washington, 1996; Tatum, 1996; Wentworth and Peterson, 2001; Willie, 2003). Identity issues regarding "the performance of race, maintaining cultural connections, and representing the race have supported a college curriculum interested in critical race, class, and gender theories and liberation pedagogy" (Ellsworth, 1992; McLaren, 1998). For black undergraduate women, this work to define their own identity requires a variety of strategies, since this work is occurring in the face of deeply rooted practices and discourses steeped in race, class, and gender bias and discrimination.

In *Overcoming the Odds: Raising Academically Successful African American Young Women* (Hrabowski et al., 2002), the authors examined the academic success of 66 black women undergraduates who participated in the Meyerhoff Scholars Program, a program designed to increase the numbers of "minority" students in the field of science and engineering, at the University of Maryland in Baltimore County (p. vii). The black women undergraduates interviewed outlined positive family influence and parental support, African American mentors—specifically those of the same gender, and religion or God as sources from which they draw strength while working towards academic success and overcoming obstacles related to their gender and race (Hrabowski et al., 2002, pp. 202-206). The women also described the development of internal resources of personal motivation, determination, pride, anger, and intelligence as crucial strategies necessary to overcome obstacles to college success (Hrabowski et al., 2002, pp. 206-208).

A common thread that runs through all of this literature is the idea that the historical and societal inequities related to race, class, and gender create conditions that require specific navigation strategies for black undergraduate women. Additionally, the challenges black women undergraduates face today are similar to those of black women undergraduates in the past. While black women are enrolling in colleges and universities in large numbers (i.e., higher than in past decades), their access to education and their successes and accomplishments are still subjects for critique and debate. Historically, the questions involved in this conversation included the physical ability to enter an institution based on phenotypic characteristics (e.g., skin color) and the relationships of these to intelligence and educational law. Today, segregation laws that denied access to education for black women have been abolished. Still, as was the case in the early integration period, movement from *theories* of educational equity to *practices* proves to be most challenging. Discrepancies in the educational preparation of women of color during high school and the low admission and retention rates in higher educational institutions that may result are often viewed as individual flaws or deficiencies rather than the consequences of an inequitable educational system. Black women (as raced, classed, and gendered beings) are subjected to racism, classism, and sexism, and their deserved right to full membership in their colleges and universities is still constantly questioned as a result (Roebuck & Murty, 1993, p. 129).

Achievement and Resilience as Strategies for College Success

As mentioned, black women undergraduates are being academically and socially successful in college despite obstacles related to the intersections of their race, class, and gender. Sanders (1997) argued that the high achievement of black students in the face of racism and discrimination shows that a "keen awareness" of how these systems work can cause students to exert more academic effort (p. 90). In academic literature, the success of black women undergraduates and other students of color is often termed *educational resilience* and is discussed in terms of why and how individuals experience success in school despite structural constraints (O'Connor, 2002, p. 855). O'Connor (2002) argued that the traditional discussion of resiliency in higher education presents the concept as an "individually determined phenomenon" (p. 855). She is calling for an understanding of the "sociohistorical and institutionally responsive processes involved in the concept of resiliency," that is, an academic discussion of resiliency that examines the structural restraints in higher education that are related to race, class, gender, and other social locations (O'Connor, 2002, pp. 857–859).

This resiliency, as discussed by O'Connor (2002), was manifest in historical conversations about blacks and their work to become educated. Like their historical counterparts, modern-day black women undergraduates face social and political challenges to becoming educated including "racial, sexual, and class oppression" (Howard-Vital, 1989, p. 180). This requires strategies to develop the skills and attitudes that scaffold achievement and resiliency. In O'Connor's (2002) study, these strategies included the following: garnering important college-going information from their high schools, tapping family members and friends who have college experience, having teachers account for the evaluations of schoolwork, and embracing descriptors like "pushy, strong, loud, aggressive, demanding, and determined" (pp. 885–890). O'Connor (2002) argued that since risks or obstacles to education are "differentially represented over time," it is important to continually examine the ways groups like black women undergraduates from multiple decades who face both covert and overt discrimination mitigate that risk (p. 898).

For black women undergraduates, this resilience, as described by O'Connor (2002), is a necessary part of their schooling labor that they must carry out in addition to their academic work. The obstacles that stand in the way of them getting an education, while "differentially represented," are always present and at work while they are in college, since the societal norms regarding their race, class, and gender infiltrate institutions of higher education.

For many black women undergraduates, the real-life consequences of intersectional oppression are played out on predominately white college campuses. Some of the ways this occurs include the following: the violence and racist remarks perpetrated by white students and faculty, the exclusion from academic study groups and mentor relationships, and the constant pressures to prove they deserve to be in school due in part to backlash from affirmative action (Roebuck & Murty, 1993, p. 129). This makes the adaptation process (described as necessary for college survival by the women in Higginbotham's study [2001]) as reflexive as taking a breath or blinking an eye for a black woman undergraduate today. The adaptation process is inherently oppressive in that black women undergraduates cannot just be students. They have the additional, constant, college work of seeking support from students and faculty who understand their position as raced, classed, and gendered beings; they must navigate additional impediments, as well.

In an attempt to offset the raced, classed, and gendered oppressions that occur in college, some academic scholarship claims that black women undergraduates should attend predominately black colleges and universities since there is much work to be done in higher education to recognize the equity and access promulgated in the theory of integration. Roebuck & Murty (1993) claimed that the academic and social success of black students at historically black colleges and universities speaks to the benefits of separate institutions. Included in their list of benefits (in addition to the higher academic success) are "more positive self-images, stronger racial pride, and higher aspirations" (p. 19); this success is attributed to a less-hostile racial environment.

Wolf-Wendell's (1998) study of baccalaureate European American, African American, and Latina women revealed that African American women may be better served at a historically black women's college than a college that is predominately white and coeducational since this "special focus institution" may provide a supportive environment that is conducive to personal growth (p. 143). This supportive, "special focus environment" should exist at every institution of higher learning. All colleges and universities need to include a wide-minded space where black women undergraduates are not viewed as a homogenous group but are able to explore and define their identities as part of their growth process.

Black women undergraduates work to define their own identities in the face of stereotyped ideas about who they are as women and as students in the midst of larger social discourses about race, class, and gender (Bowman et al., 1995). As shown, historical representations of promiscuity and emasculating, demanding matriarchs led to a higher education curriculum aimed at teaching morals and ways to serve in the home (Noble, 1956/1987). Academic curricula have expanded beyond historical representations; modern college curricula explore critical race, class, and gender theories and liberation pedagogies. Still, black women undergraduates in these contemporary classes are often faced with classmates and professors who hold stereotyped views and show little sensitivity to the lived experiences of black women. Feagin, Vera, & Imani (1996) claimed that "a common white image is of young black women as whores or welfare queens" and that "this gendered racism undergirds the misrecognition of black women as not fully human and has a very negative effect on young black female students" (p. 89). Black women undergraduates often feel compelled to challenge stereotypes that are not representative of their experiences and that render them as inferior beings. Such *negotiations* induce the development of strategies such as "actively seeking mentors, drawing upon internal resources of personal motivation, formulating theoretical frameworks to explain oppression, and dispelling myths." Note that these negotiations and strategy development must occur simultaneously with the students' academic work, thus pulling them in multiple directions as they move through their coursework (Howard-Vital,1989; Hrabowski et al., 2002; Jackson, 1998).

Black women undergraduates who do this additional work of negotiation and strategy development are often described using the aforementioned term *resilient*. In this case, the use of resiliency is closely linked to *bootstrap theory*, another ideological stance in which individuals bear the sole responsibility for outcomes connected to structural oppression with little focus on the ways they bear this responsibility or the cost of this work. Like their historical counterparts, today's black women undergraduates face challenges that require skills and attitudes that scaffold achievement. This work requires risk and, as O'Connor (2002) argued, an ongoing examination of changing contexts and obstacles, related to race, class, and gender, to see how populations of Black women graduates mitigate that risk (p. 898).

Conclusions

What is missing from the discourse on resiliency is the identification of the currency women use for college success as *cultural capital*. The black women undergraduates interviewed for this book identify how they engage in this struggle for educational equity and success. They discuss (a) some of the ways they acquire and live out motivation, (b) impacts of hierarchies of power and histories of domination (e.g., slavery) on their present-day schooling and work, and (c) how current knowledge and work expand traditional descriptions of the cultural capital needed for college success.

The varying forms of cultural capital employed by the black collective were not recognized historically—and are often not recognized today—as useful strategies for academic and social success for college. And yet, the necessity and practicality of these varying forms of cultural capital are evident in the ways blacks have gained access to education today—albeit not without oppression. The historical fight for equitable education, including sufficient resources and appropriate cultural representation, continues in contemporary times. Examination of the various forms of cultural capital in these contexts and their impacts is the focus of this book. Historically and in modern times, black women undergraduates—in recognition of the impacts of their intersecting race, class, and gender—have utilized nontraditional forms of cultural capital to overcome obstacles and get educated. Their work deserves our attention!

CHAPTER THREE

Black Undergraduate Women Utilizing the Sociological Imagination for College Success

> Alana: When I say that my culture is black, I mean that when I'm in a space and I am directly viewed as something, I have been cultured as that. For example, everything that is black in America has always been associated with this movement of bodies to America, this whole mix-up of cultures and then this whole, you know, disbursement of African Americans derived from the south. But yeah, I say that because I'm gonna automatically be viewed as a black woman, and I have been cultured as a black woman; there's just certain things you do as a black person that I know that white cultures would not. (Interview, spring 2004)

> Teena: [Black culture,] it's just this thing that comes from a history that made an environment that culture grew out of, and even, you know, in bad times—even during enslavement and the hundreds and hundreds of years of oppression in this country—that culture was an escape, and it was a means of survival. (Interview, spring 2004)

Being a black woman in America is connected to a particular history. This history includes the movement of black bodies from Africa to enslavement in the British colonies and then the United States, the northern migration of blacks in search of equal citizenship in the United States, and the development of a culture heavily informed by oppression—that culture often also provided a reprieve from that oppression. As shown in Chapter Two, this history exposes the denial of access to formal education for blacks for hundreds of years and draws attention to the ongoing fight for equitable education.

C. Wright Mills (1959) claimed that the study of the intersections of history, biography, and society are the coordinate points of the study of man (p. 143). He stated, in gendered language, that most humans are unaware of the importance of these connected features:

> Seldom aware of the intricate connection between the patterns of their own lives and the course of world history, ordinary men do not usually know what this connection means for the kinds of men they are becoming and for the kinds of history-making in which they might take part. They do not possess the quality of mind essential to grasp the interplay of man and society, of biography and history, of self and world. (pp. 3, 4)

According to Mills, it is impossible for one to know and make sense of one's own biography and current place in society without understanding the historical and social ways that one's own collective group was treated and how that informs their place in the world. Mills (1959) called this knowledge a *"sociological imagination* [that] enables its possessor to understand the larger historical scene in terms of its meaning for the inner life" and enables us to grasp history and biography and the relations between the two within society" (pp. 5, 6).

Following Mills's lead, some of the black women undergraduates in this study would be considered extraordinary in their knowledge of the existence of this *intersection of biography, history, and society* as they repeatedly named the connection when they defined and described black culture. Kimberly's comments further explained:

> Kimberly: Black culture is multidimensional, very vast because of where we're coming from. I don't even know if you can sum it up because it is so vast, and I feel my connection to it. We're all the same. It was just that one boat stopped at point B and the other one stopped at point A; and when those bodies on those boats were dispersed, our ancestors, we kind of had this connection to mother Africa. The way we [Caribbean Americans and African Americans] held onto it... The way we preserved it was so different, but we still can connect with each other at a certain level. (Interview, fall 2004)

Kimberly connected her biography to the historical, geographical movement of blacks from Africa to various parts of the United States. Kimberly realized that black people are not a homogenous group and that black culture in U.S. society is, as a result, multidimensional. As a Caribbean American woman, she explained that she feels a connection to this collective that shares a specific history of migration. She asserted that this shared intersection of biography, society, and history creates a *sameness* among black people and black cultures and yet still allows for differences among black people and cultures.

Nicole also showed an understanding of the ways history, biography, and society intersect as she spoke on black culture:

> Nicole: Black culture has strong roots in the past. When I think of black culture, I don't think of just something present that happened now and the kinds of traditions that come from now; I think of it more as back in the past, like from our ancestors in Africa and from slavery. (Interview, spring 2004)

Nicole recognized that what happened in the past (specifically, the history of enslavement) informs black culture as she understands it, particularly in terms of traditions. When asked, she defined *traditions* as "unity, being together and helping others even if they are not close to you, like family. Just because you are black, I'm gonna help you if you need anything" (Nicole, interview, 2004). Nicole's claim that black people will always help other blacks because of shared race can be challenged as a generalization, yet what is important is Nicole's identification of a social way of being that she believed exists in black culture as a result of the intersection of history, biography, and society.

Kimberly and Nicole understood that individual experience as well as the collective biography of blacks, their culture, and how they are viewed and valued in society is connected to a specific history. In our discussions, the women identified this knowledge as coming from a variety of sources including "high school, parents and other family members, books, college classes, and popular culture (e.g., *Roots*, a 1977 television miniseries)."

RGB moved the conversation about the intersection of history, biography, and society beyond a focus on historical connections. She discussed ways these interactions inform social structures, particularly the schooling lives of blacks:

> RGB: I think that in this country discrepancies in school achievement are the residue of historic situations, and you wonder why kids aren't really interested in a lot of what they're learning. It's 'cuz they can't relate to it. They spend all day in school being taught that their only contribution in history was slavery and Martin Luther King. When you are taught that over and over again, it's imagined that you would fall behind other people because you're not being taught somebody who did something of worth looks like you. (Interview, spring 2004)

RGB understood that the intersection of historic situations, societal value judgments regarding educational curriculum, and lived experiences of black children are one way to understand achievement discrepancies; this understanding is crucial in discussions of academic success and social change focused on academic equity.

Building on the idea that the black women undergraduates interviewed possessed sociological imagination, this chapter examines how a sociological imagination informs the schooling lives of black undergraduate women (Mills, 1959).

The Sociological Imagination and Cultural Capital

Knowledge of the intersection of history, biography, and society and how these interactions inform institutions such as education today is a form of cultural capital that black women undergraduates utilize to navigate success in higher education. Because of their school experiences as raced, classed, and gendered students, black women undergraduates in the United States have no choice but to deal with the material consequences of living these social locations. For example, a black woman undergraduate can never have *white-skin privilege* on her college campus or anywhere else. This being the case, she must live with the oppressions that come from having black skin. This type of inevitability pushes black undergraduate women to develop and use a sociological imagination, which becomes a form of cultural capital they employ to navigate their lives in school.

The focus in this analysis of black women undergraduates and the sociological imagination is not just *what* the women know or that they have an understanding of *how* history, biography, and society intersect, but also what having

this knowledge *allows and inspires them to do* as they make their way through social structures such as higher education. Black women undergraduates use a sociological imagination (a) to develop ways to discuss private or public issues
related to education and the black community that move beyond deficit models
and (b) to expand discourses regarding the interplay of their social locations and
their schooling lives to include intersectional analyses. This chapter focuses on
the women's descriptions of how this knowledge and discourse translate into
practices and perspectives that can foster college success.

Private and Public Issues in Higher Education: Being Prepared

> Leviticus: By 11th grade, everybody was telling me, "You gotta go to college! You
> gotta go college!" And my view of college was just that of Boston—which is like col-
> lege central—and negative. I didn't realize that there were as many options. I didn't
> realize there were colleges and universities and community colleges and specialty
> colleges; and all of that just overwhelmed me when I was ready to go to school. (In-
> terview, spring 2004)

Leviticus stated that, because of a lack of knowledge about colleges and universities, she was unprepared for the overwhelming decision of where to attend college. Public talk about the schooling lives of black undergraduate women often
centers on their being underprepared for college as members of non-privileged
groups holding multiple social locations that do not carry power. Such topics
were prominent in past discourses about black women and schooling and remain
part of current discourses.

The public, academic conversation regarding preparation, with its focus on
test scores and other quantitative measurements of academic success, operates
from a deficit model that privatizes and individualizes the lack of adequate academic grounding. Mills (1959) claimed that part of sociological imagination involves the understanding of how personal issues overlap and intersect with public
or societal issues and acting accordingly (pp. 8, 9). The black women I interviewed understood that their race-, class-, and gender-informed high school experiences may have left them, as a collective group, less prepared in some ways
for college; but as Nicole illustrated, they also understood that this is a public
issue related to history, societal values, and biography. Lack of traditional preparation may be an obstacle to college success, but it is not an unconquerable one.
Nicole explained:

> Nicole: I was a very good student in high school, I think. But the thing is, I was al-
> ways comparing myself to them [wealthy, white students]. I didn't want them to
> know I was on scholarship. I felt that they would look at me as that was kinda the
> only reason I was there, you know—because I was black and on scholarship, not be-
> cause I deserved to be there. I guess I kinda wanted them not to accept me like be-
> ing white, but just accept me as part of their school and going through what they're

going through. My thing is, I don't do well on tests, like standardized tests. I actually failed the test to get into this school, but they saw from my previous school that I was getting like straight As every year, so they realized I was probably able to do the work. (Interview, spring 2004)

In her junior year of high school, Nicole moved from her mother's home and went to live with her father. There she attended, in her words, a "very rich, white high school" from which "most who graduated went on to college." Nicole explained that her race and class, as a black student on scholarship, dictated that she had to guard her academic reputation to ensure that her place at the school was not questioned and she could be accepted. Nicole recognized that her race (i.e., black) and class (i.e., scholarship student) carried a particular meaning in this setting where differently raced (i.e., white) and classed (i.e., wealthy) students were privileged. Nicole had this knowledge regarding her social location early on in her schooling. She continued:

Nicole: From a very early age, like as far as I can remember, just because I always went to majority white schools, and so I always knew I was different. I remember every day going home—like the first day of classes—going to my mom [and saying], "I'm the only black girl again!" And she would say, "Oh, maybe you'll get lucky next year" and that's pretty much from kindergarten. (Interview, spring 2004)

Nicole being the only black girl in her class was "unlucky" according to her mother's implication that having other black students in her class would be of benefit to Nicole. That Nicole came home each year with the revelation of being the "only black girl" showed her connection to a black collective biographical history. Nicole and her mother did not name this connection, but it is clear that the consequence of it, namely the privilege of presence in the classroom, informed their exchange.

Nicole claimed that she held this knowledge "pretty much from kindergarten." When she got to high school she was aware that the traditional view of academic capital, which deems standardized test scores as predictors of scholastic success, was not an accurate forecaster in her case. After failing the standardized test to enter the school, Nicole was able to gain access because the grades she had earned at her previous high school showed she was a good student. Nicole disclosed her private struggle by saying, "I don't do well on tests." She recognized that this private struggle became a public discourse that, due to her social locations, could have inhibited her from being accepted in that privileged school setting.

For Nicole, this schooling history and biography, intersected with societal values, was connected to her work in higher education. She recognized that, just as in high school, her status as *black* and *woman* made her an object to look at in college:

> Nicole: I don't know if it is necessarily the case, but a lot of time, I feel that because I am black I'm looked at here [at Central University] as if I'm not gonna succeed and I'm not gonna do as well as my white counterparts and I'm not gonna be the CEO of a company or whatever. So knowing that is kind of what pushes me to do well, just to kind of prove everyone wrong. Like, I can make it no matter what I've been through and struggled through. (Interview, spring 2004)

Understanding that her experiences in school are connected to her history and biography and to societal values that mark her as less likely to succeed made Nicole work harder. This is an example of how this knowledge, as cultural capital, works as a negotiation that leads to strategy. This strategy of working hard to offset a lack of traditional academic preparation and the resulting discourse has paid off in multiple forms of academic currency for Nicole. These include membership in an academic honor society, successful study abroad in Spain, scholarships for conference travel, and, most recently, acceptance to several graduate programs. This payoff shows the ways alternative forms of cultural capital can facilitate the acquisition of traditional cultural capital.

Test scores that do not accurately predict her ability to succeed have also impacted Cheryl's life in higher education. She agreed that being underprepared as evidenced through testing is a limited public discourse about the schooling lives of black women undergraduates and not necessarily a predictor of college success:

> Cheryl: Where I come from and from what I know, to be successful is a black thing. I don't know one black person that would say, "I don't want to be successful." So when you apply academics to being successful, I want to be successful, so that means I have to be successful in academics. Take, for example, the SATs. I wasn't prepared for the SATs, but that doesn't mean that I *can't* be successful. To me, academic success for blacks just may be the preparation or lack thereof. They just may not know that there are outlets or how to utilize their success. For me, when I came here [to Central University] I didn't have anybody say, "its okay to drop a class if you're about to fail it." Nobody told me that. I had to figure it out myself. So I just think it has to do with knowledge. (Interview, fall 2004)

Being unprepared for the SAT exam was an impediment to Cheryl's academic success. She later explained that her economic status prohibited her from doing all the SAT "prep stuff." Cheryl was confident that, even though she was unprepared by testing guidelines, once she was accepted to her school, she would find success by "figuring things out for herself."

Cheryl moved this discourse about academic success beyond just passing or failing the SATs. She forced the conversation to include the intersections of biography, history, and society when she explained that college success is about access to valued knowledge. Cheryl recognized that black students may not have been schooled in the knowledge she addressed, such as the strategies needed to successfully pass the SAT exam and the navigation of campus academic policies.

In her analysis, the lack of this specific information is an inequity connected to race that must be overcome. Cheryl realized that black students can be academically underprepared. She also realized that black students who fit this category must work as she did to obtain the range of knowledge necessary for achievement. Cheryl's cultural capital is the insight that she may know less than other students, the understanding of why that may be the case, the confidence that she can overcome that obstacle and succeed in higher education, and the strategies she employs to "figure it all out."

This topic of black undergraduate women being academically prepared or not prepared for success in higher education is complex and informed by larger societal issues such as economic inequalities and racism. All black undergraduate women do not fit this category of being academically unprepared for college life. RGB explained that going to college had been her goal since "fourth grade when I loved to watch the television show *A Different World.*"[1] As a child, she recounted that she would exclaim, "Oh man, I'm going to college; I can't wait for that." RGB worked hard to maintain a GPA of 3.5 and above all 4 years of high school and participated in co-curricular activities like Project Bridge and the Cathedral Scholars Program:

> RGB: There was a program called Project Bridge that I was in, in high school. It was started by this group called the Korea Society. It's a year-long program where 10 students in the DC area were, every month, immersed in some kind of activity where they came together and had roundtable discussions about their cultures and their neighborhoods and go to various institutions—like the Latino Youth Center— and had roundtable talks there. Then to top off the whole program, they take us to Korea for 2 weeks. I was also involved in a summer program for three consecutive summers called the Cathedral Scholars Program. It's a program where, at the end of your freshman year, you apply to this academic program where you take classes in the summer at Washington National [Cathedral]. For the first half of the day you have classes, and the other half of the day they send you into the city on an internship. (Interview, spring 2004)

RGB outlined the ways traditional forms of cultural capital were built into her inner-city high school experiences; she had access to summer programs that focused on internships and took courses on a college campus. She possessed the established markers of scholastic capabilities with a high GPA, which she maintained throughout high school, and a record of participation in quality co-curricular activities. Unlike Cheryl, RGB felt she *was* being prepared in a specific way to navigate academic settings. Her high school experience provided her with multiple, traditional forms of cultural capital that supported her transition to college:

> RGB: So, my high school operated a lot like college in that we went off campus a lot. Instead of staying in class and reading books about primates for biology class, we

would take it to the National Zoo. We had a humanities class that, when we were studying the different areas of humanities, we went to the Smithsonian and different museums and did assignments and had lessons there. We were on the campus of a big university, and when we did research, we did our work in the college library. With that kind of setup, it just taught us to be very independent. It taught us to take control of our own learning because teachers didn't escort us to these places; the onus was on us to get there. Our learning took place all over the city, and when I came to college, it didn't feel much different. The atmosphere and interacting with people who are different from me and having independence and getting to class and things like that, it was pretty much the same, so it [my high school] very much operated like college. (Interview, spring 2004)

Visits to zoos and museums for hands-on lessons, conducting research in a university library, being responsible for getting to class on time, and traveling independently all over a major city provided RGB with tools to succeed in college. These tools included knowledge of how colleges work, academic resources available, how to gain access to college, and how to take charge of her own learning. For RGB, that part of her transition to college was "pretty much the same" as high school. RGB's description of her smooth transitions from high school to college highlights the advantages of having a lot of the traditional forms of cultural capital when entering school, in this case, familiarity with a college atmosphere, procedures around college classes, and ways to navigate campus spaces (e.g., a university library). RGB's narrative draws attention to the additional learning and navigating black women undergraduates like Cheryl must do when they are not privileged in that way.

Larger societal discourses connected to social class informed RGB's transition to college. While academics and cultural experiences were not an issue in her quest for college, paying for college was. She explained some of the ways she had to strategize in order to respond to the obstacles she faced getting to college due to her socioeconomic status:

RGB: My mother told me at the outset of my senior year [in high school]; she said, "If you're really serious about going to college, you better get to filling out some serious applications because I am gonna tell you right now that I don't have anything to give you." So, I did what I had to do as far as applying for scholarships. I applied for pretty much everything that came across my plate. It was a lot of hard work and a lot of writing, but I had to do it if I was going to go to college. (Interview, spring 2004)

RGB also explained that it was not just the labor of completing the applications but also the work of presenting herself to those in the position to give it to her:

RGB: It was never discussed [with her mother], "What if you don't get into college? What are [you] gonna do?" It was pretty much known that I was going to get into college. Now the only thing that was ever debated about was the money aspect of it. Like I said, I filled out everything and went through several interviews because a lot of the scholarships I applied for were very competitive. You had to go in person and dress up businesslike to sell yourself and tell them why you need this money. I did what I had to do. I didn't even think about it because I'm like, "Hey, if I'm going to go to college, I have to get up in the morning whether it's raining or snowing or whatever and talk to these people." And I didn't feel intimidated at all, and I didn't feel like, "What if the other person gets it over me?" I was like, "I know I need the money, and I know I'm gonna tell them why I need the money." And I'm just going to be honest and let my credentials speak for itself—you know, my academic achievement. (Interview, spring 2004)

RGB "did what she had to do" to overcome the obstacle of getting money to go to college. This included the practical steps of filling out many scholarship applications, "dressing businesslike," honestly presenting her needs, not being intimidated, and being confident in the credentials she worked for in high school. RGB's claim that she "did what she had to do" suggested that black women undergraduates from working-class or poor backgrounds, who may have had access to traditional forms of cultural capital connected to education, must still address this classed feature of their identity in higher education. Cultural capital, which is useful in the academic exchange, fuels the pursuit of scholarships, familiarity with college and university atmospheres, and knowledge expectations; it can, however, undo neither the ways obstacles related to lower socioeconomic status, intersected with race, inform the experiences of some black women undergraduates trying to get into college nor the events that occur once they are accepted. These obstacles often include how the women are seen by those in a position to offer financial support. This so-called *gaze* upon black undergraduate women does not exist outside of dominant and oppressive ideas related to race and class. Thus, RGB's strategy of "doing what she has to do" must include an attempt to counter a stereotyped ideology about who she is as a student in addition to the work of acquiring the money she needs to pay tuition. The strategies RGB and other black women undergraduates create and use to overcome these obstacles are a valuable form of additional cultural capital that fosters college success. For example, learning to overcome obstacles related to her socioeconomic status, which she described as low income, supported RGB's work at Central University as she managed financial systems that allowed her to stay in school. When asked about her contact with academic financial offices, she explained:

RGB: Because I get scholarships that take care of everything, I don't really go in there often. I go in there to get my refund check, and I go in there and make sure they get the checks that I sent to them because my scholarship checks—a lot of them—get sent to me, and I give it to them. So you know, I just make sure that they are sending off my transcript because I get a yearly scholarship, the [name of scholarship program], so I just make sure the scholarship office and financial aid office have taken care of their end. (Interview, spring 2004)

Navigating academic offices is a challenge for many students and a part of the discourse that surrounds black women undergraduates. This challenge is connected to low socioeconomic status and parents with no college experiences and thus little or no familiarity with the practices and policies in higher education to pass on to their children (Bowen et al., 2005; Constantine & Greer, 2003; Terenzini et al., 1994). RGB utilized the cultural capital she acquired while seeking financial support to come to college to ensure that she could continue. Her strategies included: not being intimidated and holding the financial offices at her school accountable for doing their part. RGB explained that she "does what she has to do." Engaging the concept of "doing what one has to do" as a drive to develop strategy is a valuable form of cultural capital steeped in black history and social discourses about race, class, gender, and education. RGB realized she had no choice but to engage in these negotiations if she was going to succeed at Central University. Her socioeconomic status leaves, in her perspective, no other option. These strategies—forms of cultural capital—have paid off for RGB. She was accepted to college, she was able to maintain the financial resources to stay in college, and she continued to excel academically. RGB maintained a high GPA and had a 4.0 the first semester of her sophomore year. She received scholarships and was active in several black student organizations on her campus.

While maintaining high academic credentials and navigating institutional financial policies and practices were "pretty much the same" in college as in high school for RGB, there were social aspects of college connected to race that she was not prepared for that impacted her life at Central University. RGB described diversity in her high school:

> RGB: It was 70% black and 30% Latino, white, Asian, and international students. But even though the school was mostly black, we had a good mixture because it was a small school; there were only about 350 of us, so we had a lot of interaction with one another. (Interview, spring 2004)

In an earlier statement, RGB indicated that she had a lot of experience interacting with people who were "different from her" in high school. She viewed this as cultural capital that prepared her for college. RGB also described how this interaction was different in college and how she was not prepared for the racism she encountered:

> RGB: So when people mentioned to me, "Central University is a mostly white school. You sure you want to go there?" I was like, "Yeah. Sure. Why not? I can handle myself." So, I didn't realize that culturally it would be so different here because, even though there were a lot of whites around and we had a lot of whites in our [high] school, a lot of the mentality of white people here [at Central University] is different from white people there. 'Cuz a lot of times here, you find that a lot of white people come from very small towns that have little to no people of color, whereas in my home city there's more blacks, Latinos, and Asians than anybody. So

they are constantly in contact with us. They have to work with us. They have to go to school with us. So it's kind of a thing like, "We're used to you, so we don't have to ask you stupid questions. We know not to single you out, and you know, treat you as if you're something different from us because you're everywhere and there are a lot of different types of people of color." So there were questions that I had to answer here that I was confronted with that I *never ever* was confronted with at home. (emphasis hers) Like, "Why don't you wash your hair every day?" One boy told me that some girl asked him, "Do black people have tails?" You know, it sounds unreal, but it is because people really aren't from the same place. [They will ask questions] like, "Why do you have organizations like Student African Society? That's racist." And you know, I was just never confronted with that kind of mentality. And so I was like, "What's wrong?" I didn't think it was going to be like this. There is all this talk about diversity, so what is going on? And that was my freshman year, you know, so I just learned freshman year that things just weren't...(pause) I always say now I'm cynical, but I'm just more realistic now than I was in high school 'cuz in high school I felt like I got a euphoric sense of what being black is like, I guess. (Interview, spring 2004)

RGB then described the impact of being unprepared for the racist mentality of white students she encountered at Central University:

RGB: So I wouldn't say I'm more cynical, but I'm just more realistic because I felt spoiled for that experience in high school, and now it's like I'm getting hit with a reality of what it's like to be black in white America. So at one point during my college career, I was very regretful of coming here because I felt so frustrated, and I felt like there was so much friction and too much ignorance. But at the same time, I think that everything is done for a reason, and it was meant for me to be here 'cuz there's some of us that do need a rude awakening—because there are some of us that are too comfortable. I'm the type of person that probably would not have grown in terms of being realistic about white America and its mentality and racism and things like that. (Interview, spring 2004)

Even though she described her high school experience as diverse, RGB was not prepared for the consequences of racism, specifically, the ignorance of white students she experienced as a black undergraduate on a predominately white campus. Her frustration with being asked what she identified as "stupid questions" and the resulting cynicism that she developed proved burdensome to her and, at times, made her regret coming to Central University. RGB used the word *realistic* to express her changed outlook on the supremacy of whiteness and the resulting oppressions (such as ignorance regarding other races in America). This word, *realistic*, operates as a code. It allows RGB a positive way to talk about her altered perceptions. Being *realistic* may take the place of being outraged, saddened, or hurt. By using the word *realistic*, RGB takes responsibility for the racist encounters and her initial reactions to events. Not being *realistic* allowed the incidents to catch her off guard. RGB felt her new *realistic* perspective would provide her with tools to allay the consequences of racist encounters in the future.

RGB put her sociological imagination to work and placed these experiences into a discourse that highlighted their relationship to history and biography. She explained that taking this realistic approach allowed her to experience the complexities of "being black in a white America" such as ignorance, racism, and racist mentalities." Applying her sociological imagination to this discourse gave RGB a way to talk about what she perceived as the benefits of these incidents, namely (a) being shaken out of a comfort zone that left her unprepared and (b) growing in her understanding of what it means to be a *raced* body, to be black in white America. Broadening this talk helped her identify her school as a place where she belonged and helped her recognize that her biography and her school setting are connected to a larger historical and social context. This is evident in her use of the words *white America*, *racism*, and *social mentalities*.

Understanding that the reasons for being underprepared for college are facets of history, biography, and society is a form of cultural capital that helps black women undergraduates find academic success. Cheryl and Nicole did not let these discourses hinder their beliefs that they can "do the work." For RGB, this cultural capital made her more aware of racist mentalities, facilitated her locating her place in college, and helped her be on guard rather than "too comfortable" in a setting that can be hostile and frustrating. The stories these black women undergraduates told broaden the discourse about preparation for college beyond forms of traditional cultural capital (e.g., study abroad, standardized test preparation) to include societal issues of race and class and the material consequences of each.

Private and Public Issues in Higher Education: So-Called Acting White

The idea of *acting white* represents a public discourse about the educational lives of black students in school settings. Latimer (2004) discussed this concept, which she described as a "casualty of integration":

> One of the casualties of integration—and this is not to wax nostalgic about "separate and unequal education"—is the loss in many schools of the black tradition of academic excellence. Somehow scholarly, academic achievement is a Black and White (and Brown and Yellow, too) issue in the minds of some young people. Some black students have bought into the notion that the good grades, honors courses, speaking well, carrying books around, and being courteous is, well ... "acting White." (p. 191)

This concept, according to some black scholars, is what drives academic achievement or lack of performance on the part of black kids in school. This concept has at its core the suggestion that academic excellence is owned by whites and that black students who achieve are selling out or abandoning a black culture that has no claims to academic rigor or distinction. According to Latimer (2004) the "fear of being taunted by other black students" and of being accused of "acting white" if they reveal that they excel academically, informs how *some* black students choose to perform in school but not *all*. She points out that academic excellence is a tradition in black culture. Latimer (2004) further claims that "some smart students have always learned how to fit in and do their work" (p.192). She explains, "They act cool, clown around, but get their work done" (Latimer, 2004 p. 193). This assertion by Latimer challenges the notion that white students have a legitimate claim on academic success and that black student do not. So prevalent is this public discourse that scholars, writing about black students in school, take it up at varying degrees in their research, recognizing that it cannot be ignored. Many, like Latimer, challenge the validity of the notion of academic success as a "white thing" by showing the traditions of academic excellence in black educational culture (Hrabowski et al., 2002; Perry, Steele, and Hilliard, 2003; Willie, 2003).

The black women undergraduates in this study were familiar with this discourse of *acting white* and how it informs the larger discourse of black student achievement. Rather than succumbing to this discourse as an academic and social reality or a dichotomous admission that, yes, this applies to some students and not others, the women presented a broader discussion of the belief using knowledge provided by a sociological imagination, namely the ways this issue is connected to a specific biography, history, and society that confers privilege on some and creates obstacles for others. Some women challenged the applicability of the argument:

> Kayla: I think that is ignorance. I don't feel that because you want an education you're trying to be white. Everybody deserves an education. It has nothing to do with your background. There are black positive men and females going to school to better themselves, [and it's] not because they want to be a part of another culture; it's because they want to get further in life. I believe it is a stereotype, too, because you are leaving out all of the Caucasians who don't go to school. So what are they supposed to be? Black? (Interview, spring 2004)

For Kayla, this discourse of *acting white* represented "ignorance," supported stereotypes, and contradicted her experiences with other black women and men in college. She recognized the racist discourse as lopsided: white privilege allows those whites who do not choose college to avoid a similar representation. Nadia and Teena also drew upon their college life to dispute the legitimacy of this claim:

> Nadia: In college, I haven't experienced that as much, but people used to say that to me in high school and even middle school—that I acted white. Maybe it's con-

nected to the way we talk or, like, how we carry ourselves or if we don't have certain things on or because I don't live on the south side. I used to really struggle with that 'cuz I'm like, "I don't think I'm acting white at all." But I haven't found that in college as must just 'cuz I think there is more of a variety of peoples, so it's not like acting like anything. You're just acting like yourself. In college, everyone knows you're there to get a degree and you're not just handed a degree in any way. (Interview, spring 2004)

Teena: In my experiences here, black students are supportive of black students who are doing great things because it's uplifting our standing on campus. So if you are doing well, then that is helping us all because you are setting an example.... And in terms of academic success being a white thing? Then that means this is something white people can excel in, but black students can't. That's not how I see it. (Interview, fall 2004)

Teena revealed a collectivity among black college students and attainment aimed at "uplifting their status as students." Implicit in her argument is the idea that she and other black students need elevating on a campus where black student academic achievement may be invisible or ignored. Nadia was accused of *acting white* in high school, but she explained the accusation in terms of class-based social indicators that separated her from students who may have had less economically, not just academically. To Nadia, having a variety of people in college makes the discourse less powerful. In college, she explained, people can be themselves since they have a shared purpose of getting a degree and working hard is the expectation, since this degree must be earned. By challenging the generalizability of the way the attitude of *acting white* informs schooling for black students, the black undergraduate women interviewed broadened the discussion beyond deficit models of academic achievement.

In this discussion on *acting white*, the black women undergraduates made use of their sociological imaginations and elucidated the ways whiteness confers privilege in higher education:

Roe: We have our own schools, predominately black schools, but they're still set up in a white system, and in some form or fashion we have to assimilate to their beliefs and ideas about society in order to achieve different goals in education—employment and things like a career. And it's according to how the system is set up. It's like a template for everyone else. How do I define *whiteness*? Wow, power is what comes to mind, yeah, power and privilege and pure white. Everything is just right if you're white type of thing, that they control everything. (Interview, summer 2004)

Roe recognized white supremacy as an infiltrating system that steers individual behavior in society. In her dialogue, adapting to accommodate the primacy of whiteness—what she called *assimilating*—is a necessary strategy to employ for educational accomplishment. Roe understood that whiteness carries the power to create a template that even predominately black schools cannot ignore in training students for degree acquisition and employment. Roe's words gave an alternative meaning to *acting white*. She implied that there are adjustments she believes black women undergraduates must make to offset the power and privilege of whiteness in education. RGB also talked about this adjustment which she called *adapting white*:

> RGB: I wouldn't say *acting white*. I would say *adapting white*. In education there are their [white people's] views. Those views of dominance and oppression dominated in education. For instance, if you look in our history books, it's not just Eurocentric; it's just all about Europe. Like, if you let them tell it, life started in Europe 'cuz that's what they open up with. They might have a page or paragraph on Africa. It's usually referred to as a country (laugh) and the country is Egypt (laugh). In Asia, you hear about the Great Wall of China and Genghis Khan and how Europeans came in and took over things. Like, everything is in relation to Europe as the focal point. Nothing about Native Americans, they're just the people that happened to be there. So I feel like education is very much a manifestation of whiteness. (Interview, spring 2004)

RGB recognized that whiteness infiltrates the way history is taught in schools in the United States, and she described this curriculum as "dominant." While it is clear that RGB does not have access to every history class being taught in U.S. school systems or even at Central University, her familiarity with the texts used in the history courses she has participated in has left her with the perception that "education is a manifestation of whiteness." Her reference to adapting to whiteness implied that she, as a black woman undergraduate aware of multiple histories but having limited power in the classroom, had to participate in this education in a particular way in order to succeed. That is, like white students in the class, she had to read that history as it was presented, discuss it in class, and write about it in assignments. Her additional, invisible work, tied to her biographical and racialized connection to history, was to do this while negotiating it with how she felt about the exclusion of people of color from this core curriculum. RGB's struggle was evident in her laugh, not that she felt what she was saying was a laughing matter. She used serious terms such as *dominance* and *oppression* to name what she was describing, yet she laughed when she mentioned the misunderstandings she felt others have about Africa. Her laugh was an attempt to make the exclusion and what it represented, namely white supremacy in education, lighter than what, to her, it really is. Perhaps for RGB, it is a way to lighten the personal burdens connected to "adapting white."

Nadia described an additional type of privilege she feels comes with whiteness and what it means for black undergraduate women:

> Nadia: I think part of white culture is also affiliation in who and what you know. I know it's not necessarily nice to say, but when it comes to academics that's what pulls them through, and the simple fact that we don't always have this is why we

fail. We can all be on the same intelligence level, but just because you might know
the right people, you can take it to the next level and we'll just stay right here. (Interview, spring 2004)

Nadia may or may not have recognized that all white students do not have what
she called *affiliation*. That is, they may or may not have allies, networking systems, and other important contacts to help pave their way through college. This
is the case with many first-generation college students. While I wish I had asked
Nadia more about this belief, what is important in this discussion is that, right or
wrong, this idea of "who you know," for Nadia, is one of the ways whiteness
works as privilege in higher education. This is her way of narrating the discrepancies in the college achievements of black students and white students. Nadia
made it clear that she and other black students are intelligent. Yet in her understanding, for black students, intelligence is not enough. They have to find a way
to overcome the advantage of "knowing the right people" that she believes white
students have to help them make it in school.

This sophisticated comprehension of whiteness and privilege helped the
women connect the idea of *acting white* to powerful societal structures. Expanding the use of the sociological imagination and the understanding of frameworks
black women undergraduates use to understand the *acting white* discourse,
Cherry and RGB explained that this idea is connected to a particular history
where white people illegitimately claimed ownership of education and blacks
risked their lives for it:

> Cherry: A lot of black people feel that once they do [well in school], they deny who
> they are, and I don't get it. That makes no sense to me. Like, just because you got
> an education doesn't mean you forget where you came from. Historically, blacks
> couldn't get an education. It wasn't that we didn't want it. We just couldn't, and
> during slavery, if we even knew how to read was to get killed, so those things are
> still affecting us today. (Interview, spring 2004)

> RGB: To some people, acting white would be getting a good education, and that
> can be explained by our history here of being denied an education and white people
> being considered supreme so they got all of the supreme things. So to some people,
> any black person who has access to education and things like that would be acting
> white. I think that's a very archaic way of thinking. We come from greatness, so
> greatness is not white, you know; it's human. (Interview, fall 2004)

Cherry and RGB acknowledged that the history of slavery in the United States is
directly manifested in the way black students are educated today. According to
the women, it also explains why the talk connecting education to whiteness exists
in black communities today. Cherry alluded to the importance of not "forgetting
where you came from." RGB expressed the idea that "black people come from
greatness." Both of these ideas, in this conversation, signify that the discourse of
acting white in black communities is broader than just a disparaging of educa-

tion. This conversation is a manifestation of the ways white supremacy separates black culture from educational attainment and success. It represents the desire of a community to assert their worth outside of whiteness. In other words, "where you came from" is a valued space or, as RGB described, a "place of greatness." Thus, altering this discourse of *acting white* is one way of rejecting anything that appears to devalue that greatness.

This understanding of whiteness and privilege in education and its connection to history was crucial in challenging the discourse of *acting white* as deficit behavior on the part of black students. It gave the black women undergraduates in this study a way to discuss the accusation when it is hurled at them or others. Several students explained this from their perspectives:

Kimberly: Sometimes I feel like we've been brainwashed to think that only white people can be professional. Only white people can have a certain type of vocabulary or can be professional. I think we have been taught to think the worst of ourselves; so anything positive or different, we attribute to the white race. So then when we see our brothers and sisters maybe getting a degree or doing something, [we say] "Oh, they're acting white." because we feel threatened by it. And it's really sad because it limits us. Like, even with my experience in New York,[2] one of my students was like, "It's great that we have three black girls, but it doesn't really matter because you guys all act white." And I was like, "What does that mean?" I was in a professional environment. "How do you expect me to operate?" And it's just sad because we limit ourselves. Our kids are just limiting themselves because they feel they can't tap into this because it's not for them. (Interview, spring 2004)

Malikah: When I go back home, you know, because I am trying to get my... My goal is to get my masters eventually, possibly my PhD. So yeah, some black people call me, "Oh, she thinks she's white." when I go home. I don't think it is. I mean, we should all get a great educational experience. We should all have it on our agenda just like whites. I don't think that should be *whiteness*. When I hear that when I go home, I know that they didn't have the motivation or possibly the support that I have to come out of the crab box, so I just try to motivate them to do something, (pause) try to at least get a GED. That's not *whiteness*; it's just, you know, getting out of poverty. Education is one of the keys to success (Interview, fall 2004)

Lisa: On my mother's side, she was the only sibling that attended college. My aunt, she got pregnant at 16 and dropped out of high school; and her brothers didn't attend either. And they were always like, "Oh, she's a white girl." I don't know, it kinda bothers me. We want our voices heard, and if we're judging each other like that over ignorance, it's a shame. I mean, you want to help your people, but they'll reject the help you're giving them. Like, "Oh, you ain't from the hood; you just want to be white." or whatever, you know.

Interviewer: Why do you think they associated what your mother was doing with whiteness?

Lisa: I guess since the fact of slavery, 'cuz slaves couldn't read, it affected us as a whole. She probably had to go through even harder things, even compared to me, back then just to get to where she is. Even up to now because of the economic and social status of African Americans 'cuz it's really hard to go to college and pay for it. (Interview, spring 2004)

For Kimberly, Lisa, and Malikah this discourse of *acting white* is connected to issues of race and class, and getting a college education is a way of ensuring economic progress. They recognized that some Black individuals in their communities at home feel that a college education provides access to a lifestyle and a way of thinking and learning that systematically excludes black culture and that their commitment to obtaining a college degree is seen, by some, as a way of *acting white*.

When Kimberly, Malikah, and Lisa were accused of *acting white*, they felt the sting. This was evident when they spoke of trying to "help your people and having them reject the help" and of the "shame and sadness involved in the ways black people judge each other around education." These black women undergraduates also understood that the collective history of blacks, including the simultaneity of race and class oppression, informs the judgments made. This knowledge, combined with their lived encounters, gave the three black women undergraduates a way to understand that this discourse and those subscribing to it are part of a collective, social, and historical biography. This knowledge also elucidated the complex work needed to undo the negative material consequences of this issue, namely, an educational culture that offers only limited resources to black students, particularly those who are poor. This multifaceted and strategic work is a form of cultural capital that helps black women undergraduates traverse their place in this idea of *acting white* and highlights their efforts to succeed in school. Kimberly shared some of the complexity of this negotiation when she elaborated on her struggles after describing the earlier experience in New York:

Kimberly: Sometimes I feel like I do have to prove myself to white people. I do feel like my intelligence, my integrity, is questioned even before I open my mouth. So I feel like I'm definitely always in interview mode here. When it definitely shouldn't be like that, you know what I mean? Because I definitely feel I have to prove to the other. I know I should be here, but I have to let you know that I should be. I guess we really have to work on changing the culture of our institutions. I think a lot of our kids want to do well and some of them don't have the resources. Some of them don't even understand why they should be doing well, so we definitely need to deal with all aspects, not just the white man. Like it's really not that simple, you know? It's much deeper than that. (Interview, fall 2004)

Black undergraduate women in this study understood the complexity and depth of the attitude of *acting white*. They recognized that this conversation exists on a continuum of written dialogue about blacks and schooling. Rather than just being a general mindset subscribed to by black students to explain individual student behaviors, the women confirmed that this attitude exists in a history, biography, and society that is connected to race and class oppression. This knowledge led for a call, from Kimberly, to examine and change institutions that limit the success of black students.

Intersectional Talk and the Sociological Imagination

> Kimberly: Race and economic status is very important to me. I understand the issues of gender, but I'm focused more on race and education because I feel like, even though being a woman in today's society is like, maybe, a double negative. I feel being a black woman or being a black woman that comes from a poor family is an even greater burden to carry. (Interview, fall 2004)

> RGB: I find that me being a person of African descent, especially being on this campus, is more highlighted within this particular setting. Now, when I am in [my hometown] where everybody is black, then you know, me being a woman is more of an issue, but here it is definitely being black *and* being a woman. (emphasis hers) I don't necessarily let it intimidate me, but it's frustrating because either you are over-looked or looked to be the point person whenever people want the black woman's opinion. It's like, "There you go." (Interview, spring 2004)

Examining, with my prompting, academic discourses about preparation and *acting white* is not the only way the black women undergraduates in my study used their sociological imaginations. As seen in Kimberly and RGB's comments, they also used this cultural capital to develop an *intersectional* language to discuss their experiences in higher education. Even though they didn't name the talk as *intersectional*, some of the ways they narrated their stories showed their understanding that multiple features of their identities came into play simultaneously in their schooling experiences. Collins (2000) claims that, for black women, the knowledge that comes out of this intersectional understanding (a) provides empowerment based on our own experiences and (b) activates epistemologies that criticize prevailing knowledge and that "enable us to define our own realities *on our own terms*" (pp. 273, 274). For black undergraduate women, this talk also helped them identify the specific challenges of their journeys, which were connected to social locations; Kimberly identified these challenges as "a greater burden to carry," and RGB used the word *frustrating*. The next section will show how, in turn, this assists them in developing strategies and skills to navigate their way in school.

Race, Class, and Gender

Malikah relayed a story that showed one of the ways her socioeconomic status and race simultaneously impacted her schooling experience. Malikah was the only black woman in the nursing class she discussed:

> Malikah: This Saturday, I had class from 8:00–12:00 at Mercy. It was our first week, and I couldn't get there because the bus doesn't start until 9:00. I had planned to just walk because everyone I called [for a ride] couldn't do it. So I called public safety, and they said they would come but not on time. So I called my instructor to tell her that I'm gonna be late. Being that they're so strict in this program, it did look bad on me. But I know they [white nursing students] have cars. Their car is not broke down, and if it was broke down, they would have been able to fix it in a week or less because of their privilege, because they're more economically stable than I am. They're able to get there early, but because of my circumstances, I was late, and I know right then and there they are looking down at me to say, "Oh, she's black. Black people are always late." But I know that it goes further than that. I didn't have money to take a cab. There are no buses. I tried contacting people for a ride, and people couldn't make it here that early in the morning. I know next Saturday, I'd better be on time because, being that I am black, they watch every itsy-bitsy thing you do. I just want to be seen as another individual, but I'm not. I felt terrible that I had to be late for class because I know what they're saying. But I know it goes back to my car being stuck in that parking lot, and I can't fix it because I don't have no money to fix it. (Interview, spring 2004)

Malikah's class was located off campus and scheduled to start at 8:00 A.M. on a Saturday morning. This was a challenge, since Malikah did not have transportation. Her car was not working, and she did not have money to fix it, nor did she have cab fare. Malikah carried the extra burden of realizing that her lateness may be connected to her blackness in the minds of her teachers and classmates. She felt she was more noticeable, since she was the only black student in the class. She realized that the assumption that "black people are always late" was not accurate in her case but feared she would be read that way despite the inaccuracy. Malikah knew that she worked hard to get to class by "calling for rides and finally walking," and she also knew that the scrutiny of every "itsy-bitsy" thing she did as a black student put her in a precarious position for the next week.

In Malikah's perspective, her race and class do not render to her the privileges that she believes the race and class of her classmates render to them. Her race and class are simultaneous features of oppression that impact not just the practical aspects of her schooling life (e.g., getting to class) but also concurrently inform the social attitudes connected to her specific biography and history (e.g., that her lateness would be viewed as a racialized deficit).

Malikah further explained that the expense of college has been a burden for many of her friends of low socioeconomic backgrounds:

> Malikah: I've seen so many people that started out here with college who have dropped 'cuz they have faced financial issues. Like this whole floor [in the dorm], my friends are all gone because they weren't able to pay the tuition, and it's sad. They were all African Americans, too; four of them on this floor that weren't able to come back. (sigh) (Interview, fall 2004)

For Malikah, there was significance in the fact that her four friends that left school are all African American. Implicit in her talk is the understanding that the socioeconomic status that does not allow them to return is connected with their racial status. She understands that a lack of resources is most often connected to brown or black skin, just as she articulated the privileged economic status she assigned to white students who can get their car fixed right away. Malikah understands that in this instance the simultaneous and multiplicative convergence of race and class, as "interlocking forms of oppressions," forced these black students to withdraw from college. Her physical sigh indicated the collectivity of this burden.

Teena shared Malikah's sentiments that at times it is clear that her social class and race intersect to cause burdens in college:

> Teena: Sometimes it can be disheartening. There are a lot of things I wish I could have. Like right now, I don't have [a] car, and it's hard. Well, I will have one soon, but just like during school, it's been really hard for me because I am a journalism major and I do have to get up and go shoot stories; and so sometimes like, I'm like the only person or I'll be one of two people in my whole class who doesn't have a car, and then it's kind of like an inconvenience and so, um. I don't like to feel in anyway like behind anyone else in class or anything like that. So, that I think a lot of times, most of the time that is what reminds me like, man, you know. 'Cause, you know, my mom is doing everything that she can; like, if we had the money then I don't think it would be a thing. So, that's one thing that I deal with in terms of race. (Interview, spring 2004)

At first, it appears Teena is talking about a social-class issue related to her major; she acknowledged that she is not the only student in the class who does not have a car when she said, "I may be one of two." Teena's final comment, however, confirmed her understanding of the multiplicative nature of race and class. She stated that this challenge, which she discussed initially in classed terms, was an obstacle she deals with in terms of race. This injection showed that Teena believed that her not having a car and her mother's working to provide all she can and how this plays out in her course is about race and class and [is] connected to a collective biography and history.

Intersectionality refutes the idea that black women undergraduates live the same lives because they share social locations. Rather, it illuminates the complexities they live and negotiate as students. Shonte's discussion about race, class, and gender exposed some of the complexities:

> Shonte: Your race and gender stop you from doing a lot. Even though they try to say that it doesn't. You know with jobs, like; for example, I was just applying for a job for the summer and like a[t] one of the… It was a hotel job, and one of the hotels said, "We are seeking females." in bold letters, you know, "Female, Energetic." I'm like, "It shouldn't matter." but that's the effects; and of course, when you're black, you're always considered a step down, you know, always underneath other

people. And then, classism is something that's huge on this campus, and you know, *you know* your place. (emphasis hers)

Interviewer: How do you know your place?

Shonte: When, you know, I don't walk around with like a $500 bag and, you know, I'm struggling to buy my books, whereas other people just, their tuition is paid for. Even people in my race, they just, their parents can just write checks for their tuition, full checks for their tuition, and they still can go on vacations and things like that. They don't have jobs, you know, so I kind of knew, "Okay, this person is pretty much rich, and I am not."

Interviewer: How important are these issues in your educational life?

Shonte: I get a lot of grants and money from my school, you know, like there are a lot of programs out there. Maybe it's sad, but I reaped all of that because… I think it's wonderful that there are a lot of programs and all types of aid and things like that, that has basically made my college life a lot easier and a lot, a lot less stressful as far as finances are considered. (Interview, fall 2004)

Shonte recognized that race, class, and gender all come into play in her financial access to school and her relationships with students who have more material assets than she has. Shonte also understood that not all black undergraduate students have the same schooling experiences. Some may share the social locations of *black* and *woman*, but their social class may grant them privileges that she does not have. Adding to the complexities of an intersectional life is the revelation that, while Shonte recognized that she cannot "carry $500 bags or have her parents write checks for her tuition or go on vacations," she admitted that her social class made her eligible for financial aid that allowed her to get her college degree at a private university. The intersections of her social locations—particularly the "sad" state of "not being rich"—bring academic financial rewards that smooth certain aspects of her path in education (e.g., paying tuition) and simultaneously make some aspects of her schooling life harder (e.g., buying books, relating to students with more wealth). The conflicting consequences of low socioeconomic status that Shonte experienced as well as the challenges Teena and Malikah outlined support the idea that intersectional talk allows space for black undergraduate women to address the obstacles, intricacies, and contradictions of their schooling lives in their own terms. This expansion of dominant discourses is a form of cultural capital that motivates black women undergraduates to specific attitudes and actions. Malikah continued this discourse:

Malikah: That's been my life and the obstacles, I'm overcoming them and I'm gonna get there. Some people are easily turned away by their obstacles you know, but through the struggle, I've been keeping up with my grades, and I've been still pressing, and when you get a chance to look at this [her portfolio], you'll see how far I've been and how I just… I'm very determined. One of the keys to success, too, is just being determined and persistent, and that's what I've been. I don't care what happens, I'm holding on till I make it. It just makes me a stronger person, you know? And if you look at… This is my favorite quote: "Success is to be measured not so much by the position that one has reached in life as by the obstacles which he has overcome while trying to succeed." It's a Booker T. Washington quote. (Interview, fall 2004)

The academic language that allows for the simultaneity of oppressions, a deeper understanding of lived experiences, and the resulting strategies black women undergraduates use to maneuver school settings are a form of cultural capital that fosters success in higher education. As Nadia stated, "I really value that I am African American *and* that I'm female, and I will use my advantages to the ump-teenth power to prove that I have my stuff together."(emphasis hers)

Conclusions

Black undergraduate women showed that their sociological imaginations en-hanced their understanding of their experiences and their place in higher educa-tion. It was a theoretical framework that guided their way of thinking about educational inequity (Mills, 1959). This idea allowed them to understand that their biographies—their lived experiences—are situated in a specific historical and social context in which their overlapping social locations can simultaneously produce privilege and oppression. This knowledge gave them a way to talk about public and private issues as related to their educational lives that does not focus on them as deficient. It also provided ways for the women to identify and discuss aspects of cultural capital that higher education institutions often ignore but that the women find necessary to succeed. By expanding academic discourses about their lives as undergraduates, they claim their place as contributing members of academic communities.

The black undergraduate women presented in this chapter realized that there were ways in which they were not prepared academically for life in higher education. They discussed this as a systemic issue that reflected the material con-sequences of their collective history and biography with other blacks who, for years, have been denied the privilege of equal access and equal resources in edu-cational settings. These women hold their institutions accountable with their critique. The women also took responsibility and were willing to do their part and "work harder" to make up for inequity. They did not believe this discourse to be an automatic referendum on their desire or ability to succeed.

The black women undergraduates explained that they saw academic success and educational excellence as black cultural realities, not as something belonging only to whites. They presented sophisticated talk about the attitude of *acting white* and explained how this attitude is situated in a collective biographical, his-torical, and social context that makes it racialized and classed in intricate ways. The intersectional talk of black women undergraduates made it clear that they understood that this context underscores the notion that oppressions are simultaneous. This chapter revealed that the multiple ways black women undergraduates utilize sociological imagination to facilitate strategies for college success are indeed a form of cultural capital that supports their success in higher education. Nicole's words describe this revelation:

> Nicole: I think just knowing like the history and where we've come from and seeing that through all the struggles we have made throughout history, we're kinda still here standing you know, despite everything. So, it's like I have pride in being a part of a group that's gone through so much and hasn't given up and that's still willing to fight. (Interview, spring 2004)

CHAPTER FOUR

Cultures Clash

Black Women Undergraduates Negotiate Oppression

> Lisa: I just think we have to promote ourselves as much as we can and break those stereotypes and those assumptions about who we are. We're not lazy. We're not uncouth and things like that. (Interview, spring 2004)

> Kayla: If we don't do it [challenge negative stereotypes about black students] who will? I mean somewhere we have to be recognized because as long as you, I mean, there are so many people who complain why we're not there. If you don't do something, you're never going to get there. If you don't open your mouth and speak your feelings and stand strong on it and don't worry about what the next person feels about how you stand up for you and your own people... If you're gonna complain, do something. If you're not going to do nothing, stop complaining. That's how I feel. We need to let people know that we're just as good as you feel you are. I'm not gonna say better, we're just as good, and we're just as smart. We're just as dedicated to whatever it is we want to do. So they need to know. They need to know our culture. They need to know what we stand for. So it's just that we need, we want to be heard. But you have to speak up. I feel it's important to speak up. If you don't speak up, it's a waste of time complaining. (Interview, spring 2004)

Kayla and Lisa responded to the questions, "Why do you believe participation in black student organizations is important?" They both explained that having a forum to "speak up without worrying about what others think about you" is necessary to combat stereotypes about black students. In Kayla and Lisa's perspectives, black students cannot just go to school and ignore the prevalence of racism. Kayla and Lisa both described an atmosphere of *us* versus *them* that puts a particular type of pressure on black students to perform. It is Kayla's belief that black students must speak up for themselves; if no one else will take on the responsibility. She proposed a way of speaking out that shows that black students are "just as good and just as smart" as white students who attend their colleges and universities. Kayla's suggestion also called for the presentation of knowledge about black cultures and values to those who "need to know," namely, white students, faculty, and staff.

Kayla and Lisa are not alone in their adamant stance that black students have to "stand strong" and "promote themselves"; they "want to be heard." For black undergraduate women, the intersectional nature of their lives—that is, the way their race, class, gender, and other social locations converge and intersect with history and society—makes their challenge to "stand strong" and "be heard" both complex and specific in their higher educational settings. Black under-graduate women face challenges from oppressions (e.g., negative stereotypes) that stem from society's definitions and depictions of who they are as humans and as students. Their work in higher education calls on them to negotiate and strategize their way through a system, which by design, devalues them and does not recognize their culture as significant. The women must navigate and maneu-ver through the resulting cultural clashes.

I am using the term *cultural clash* with intent to describe the negative ideolo-gies, attitudes, and resulting exchanges black women undergraduates encounter in school that are related to their race, class, and gender. These cultural clashes demand that these women choose to challenge racist beliefs and approaches in classrooms and curriculum, find ways to deal with bias incidents on campus, and live with the consequences of campus diversity polices. These choices have spe-cific consequences. The ideals, standpoints, and interactions that fuel the clashes are steeped in the history of enslavement and prohibitions for blacks seeking education, in a social climate that renders black students inferior, and in the black women undergraduates own biographies. Cultural clashes present oppres-sive obstacles that the informants in this study explained they must overcome to succeed in higher education.

Speaking Up and Being Heard

Kayla, in the earlier quotation, indicated the need for black students to speak up and help white people learn who black students are as individuals, learn about black culture, and learn truths to combat stereotypes about black students in higher education. Nicole explained that being in college with black students who have accepted this call has helped her learn this strategy:

> Nicole: I've learned to stand up for myself as being black. Having more blacks around me, it is more accepted, and I have more of a support system in doing it whereas in high school it's just me standing alone. So I guess a lot of the time, I was afraid to stand up. Here, I have more people who are willing to stand up along with me.
> Interviewer: In what ways do you support each other?
> Nicole: I think just as far as being there when anybody needs anything, you know? Any time there is a bias-related incident, everybody's always willing to rally and it's not just one or two people. It's always a lot, at least 100 students who are willing to stand together and fight for something or fight for the rights they feel they have on campus. (Interview, spring 2004)

The support of other black students on campus, who took on the responsibility outlined by Kayla, to "speak up, teach others, and stand strong," helped Nicole learn how to "stand up for herself as a black student." For her, the answer to the question, "If we don't, who will?" was clear. As associates on campus, Nicole chose black students who accepted this challenge and who, she later explained, taught her "more about her black culture than she learned in all of her years of schooling at home."

The black women undergraduates in this study gave multiple examples showing the ways they accepted the responsibility to "speak up, be heard, and be strong." Their stories also show the complexity of this process. One of RGB's chances to speak up came when a teaching assistant in a recitation section for a fine arts course singled out RGB and a Latina woman undergraduate for a particular conversation after class:

RGB: Oh! Freshman year I was in arts class, Fine Arts 106. It was me and maybe two other black people. In my recitation [section], I think I was the only black person in recitation and then there was a Latina girl.

Interviewer: Out of how many?

RGB: In my recitation [section]? Maybe 20 people in my recitation, but in the actual class it was mostly white and there was maybe 10 blacks and Latinos and that's out of about 100 students. So in the recitation [section], our teacher was what I call a white Latino. He was blond haired and blue eyed, but he was Puerto Rican. And this was in the second semester of my freshman year. After the recitation was over he asked both me and the Latina girl to stay after to talk to him. He first started off by saying, "You know, you two are some of the top students in my course, and you are doing very well; but I don't see that happening with the other black and Latino students that we have in our class and that I have in my recitations, and I wanted to know why that is."

And at the time I was very, very, very naïve.... I started explaining, and I was like, "Well you know, I think it's mainly because, well first of all, this class is call[ed] Fine Arts but its only fine arts for Europeans. Nobody else is included in this, and so a lot of times when we don't feel included, we're not interested. And so there may be some ways that you can incorporate art from Africa, art from black America, um art from Latin America, that would, you know, interest us better because, you know, we're just, a lot of us aren't interested." And the girl next to me, I noticed she was pretty silent, and because I was always into explaining things to people, I felt the need to do that with this professor, and it wasn't until after I left that I was like, "What he did right now was really wrong!" And I just felt so stupid because I should have just called him on it but I was just, I was just very naïve.

He never addressed it again after that because I think he realized from our demeanor and my response to him that this wasn't necessarily a problem with the black students in the class, and that it was a problem with the curriculum itself and the mindset of the professors. And I guess he wasn't willing to deal with that because, you know, the class just went on as usual. Afterwards, I approached the professor and I told her, not in particular of that incident, but I told her, "I really feel like there is a lot missing from this class, and if you're gonna call it Fine Arts then you should cover fine arts from all peoples you know, not just European people." And she was like, "Yeah, that's something that's being debated in the art world and is currently being discussed in the art world." And I'm like, "Debated and discussed?

What is there to discuss?" She never really gave me a straight answer, and she was just like, "I understand what you're saying" and just kept up with the class.

Interviewer: You said that you felt like with this particular teaching assistant, you should have confronted him. What would you have said?

RGB: I would have probably told him, first of all, "I think it's very unprofessional of you to approach two people in such a manner and ask about why other people of our particular background are not doing well in your class. We don't have recitation with those people and I think it's very unfair to us for you to ask us such a question. And if we… If it was the other way around, if it was a mostly black class and you had a handful of white students, would you have confronted one white student and asked why the rest of the white students aren't doing well? Just think about things and the position that you put people in when you ask those kinds of questions." And I mean I wouldn't have necessarily been disrespectful. I would have just let him know it made, it made me feel very uncomfortable and put us both in a position where we felt singled out and like we had to speak for other people who were not doing well in the class. So to act like the fact that we weren't doing well had something to do with us being black or Latina, you know; in the large scope of things, it did because we're not being represented in the curriculum. But in the way, I don't think that he, he didn't even think of it from the sense of "we're doing something wrong and that's why." He just thought of it as being deviant, not smart enough, and you know and "You two seem to be getting it, and I don't know what's wrong with the rest of them." You know? It was that kind of tone, so I would have—knowing the kind of person I am now and how outspoken I am now—I would have confronted and responded to him in a different way. (Interview, spring 2004)

In Fine Arts 106, RGB and her Latina classmate were given the added pressure of being representatives of their race, not just students enrolled. RGB indicated that at the time, she felt she *had* to talk to this teaching assistant who pulled her aside and "confronted" her about the progress of other black and Latino students. Her use of "confronted" to describe the encounter made clear her assessment of the encounter as hostile. RGB connected the questioning and her need to respond to race and power. She described the teaching assistant as a "white Latino" and specifically noted his blue eyes and blond hair. The physical appearance of this authoritative figure was significant in RGB's narrative. She wanted to make it clear that, even though the teaching assistant was Puerto Rican, he had *white-skin privilege*. RGB told this part of her story in a way that showed she believed this privilege informed his behavior.

RGB had to negotiate her response when she was asked by her teaching assistant to "explain why other black students in her fine arts class were not performing well academically." RGB's cultural capital, namely her ability to tie the issues of academic success to larger societal issues, allowed her to "speak up" to this teaching assistant and, soon after, the course professor. She spoke to each of them about the lack of representation of groups other than whites in the course content. Later RGB felt conflicted about this encounter with the teaching assis-

tant. She contends that "knowing the person she is now, she would have spoke
to him about how wrong it was for him to single out both her and the Latina
woman for this discussion." RGB's experience confirms that the process of
"speaking up and being heard" can be complex and dynamic. As a black undergraduate woman, she cannot just go school and be a student. The positioning of
her race, class, and gender on her predominately white campus, as intersecting
features of identity, means that she will always be a representative of her race on
her campus. RGB understood why this particular *gaze* occurred and tied it to
racism; that is why her teaching assistant asked her and the Latina student to
speak for others of the same race. Her work was negotiating that gaze with her
desire to "speak up and be heard" and her sense of fairness.

Earlier, Kayla explained that part of "speaking up and being heard" for black
students involved letting others "know what you stand for" since black students
are often placed in a perceived position of defense by the materializations of racism. Kimberly described a cultural clash related to race that caused her to speak
up and defend the dignity of black students:

> Kimberly: Something I could talk about is just the fact that people that work in ad-
> ministrative positions at Central [University] have a problem with black students.
> They really do. They don't know how to talk to us. They often talk down to us until
> we put them in their places, and then they say, "Oh, you have an attitude." And it
> annoys me because I feel like, oh my gosh, like, we went to a [named campus build-
> ing] party on Saturday and they treat us like animals. I really believe so. Do you
> know how many cops were out there?... And so everybody goes to [the food court]
> afterwards. You have to cross the street to go there. This white cop yells, "Get out of
> the street!" This was his first time saying it, so it wasn't like he said it before and we
> ignored it. So I went up to him, and I'm like upset, and I went up to him, and I was
> like, "You know, sir, I really don't appreciate the way that you're handling us. We're
> not animals. We're students here. We pay tuition, as well, and we didn't disrespect
> you or your authority, so there is no reason for you to treat us like that." [He said,]
> "I'm not here to be nice, da, da, da. I have a job to do." I was like, "I'm sure, but I
> really believe that if you are on [a local street where white students at Central Uni-
> versity congregate] you would not have treated students with that kind of disre-
> spect." And he just walked away, and I said, "Don't just walk away from me. That's
> very disrespectful. If I did that, you would be totally offended, and I'm offended."
> And it just took me right out of party mode. I don't know. I'm just angry all the
> time. (laugh) That's my problem.
>   Interviewer: One student told me they bring police dogs to the parties.
>   Kimberly: Yeah! I wonder what can be done. I was just actually thinking about
> that. Like, who can I speak to? The chancellor is meeting with [scholarship recipi-
> ents], and I am going to ask if I can speak to her about it. (Interview, fall 2004)

To Kimberly, the police officer's actions and words were degrading to the black
students involved in this incident. She perceived the officer's treatment of black
students leaving the party was related to race and class. She believed that white

students, in a similar situation, would not have received the same treatment and, as a result, felt the need to defend the rights of black students on campus. For example, Kimberly told the officer that the party goers did not behave in a way that was disrespectful, indicating that the students had done nothing to warrant being yelled at. Additionally, Kimberly said to the officer, "We pay tuition here." She used this class-related defense to challenge an assumption that all black students are educational charity recipients benefitting undeservedly from affirmative action and government funding, an argument used to make their presence on campus seem less powerful or valuable. The officer may or may not have held this common conjecture. What is important is that this assumption *must* be a part of Kimberly's defense. Her race and class do not allow her the luxury of pretending these ideas do not inform every experience she has at Central University, particularly when they are oppressive. Kimberly felt a need to let this officer know that she and her black college-mates deserved as much access to campus settings without harassment as any other student who had paid to attend. She took a risk and spoke to the officer. Since the officer did not indicate that he would change his behavior and instead "walked away," Kimberly elected to "stand up and be heard" again by taking the matter to the school's chancellor.

In Alana's narrative, answering the call to speak up included addressing a classroom curriculum that fostered inequities. She explained:

> Alana: In a lecture hall of 160 people and I'm the only [black] person there and the only voice and the only [black student], you know, and we're skipping over the fact that the Dutch colonized so many places. Why are we skipping over that? That is history, and it is European history whether it's wrong or it's right, it still is, you know? And you're expected not to be smart enough to get that.
> Interviewer: So what do you do in those settings?
> Alana: You're that role piece. It's up to you.
> Interviewer: What do you do?
> Alana: I am that voice! I will get up and say what I have to say. It took me a while though. I'm not gonna say when I first got here I was able to do it 'cuz it's a mind game. If you're not able to play the mind games, then you won't make it. (Interview, spring 2004)

One of the roles Alana chose while a student in this classroom was to verbally address classroom curriculum that ignored the ways European dominance has historically informed the lives of nonwhite groups. Alana was affronted by the "skipping over" of historical cultural knowledge, claiming that the reason it happens is because she, as "the only black student, is not expected to be smart enough" to know the exclusion occurs. In Alana's view, this omission was not just about the professor's skin privilege, the professor's choice of material to include in the course, or the Eurocentric curriculum in this course at Central University, even though each of these could be an analysis of what was occurring in her class. Alana believed the exclusion of particular histories was a symptom of a larger issue. She connected this to a discourse regarding the intelligence of black students and, similar to Lisa and Kayla, indicated an *us* versus *them* atmosphere that dominated her classroom. Alana believed that white students or professors perceived that she, the only black student in the class, would not have the knowledge and skills to recognize the omission. Contained in Alana's perspective is the notion that the omission is deliberate, and her white professor and classmates are not concerned with the absence. In fact, there may be white students who are just what Alana fears she will be perceived as: they may not know an omission is occurring. What is important is that Alana read this in these raced terms. This reading drove her to action and Alana spoke out. Speaking up may have forced those in her class into a more inclusive consciousness around history, but for Alana, it proved that she, the only black student in the class, is in fact a smart student. Alana explained that she learned to "play this mind game" out of necessity. It is what she must do to "make it" in higher education. For Alana, this speaking out was about more than the exclusions in history class. It was a strategy she used to defy stereotyped ideas about black student intelligence and to challenge educational curriculum that was not inclusive.

Alana later explained that making this choice to speak out had consequences:

> Interviewer: So what happens when you stand up in this class and say what you have to say?
>
> Alana: You get a lot of different reactions. You get the "big mouth girl" or you get the "Wow, I didn't know that." You get a lot of different reactions. Like, you know, you almost feel the heat as soon as you open the door and you've had classes with these people before because they expect you to be that person who will say something, for you to be the person who will either disagree with the teacher or professor or only speak on certain issues that involve either Africans or people for West African, East Africa, South Africa, you know, what I mean, Brazil all these places. And they're like, "Oh, well, she only speaks about issues when it has to do with race or ethnicity or culture." (Interview, spring 2004)

Choosing to speak at times caused Alana to be labeled as a "big mouth girl." In some instances, her classmates expressed an appreciation for the information she provided, but they also made it clear that they *expected* her, the only black woman in the class, to speak in classroom conversations about race, culture, and ethnicity. Alana implied that speaking up about these particular issues made any other talking she did in class invisible to her classmates whose naïve assumptions were that these issues were about the other, in this case, Alana and not themselves. Alana sensed that the students labeled her as a "big mouth girl" because she was always outspoken when issues of race, culture, and ethnicity came up in her class. Her speaking out forced them to consider topics they may otherwise have ignored.

Roe described another situation that included the decision of whether or not to speak up in class when there was a conversation related to race, ethnicity or culture. She explained this complicated decision:

> Roe: Our professor was a person of color. She was from India, and we had a conversation about different clans and caste systems and things like that. And one of the white students said "Oh, I would be part of the Brahmin caste." As if, because she was white, she assumed that she would. She's that caste automatically, and Brahmin is one of the highest casts in the Indian system.... She was presenting it as, if you were nonwhite, you would be in a caste under that. So I was like, "Okay." And those are the things that we come across that are sometimes difficult for me to deal with, and I had to really think about how I respond to situations like that because it not only... (pause) The thing about being black is that you don't get to represent yourself; you represent everyone else, you know, in your response.
> Interviewer: Did you respond?
> Roe: I didn't because I have issues with, um... I'm working on being tactful. (laugh) So, sometimes in some situations, I deem it unnecessary for me to say anything because I know my response will reflect on every other black, African American woman that comes behind me. They always think, "Yeah, ignorant black woman." And then that stigma just seems to hang around, and it just passes along. You never view the individual. They view us as a group. That's a problem for me; it really is. (Interview, summer 2004)

Roe's perception of "representing the entire black race" when you speak is common in discussions regarding black students speaking up in college classrooms (Feagin, Vera, & Imani, 1996). Roe claimed that "speaking up" in this class was connected to issues of race that made her experience in her class "difficult." It is clear that Roe felt a need to speak. She identified the white student's hypothetical claim of membership in the highest caste in India as a postulation steeped in entitlement and white privilege. Roe also felt the responsibility of representation. She believed that her reaction would have been read as the response of the collective, and that if she was not tactful in her comeback, this would also reflect on "every other African American woman that came behind me." This quagmire caused Roe, in this instance, to remain silent. Roe later explained that when she does make the choice to speak up, it is because she accepts this role as part of her work at a predominately white university:

> Roe: I can choose, it's a choice in whatever I do in my life, and I've chosen to attend a predominately white university knowing that it was not going to be an easy role to fulfill. And it's not an unbearable one, and it's acceptable if you choose to deal with these situations that may arise. (Interview, summer 2004)

Roe tied this acceptance to the responsibility she feels she has to the black community that is different from the representational responsibility ascribed to her in the classroom:

Roe: I know that if I look at me as being a single black woman in a white society, this is how I will move forward. This is definitely a way I can do that, [get an] education in a prominent university, obtain a degree and hopefully open doors for other black women that are coming through. Although I'll have to go through some things to achieve what I need to achieve to help others; I can open doors for them. (Interview, summer 2004)

Making the choice to attend a predominately white university placed Roe in a setting where the challenges to speak up are a large part of her college work. In her classroom, deciding whether or not to confront privilege is a dilemma she must negotiate. Roe was angry with the racist and class-based presumptions made by the white student in her class. Roe must balance that anger and her desire to challenge white privilege with her need to protect the collective reputation of black undergraduate women. Learning this skill of choosing when to speak out and challenge inequity or oppression and using it strategically is a form of cultural capital that draws upon the sociological imagination. Roe recognized that because of racism, the bodies of black students and Black student behaviors are read in specific ways, and that, in this instance, an angry response would reflect negatively on her and other black students who come behind her. Roe understood that her body is part of a collective community that has worked hard to establish a place in educational institutions and that participation in the institution is challenged by issues of race, class, and gender.

In this instance, Roe chose to remain quiet. This choice was one she felt would facilitate her desire to break down doors for others who come behind her. This choice also limited the power of the "responsibility of representation" ascribed to her by her classmates. When she speaks, it is for her own reasons, not theirs.

Malikah, too, described an encounter related to her race and class that caused her to speak up to defend what she felt was "her right" as a student:

Malikah: I had a big incident when I went to the bookstore. I have a bookstore account so I didn't pay for it [the bookstore account] completely. You know, [I didn't] pay the total before the semester started. So even though my bookstore total wasn't paid for, I had already notified financial aid to pay for it. So, usually when you have a bookstore account, you can get anything you want at the bookstore. So I went to get two [school] book bags that were on sale. When I went to pay for the bags, the card declined, so the lady at the cash register called upstairs at the bookstore account[ing] [office] and [someone there] said, "Her card expired." And I said "No! I want to talk to her on the phone. The card is under financial aid, and they're gonna pay for it, so can you please put this through?" So I guess she called financial aid and [someone in] financial aid said, "Yeah, we're gonna pay for it." So the woman [from the accounting office] ordered the lady at the cash register, "She can only get books. Don't give her anything but books." So I rushed upstairs and said, "These bags are on sale. I need them." She said, "Nope, you only get one bag." I said "No." I had to call the supervisor.

Interviewer: Why?

Malikah: Well, I said, "Excuse me, I want two bags. Why should I be restricted to just one bag?" [She said,] "You didn't pay your bill. You had all summer to pay your bill, and you didn't pay your bill," talking to me like I was a criminal. "You didn't pay your bill, so you only get books." I said, "Ever since I've been here, when I have a bookstore account, I pick up books and pens or whatever. That is what the bookstore account is for." And I had to call the supervisor of the whole building because I was like, "This is not right. I'm not going to go through this, and after that [the lady at the register] put it through." She said, "Go ahead and get your two bags." And I called the supervisor and told her that she was talking to me as if I were a criminal.

Interviewer: And so what did the supervisor say?

Malikah: She said that she would talk to her about her conduct. That [the cashier's] behavior is not acceptable, and she would talk to her about it, and I guess she did.

Malikah: She was a pig. You should have seen the way she was blowing at me and talking to me. You could see the racism there. I was like, "Oh no, not because I am black. I am a respectful person. Don't talk to me like that, and I *will* (emphasis hers) go get my two bags." That hurt me so much. (Interview, fall 2004)

Like many students at Central University, Malikah relied upon her financial aid to help her buy the materials and books she needed for school. Often students like Malikah need the supplies before the aid shows up on their financial record. The financial aid office often approves a purchase for a student based on the knowledge that the funds to cover the purchase will be available, just as that office did for Malikah. To Malikah, the woman at the register who tried to prevent her from buying her bags was overstepping her bounds and trying to control and punish her for not paying her bill at the bookstore. Malikah connected this control to racism and class oppression and felt the need to defend her character as a black woman. She described herself as "respectful" and "not criminal" indicating that only a disrespectful person or one who committed a crime deserved that kind of treatment.

Malikah felt she was being thrifty by buying the bags she needed to carry her schoolbooks while they were on sale. Yet, Malikah had to negotiate her right to make decisions about her own finances and need as related to her schooling with the cashier's implied discourse about her race and class, namely, that she was neglecting her bill and trying to buy something she did not deserve. Despite the "hurt" Malikah felt during this encounter she chose to speak up for herself and spoke with the bookstore supervisor. Malikah also decided that she was going to get her two bags because she knew she deserved the opportunity to purchase them. She would not let the cashier's opinion of her take that knowledge away from her. Malikah was determined not to let what she saw as the cashier's race and class bias control how she felt about herself.

Black undergraduate women in this study have taken the challenge to stand up, be strong, and be heard to combat cultural clashes they faced in higher education. The women recognized that there were risks involved in doing so, including being "invisible and labeled as a big mouth, being ignored, and being hurt." They also recognized the benefits of having each other as a support system to teach the skills involved in speaking up. As black undergraduate women grow and progress, and as they practice speaking out, *how* they do so will continually change. The skills they accrue and the strategies that evolve as they make decisions associated with this work are a form of cultural capital that supports their success in school.

The women spoke up and were heard in multiple ways and with multiple goals. Each woman's story recognized this process as part of her work as a raced, classed, and gendered being that must deal with cultural clashes in higher education as they occurred. This was described as a way to "make it" in higher education and a way to "smooth a path for other black students that will come behind them." This analysis of the encounters they described reveals that these women can never just be students. Their attention to discourses about them and their negotiation of oppressive encounters that led to their taking the risk of standing up and speaking out, was a strategy they used to successfully navigate the racism they faced. This is a form of cultural capital necessary for their social and academic success. Roe explained that these skills "help you through because you know when you leave here you definitely take some things with you. You know what you've gone through and you also take a little piece of paper that says, "Yeah, I made it through" (Interview, summer 2004). The skills associated with speaking up and being heard proved useful as black undergraduate women described the ways they tackled critical systems related to diversity and multiculturalism in their schools.

Talking about Diversity and Multiculturalism in Higher Education

> Kimberly: You don't need a diversity pamphlet if you have diversity, so let's not kid ourselves you know what I mean? I feel like we have the ingredients for a nice-tasting meal here, but we haven't figured out how to put it together. (Interview, fall 2004)

Institutions of higher education, for the most part, recognize there is diversity among the students they are commissioned to serve. This diversity includes race and ethnicity, ability, socioeconomic status, sexual orientation, and other identity markers. Like Kimberly explained, the differences are like "ingredients for a nice-tasting meal." Colleges and universities attempt to address this multicultural condition in their practices and policies, particularly since affirmative action laws demand not only equal access to education but also equal resources, equal quality, and equal support to scaffold college success (Duarte and Smith, 2000; Bowen et al., 2005). To meet this lofty goal and in an attempt to "put together a tasty meal," colleges and universities often implement programs, policies, and activities designed to support the needs of an assortment of learners both academically and socially. These practices, policies, and activities often carry in their titles and themes the terms *diversity* and *multiculturalism.*

The black women undergraduates in this study explained ways the institutional use of multiculturalism and diversity initiatives informed their work in higher education. They provided their definitions of the terms *diversity* and *multiculturalism.* They also outlined the ways they felt those definitions inform their schooling lives. The black women undergraduates also provided critiques as they evaluated the intended goals of multicultural and diversity initiatives at their schools and as they compared these initiatives to their real-life experiences.

Defining the Terms

The term *multiculturalism* is used in multiple ways in academia (Banks & Banks, 2004; Duarte & Smith, 2000; Grinter, 2000). In this study, the black women undergraduates provided their own definitions of the term when I asked, "How do you define *multiculturalism?*" Their responses ranged from simple ideas of acceptance to more complex ideas connected to larger societal issues:

> Jessica: I would say just being open, I guess, to other cultures and accepting other things; not being just self-centered, into one culture. (Interview, spring 2004)

> Alex: Many cultures—a big ole bowl of cultural soup. (Interview, summer 2004)

> RGB: I believe that, in this society, *multiculturalism* means people from different backgrounds coming together and saying, "Oh, you eat rice and I eat chicken, that's cool. We're together because we like different foods," and not acknowledging the history and the oppression and the plight of people along with that. Just highlighting the good and singing "We Are the World." It's a very *Sesame Street* kind of thing. It's like, "The only thing that makes us different is that you're a different color from me, and that's it." I believe that, you know, race in itself, this whole idea of different races among humans is unreal and is a construction; however, the effects of that idea are with us today and they affect how we live, how we interact with one another, and oppression. So oppression is very real; so to just act like, you know, to just talk about the good things that differentiate people and just ignore the bad parts of history and ignore the fact that we still live in a white society that promotes white culture and white ideas and Eurocentrism in every aspect of our society, is not truly being multicultural but just putting a Band-Aid over the bigger problem. Lots of times in uplifting multiculturalism, people play down pro-blackness. (Interview, spring 2004)

> Leviticus: Like, especially at this school, you hear *multicultural*, you hear *diversity*, and that just means they have one person from somewhere else, and that makes the

school special. *Multiculturalism* and *diversity*, they just use them as keywords to say, "We're not just white people." To me, that's all that means. When they say it in vice president[ial] addresses and chancellor addresses and school initiatives, they are just saying, "We're just a bunch of mixed-up folks, and we have more than just white folks here, so please come to our school because (sarcastically) you'll find your kind here." (Interview, spring 2004)

Kimberly: I would say being in a state of mind where you're accepting and open and able to integrate. Not even really integrate, but being able to respect different people's culture and different perspectives. Not necessarily saying, "I don't even feel like you need to incorporate it into yours because then I feel like you lose your culture by this," but just respecting and having appreciation [for other cultures]. (Interview, fall 2004)

An examination of the definitions revealed that the women recognized that the term *multiculturalism* can simply mean "more than one culture." Most of the women defined the term as "a coming together of cultures that involved respect and appreciation for others." Kimberly and RGB also explained that this "coming together" should not include integration that forces black culture to the margins and allows it to be lost. Teena echoed this idea of black culture being lost in multicultural initiatives and gave an example of how this phenomenon informed a facet of her life at school:

Teena: *Multiculturalism* is—I tend not to like that word at all. I just don't like that multiculturalism thing 'cuz sometimes I think this whole multicultural rhetoric is just like, "Okay, bring in everyone. We can have black people and Jewish people and Asians, and we're all going to come together, and it's gonna be great." And what it is, is fusing everyone into this kind of dominant culture here. So you have all the groups represented, but then what they are losing is that kind of multiculturalism because they [various groups] lose things in order to appease the whole idea behind multiculturalism. Like, everyone can come together, and this is great.

But you know, some things need to be, I don't know, I just think that sometimes we need to be separated. Not separated in terms of, I don't know I just, like, we need to be, to define ourselves so that we don't lose what we gained in history. I will give you a perfect example. I'm the co-coordinator of [a campus dance company]. Now when [the dance company] on this campus was founded, it was a black dance group. Why did we need a black dance group? Because the dance groups that were here were not addressing the needs of black dancers. They wanted people who were doing ballet only. So we needed this black dance group so that the people who wanted to dance African, who wanted to dance to hip-hop, who wanted to dance jazz, and different things could do that. They have a space to do that. Now, over the years, people well. One thing about [the dance company] is it's getting whiter, and you have to constantly remind people in this group that, even if you are a white person and you were accepted into this group because you do that well, you have to remind them, this is not becoming a multicultural group for everyone to do their own thing. *This is a black dance group.* (emphasis hers) We have had to do this because historically we just... You know what I mean? Like, why we all want to be multiculturally together now? Do you know what I mean, like, "No!" (emphasis hers) Based on our history, we've had to organize and have our own separate group so that our culture could flourish and grow and have a place to be shown and seen.

So now, because some white people who consider themselves to be liberal minded or race conscious or whatever decide that they want to join this group; that doesn't mean that our goals are going to change. Because then what happens is you have a group with this diverse group of people, and what happens to the black dance? Then you don't see black dance, anymore. You see a fusion or a mesh of a white to rock-n-roll or ballet. Then black dance is lost. So, it's important to me 'cause I don't really buy into the multiculturalism thing because it's like saying that "one day everyone's going to be the same." I think that's what's underlying this whole *multi*-thing. I don't think that everyone will have a place. It will be, you know, some groups that will and others that won't. (Interview, spring 2004)

For Teena, the idea of multiculturalism diminishes features of blackness and has a goal of "everyone being the same." In Teena's estimation, this sameness would be an absorption into a dominant white culture. She explained that historically and in her time at school as the coordinator of the dance group, black people have had to carve their own space in order to let their culture thrive and be visible. Teena understood the power associated with whiteness and felt that multiculturalism, in this case, forced an integration that resulted in a cultural clash. This cultural clash required her to stand up and be heard. She had to remind white dancers that the "unchangeable goal of this particular dance group is to promote and support black dance."

In their definitions, other black women undergraduates acknowledged that the use of these terms by institutions of higher education was connected to larger issues of race and privilege. The ways their schools used the terms often facilitated whiteness as supreme by ignoring "history and the Eurocentric focus of society by just focusing on good things that differentiate people like foods or skin color." For Leviticus, the terms *diversity* and *multiculturalism* represented an advertising pitch to get nonwhite students to come to her school. Her response revealed a necessity to assure nonwhite students that they can "find their kind" in a setting where this may appear unlikely, like her predominately white school, Central University. At Central, the tenets of multiculturalism inform another event the school uses to draw nonwhite students. The event is called Multicultural Weekend.

Multicultural Weekend

In response to this connection of *multiculturalism* to issues of race and privilege, the black women undergraduates also critiqued schooling initiatives tied to the term. Their talk reveals cultural clashes that occur between the intended purposes of initiatives provided by their colleges and universities and the real-life experiences they live daily. For example, at Central University, Multicultural

Weekend is an event sponsored by the Admissions Office. Nonwhite entering students are invited and strongly encouraged to attend. At this event, they are introduced to a variety of university settings and events designed to showcase the university's commitment to diversity. The black women undergraduates in the study discussed Multicultural Weekend at Central in different ways:

> Leviticus: Another way they lie, they say this place is diverse. They bring you up here on Multicultural Weekend, and they show you all the things you can do—and I mean this is a common complaint, I guess, of black students on campus, and I feel especially feel bad for, like, the Latinos 'cuz there's even less of them—and I'm like, you come up here, and you see like the performances and all these students, and what you don't realize is that you see a lot of high school students. You're not seeing that many college students, and when you do get here it's like culture shock. You get really depressed because you see so many white people, and they just do all of these things that are unheard of to you, and they say things that are hurtful, but you don't (pause) you don't immediately recognize them, therefore you don't know what to say or do. (Interview, fall 2004)

> Teena: I came up here to visit and I loved it, you know, because I came up here for multicultural weekend—quote–unquote Multicultural Weekend—and so they pull it all out for you. They pull out the red carpet. I was just like, "Oh my!" I was like, "There's so many black people, and everyone likes each other, and they're partying, and they do all these things. I saw these groups, and they dance, and they do all this stuff. Oh, this is the place, I love this place." Like, they bring the students here, and you make them think that there's something going on. And I think, if you ask any student that went to Multicultural—and I don't know if, if it's even as big as it was before—but any student that went to Multicultural Weekend, they'll tell you. They bring you here, and they put on an act for you. Like this institution is for you, and that's just not the case. (Interview, spring 2004)

> RGB: Anything that's self-asserting to a specific group—so you have something that used to be Black and Latino College Weekend becomes Multicultural Weekend, you know? Because we can't just have blacks and Latinos doing anything, it's like scary. And the thing that kills me is it's white people who push that agenda, but they don't push it on themselves because they're considered the norm and the rest of us colored and ethnics are weird people, so we have to be all mixed-up in this amalgamous [sic], amorphous group of nothing to make them feel comfortable in just being white. (Interview, spring 2004)

For Teena and Leviticus, coming to their campus for Multicultural Weekend gave them a sense that the school was "a place for them." Their words, however, also revealed that they felt their school duped them. Teena refers to the "quote–unquote Multicultural Weekend" indicating her skepticism of the event. She later explained that what she saw on Multicultural Weekend, namely the events and discourses designed to make students of color feel as if they belonged, was not the same once she arrived on campus.

Leviticus called the performances on Multicultural Weekend "a lie" that promoted the myth that her campus was more diverse than it actually was. For her, one consequence of the lie was a "depression that stemmed from negotiating relationships with white people on her campus." In RGB's eyes, white people who promoted multiculturalism assigned the work of integration as a task to blacks and Latinos, but not themselves. She felt a "fear and discomfort around blacks and Latinos doing anything without their inclusion drives white people to push this agenda." Clearly the realities the women faced around Multicultural Weekend were more complex and far reaching than the initiative's intent.

Diversity Policies

The black women undergraduates in this study discussed their school's diversity policies and the impression of these policies on their schooling lives. Some of the women were unaware of their school's diversity policies:

> Interviewer: How do you feel about your school diversity policies?
> Jamie: What do you mean?
> Interviewer: How do you feel about the things your school has in place to deal with difference on you campus?
> Jamie: I don't know. I'm not really connected with that. (Interview, spring 2004)
> Interviewer: How do you feel about your school's diversity policies?
> Alex: What is their policy, man?
> Interviewer: Are you aware of them?
> Alex: No. I think we went over them one day in class, but I don't think I was really paying attention. (Interview, summer 2004)
> Interviewer: How do you feel about your school's diversity policies?
> Cherry: What do you mean?
> Interviewer: Most schools have policies about handling difference. How do you feel about Sunshine's?
> Cherry: I don't know. They probably gave it to us if they do have one. I just really didn't pay attention to it. (Interview, spring 2004)

The women above attended University of Borders and Crossings, International Community College, and Sunshine State University, respectively. From their comments it is clear that they were not, at the time of the interview, connected with the diversity policies promoted by their school. They did not recognize these polices as critical to their schooling experience. This reaction could be based on their status as first year students. This area of discussion provided one clear difference between women who attended predominately white Central University and the women who attended the other institutions. The women attending Central University were very aware of the ways diversity policies informed their lives at school:

> Interviewer: Talk about the school's diversity policies.

Shonte: They're crap. They suck. They should not exist because they don't follow them at all. They do not follow them. If they implemented them the way they
should, bias-related incidents would not occur. It would not be tolerated. You
wouldn't have the school newspaper writing some of the things they write and disre-
specting some of the people that they disrespect. [The graduation speaker] was the
guest speaker regardless if she's credible to you or not. You don't disrespect the
woman in the school newspaper.
Interviewer: What was said about her?
Shonte: Calling her all kinds of names, and there was a cartoon making fun of
her as someone not worthy of being the speaker. I mean, it was just horrible. I
mean, if the President came to speak, they wouldn't have had much to say. And no
one stepped up. No one stepped out and said, "This is wrong." Why would you
write something like that? No one stepped out, and I just think that the diversity
policies really should be revised. People need to sit down, and it should be revised
by, like, the students on campus. Basically the students of color should revise it because we're the ones you're hurting, but I guess no one sees that. (Interview, spring
2004)

Shonte felt that Central University's diversity policies were not reflected in the
response to bias incidents that occur on campus. She feels students of color are
being hurt by policies that exist but that are not carried out. For example, seeing
her school's student newspaper disrespect a black woman graduation speaker
angered Shonte. She believed that no one in "high places" took a stance to defend the black woman graduation speaker. While someone in the administration
may have indeed responded, it was not a part of Shonte's knowledge. Her perspective caused her to decide the diversity policies at the school needed to be
evaluated and revamped in such a way that this would not be allowed to occur.

Like Shonte, Leviticus also felt frustrated over the lack of implementation of
the school's diversity policies:

Leviticus: I think the diversity policies are bull, and they're just words, they're just
words. The people that sit there and try to uphold them, no offense to the people in
[the Multicultural Affairs Office], but they need to realize that this university is not
with them.... Other people say, "This is a core value at Central University." But
there is so much racism here. Like, you can get suspended from school if you plagia-
rize, but someone that comes around in blackface, they just get, (sarcastically) "Oh,
you can't be in the fraternity anymore. Let's have a meeting and talk about it." No!
(emphasis hers) You can copy someone else's work and get expelled. You come out
in blackface, that is a historical no-no, and you go parading around this campus, and
it's just like, "Oh, we just need to understand each other better." So, I just mean the
university's diversity policy reflects that. (Interview, spring 2004)

The racism that was manifest on her campus through blackface incidents that are,
in her view, punished lightly compared to other academic wrongdoings, led Leviticus to conclude that the diversity polices are "just words." Alex, Cherry, and
Jamie, in earlier responses each told me that, as first year students, they had not

faced any racist incidents on their campuses. Black women undergraduates at Central University, like Leviticus, mostly critiqued diversity claims and initiatives *in reaction* to racist incidents that occurred on their college campus:

> Nicole: I would definitely say we've had a lot of cultural clashes as far as the bias-related incidents that happen here. They try to stress that they're really big on diversity. I remember applying to this school; we had to write an essay on how we would fit into the diversity, and you know, that was one of the core values. But then when you actually—when the school actually has issues that rise as far as bias-related incidents that come up, it's like, what happened to "we're so big on diversity"? They don't do anything about it, you know. It's kind of like, you say you're big on diversity, but you're not showing us you're big on diversity.
> Interviewer: How are you impacted by this?
> Nicole: It's not a direct impact, but just knowing that someone thinks they could do something that offends me and my culture; it saddens me that you can have people that are so ignorant to do it, and then it saddens me that we have a school that, in a way, is allowing it to go on. (Interview, spring 2004)

Nicole's perceptions of the ways Central University "allowed" bias incidents, like white students wearing blackface, to take place caused her to question the commitment the school claims to make about its commitment to diversity. While she states there is not a direct impact to her when students who engage in racists acts are seemingly not punished severely, she does state that these occurrences and the attitudes that allow this to go on "sadden" her. I wish I had asked Nicole why she felt sadness was not a direct impact but I did not and so have no analysis of, what seems to me, a contradiction.

During this part of the interviews with the women at Central University, I provided them with a copy of the *Diversity Digest* to peruse as they commented on diversity policies. *Diversity Digest* is a magazine created at Central University to "provide information about the many programs and activities on campus that support diversity and to stimulate further discussion and education on this critical issue" (*Diversity Digest* Committee, 2003, inside cover). The issue I provided to the women during the interview was the first volume printed. Perusing the magazine informed the responses of the black women undergraduates who attended Central University on the issues of diversity:

> Teena: Oh yeah, (reading) I do realize diversity is a core value. I forgot. Don't you love how they just, how the pictures, they're just perfect [in the *Diversity Digest*], you know what I mean? They just pick out all the... They can pick pictures of all the black people; look, see how she's in the middle. You see the white people; it makes it *seem* like, like she's not the only one in here (pause) There's a good chance she is. I never actually saw this before. But anyway, I think in terms of the diversity policy, I think it sounds good. The diversity rhetoric sounds good. You have to say that these days. You know what I mean? You have to say that you're for diversity and all of that because it sounds good and because you're supposed [to be. (Interview, spring 2004)

Teena was cynical as she examined the photos and ethos of the *Diversity Digest*. Her cynicism was a reflection of her experiences at Central. She knew that racism existed on the campus. She also understood that society deems the appearance of equity in its institution as a desirable feature and that Central University doesn't exist outside of this political discourse. Teena's sarcasm depicted how that knowledge informed her critique of the magazine's mission.

Blue also critiqued the diversity initiatives at Central University in relation to the racism she lived with as a student there:

> Blue: I think for a school that claims to be so diverse and so understanding to all types of populations, they don't do enough to prevent people from being as ignorant as they are. I think, like it says here [in the *Diversity Digest*], like one of the values of the school is caring, and there's so many people who don't care about the people around them. It's a community. So you should care about your community and the people in it, and then for someone to do something like that; they're not caring.
>
> Interviewer: What do you think the university should be doing?
>
> Blue: I don't know. (sigh) They could be doing more, something that is proven to work. Not just Judicial Affairs forcing them to do something they won't really care about, but having them do something that would help them learn something. (Interview, fall 2004)

Teena referred to the *Diversity Digest* and its message as necessary rhetoric in a society that claims to resist racism. Nicole and Blue alleged that what Central claimed about diversity and what it did about it were two different things. Nicole stated that she was saddened by bias incidents and explained that, in her perspective, the school's commitment to diversity was not evident when these things happen. Blue proposed that students who commit these acts should be "taught something" in order to support the school's claim of a caring community.

It was evident in the study that the cultural clashes around diversity issues had an emotional effect on black women undergraduates at Central University. RGB and Teena outlined the emotional impact these cultural clashes and the school's handling of them had on their lives:

> RGB: I'm very much impacted because I feel like, even though these things didn't happen to me directly, that doesn't matter to me because, you know, like, black people when something happens to one of us like, we feel like it happens to all of us, and that's just how I feel. Like, with blackface incidents and things like that. I never in my life experienced that, ever. I've never seen that in real life. I've never dealt with that in my upbringing. So to come here and have to deal with that, to me, was just uncalled for. It was unfair. It was scary to know that there's people in this world that, to this day, think that that's okay. And it was just really frustrating. It depresses me sometimes. It makes me feel powerless at times. It makes me feel disrespected and unworthy of, of humanity and humane treatment when these types of things happen. Because it's also not just the person who does it but the way that the University handles it. The way they just, they just kind of write it off as, "Oh, this is a kid being stupid." You know, they don't understand, or they don't address the

deeper underlying issue that this campus has an atmosphere, breeds an atmosphere where people do think this kind of thing is okay. They're not taught in history classes about this type of thing, and they don't know. The only way they would know about it is if it they took an African-American studies course. How many white kids, just on their own, take African-American studies courses? So that, you know, it, it just, it drives me towards action, but it also, a lot of times, makes me feel very powerless. (Interview, spring 2004)

Teena: When I was a freshman and lived [in the dorm] there were two black people on my floor. There was a girl who lived a little close to me, she lived right across the hall, and she had a picture on her door, and it was her and her roommate was white, and when she woke up one morning because, you know, those kids in there they would be, in that dorm they would be walking around drunk. They were so filthy drunk, like it was just disgusting. We woke up on a Sunday morning and someone had wrote nigger [sic] on her picture, and I had never, never, like I'd never experienced anything like that in high school so, I, I didn't know how to react to that. I was so mad. I went to the gym because I used to go to the gym when I mad. I went to the gym. I swear I did like 150 sit-ups. I was just doing sit-ups and I was riding a bike. I was furious.

It was still early on in the year so, you know how they sweep those things under the rug? I'm sure people came to talk to her and she was upset about that and we talked about it at our floor meeting. But that was it, you know? And then after that, there was the blackface. The first in my career, the blackface thing where the guy was on Marshall Street dressed up like Tiger Woods in a blackface. That was at the end of the year, and I remember I was getting ready to go. I think I was leaving to go home the next day when that happened. They [black students] had like a meeting or whatever, and we talked about it, and everyone was upset, like, "What are we going to do? Let's go over to the lawn and stand." Everyone was just really upset and heated. And then after that, I had to leave. So, I knew they had done some stuff, like I know they sat at the chancellor's office and stuff, but I was already gone. I found out about it after. My whole summer, not that I was sitting at home thinking about it the whole time, but that kept coming up in my mind, for real.

Like, it kept coming back, and that's why—I don't know if you knew that—but when I got back my junior year after that happened, I made up a dance that was showed [sic] at the [dance] show last year. In the middle of the dance, the dancers stopped, and there was like a PowerPoint presentation of just pictures of the black-face incidents on this campus. There was a like a rash of blackface incidents that were happening, and people dressed up like Ku Klux Klan and stuff like that. So, I had like just those images, images, images, and then the dancers were dancing. It was a really angry dance. It was just extremely angry, so I think that's how I got that out.

Things are happening all the time, and I almost feel like I'm desensitized to it because I expect them to happen now. That's the difference between now and how I was a couple of years ago. I didn't expect that, but now I expect those things to happen, and the people that do this are the people that you interact on an everyday basis, and that's the thing that kills me 'cause you don't know what these people do. You don't know what they say. You don't know what they say; you don't know what they do when you're not around, and it just reminds me to always be on guard because those are the same people who are smiling in your face. (Interview, spring 2004)

From RGB and Teena's standpoints, they did not experience the kind of climate the university's *Diversity Digest* promoted. They felt that racist incidents were allowed to occur with little consequences to the offenders. While it can be shown that Central University did, in fact, speak out strongly and punish students involved in some of the blackface incidents, what stands out in the perspectives of these women is that whatever is being done is not enough to combat what they define as the source of the problem, namely ignorance.

RGB and Teena indicated that the emotional consequences of these racist incidents reached far beyond the time of the actual occurrences. For RGB, the racist cultural clash made her feel she had no power. She felt "disrespected and unworthy of human treatment." For Teena, the clash she described resulted in an anger that followed her home and infiltrated her summer break. Both women explained that these events motivated them to act. Teena specifically named creating a dance about what had occurred. This gave her a creative outlet for her anger but also infused her social and creative outlet at school with the burden of racism. Teena further explained that she is more guarded in relationships with white students as a result of these encounters. This additional work is evidence of the ways racism can cause oppression in the schooling lives of black undergraduate women and the ways they must traverse the oppression so as not to be overcome by it.

These examples suggest that the black women undergraduates' abilities to critique systems connected to diversity and multiculturalism on their campuses provide a form of cultural capital that supports their college success. At Central University, the women understood and identified the discrepancies between the intent of the Multicultural Weekend initiative and the way they experienced it as *raced* beings. They offered a critique of this cultural clash that looked beyond the intent, which appeared to be noble. The women outlined the impacts these types of events can have on student schooling lives if real issues, like "how multiculturalism can push black culture to the margins," are not addressed.

The black women undergraduates also critiqued diversity policies and provided experiences that showed discrepancies between the atmosphere diversity initiatives at Central suggested exists and what the women came across. The women challenged their schools to do a better job of addressing racist incidents if the institutions are truly committed to diversity. In this chapter, they delineated the ways the policies and practices of diversity and multiculturalism can mislead students and the ways they negotiated the consequences that result.

Negotiating Stereotypes

> Kayla: I feel there is not one person in this universe that is never stereotyped. I don't like how black people are stereotyped, period. It gets me more upset in black women. But every, anywhere you go, any race, you get stereotyped. People look at you in a certain way, and they'll automatically put you in a category that you may be a part of or you may not be a part of. So the way they stereotype black women is black women are known to be, you know, attitude and snapping their necks. It doesn't bother me because I know who I am and where I put myself. (Interview, spring 2004)

Kayla believed that in American society stereotypes exist for every racialized group. Framing this discourse this way worked in multiple ways for Kayla. First, it is a type of verbal shrug that attempted to minimize the impact of a part of her raced experience and to be fair to other groups who experience this same thing. Second, this framework allowed her to separate out one aspect of stereotyping she felt connected to without taking on the entire discourse and appearing too biased. Kayla asserted that she was more upset when she encountered stereotypes about black women. By using the framework that everybody is stereotyped and then asserting her anger when it happens to black women, Kayla attempted to normalize stereotyping and gave the appearance of being fair in her analysis while still maintaining the right to recognize stereotyping as oppressive for black women. In other words, in Kayla's perspective, stereotyping happens to everyone, but in this case, in her lived experience as black and woman, it is most infuriating.

In a seeming contradiction, Kayla stated that she did not let the stereotypes bother her since her strong sense of self provided protection. A close examination of Kayla's comments raised several questions. Does Kayla's anger when black women are stereotyped mean that, despite her protests, stereotyping does bother her? What insulation does a strong sense of self provide against stereotyping and race and gender oppression? What is included in the idea of a strong sense of self?

Other black women undergraduates in this study shared Kayla's realization that stereotypes about black women exist. Lisa also showed that she was fair-minded by acknowledging that everyone was stereotyped. She then connected the stereotyping of black women to popular culture:

> Lisa: Everybody is stereotyped. I mean black women at first were considered demanding, then, you know, the sexual role—she had no preference in men. We had the over-sexed female and the attitude female like Omarosa on *The Apprentice*. You have to have a strong sense of self to break through those stereotypes and know that you're not that person. (Interview, summer 2004)

Like Kayla, Lisa believed that a strong sense of self helped her skirt the impact of stereotypes about black women. Each woman stated that they did not let the stereotypes they outlined that are attributed to black women define them or stop them from reaching their goals. Like Kayla and Lisa, many of the black undergraduate women in this study acknowledged that stereotypes about black women exist. During the interviews they highlighted that stereotypes infiltrated their lives in higher education. The most popular discussion surrounded the stereotype of the *angry black bitch*.

> Kimberly: I was in New York, and I'm dealing with my colleagues that I'm working with that are mostly Caucasian, and even the way I would speak to them, they'd be like, "Oh my god, I want to cry." They get so offended because they don't understand my point of reference. They feel like I'm rough. I'm just very much, like, to the point. Like, "I don't like when you do that. Don't do it again." And they're just like, "Why are you so mean?" Sometimes I just feel like a lot of the times I'm viewed as, because when I think of black women, I think of strength. And a lot of times, I feel like a lot of people are intimidated by our strength, and for me, I always feel that I'm being viewed as the *angry black bitch*. To be frank, that's how I feel. Because I have an opinion, and I'm not afraid to express it, and so I feel like a lot of times, I have to walk on eggshells because other people are going to get hurt, but other people don't take account of my feelings. So I've just decided that I'm going to say what I want to say, and I don't really care anymore. (Kimberly, fall, 2004)

Earlier in this chapter, in her discussion about confronting the police, Kimberly claimed that when it came to injustice, she was indeed "angry all of the time." Here she explained that her peers response to her direct, verbal approach made her feel like she was seen as an *angry black bitch*. While Kimberly claimed her anger in the earlier example, in this case, she rejected anger being thrust upon her. Instead, strategically, Kimberly embraced the idea of strength to account for this experience and refused to be silenced. This strategy enabled Kimberly to negotiate the stereotype and still find a place for speaking her mind.

For black women undergraduates in this study, *speaking up* often facilitated the stereotype of the *angry black bitch*. This occurred because black women who spoke up were often accused of attacking teachers and classmates. One student explained:

> Shonte: I was in a race, class, and gender class, and one of the girls, a Jewish, rich Jewish girl and she was like, "You know, I've never been to the ghetto, and I just— those people scare me." [I said,] "What! We're human beings. What's wrong with you?" You know, not saying that maybe crime is, you know—how do we know crime is higher there? Why, because in Long Island they don't report it, you know. Oh, she just pissed me off. She made me so mad; I was like, "What do you mean, those people scare you?" And she thought I was *attacking* her, and I'm like, "No. Explain what you—what do you mean?" I said, "What? What do you mean, we scare you?" [She said,] "Well, it's just like, you know, you people are always outside." [I replied,] "Who wants to be in the house? Like, what's wrong with that?" You

know, "I've—I've gone to 125th Street, and there are just so many black people." [I replied,] "So what? I've been to Long Island and got scared, too, 'cuz so many." You know? So, I just, just don't disrespect where I am from. What's wrong with you? That's like me saying that every white person is a serial killer. You know, that's like me saying that; I would never do that. And I just, the level of respect, like I mean, there was none in that class, and the teacher didn't even curb it. I was like, "Wait a minute, you're a sociology teacher. There's a level of oppression everywhere, and you didn't even step in and say anything." She just disrespected where I am from, and she just made it seem like anyone who was in the ghetto can't be educated, and so I guess I really *had* to attack her. (emphasis hers). I really had to. (laugh) (Interview, spring 2004)

What is an attack? Shonte spoke up in response to the racism and classism she perceived evident in a series of comments made by a white, Jewish student in her class. It was important to Shonte to identify this classmate as white and Jewish since she felt this interaction was being informed by race and class stereotypes. Using this identification showed that Shonte's way of thinking about this incident was also informed by stereotypes about race and class. This student was not just a white woman; she was white and she was Jewish. A common stereotype about white people who are Jewish is that they are wealthy. This assumption informed Shonte's response whether she was aware of it or not since she assumed this student's comments were connected to that discourse on race and class.

Shonte felt the woman took her strong response as an attack and supported this claim by discussing the email this classmate sent after class about her displeasure with the attitude Shonte displayed toward her. At first, Shonte rejected the idea that she was "attacking" this student in her class. She claimed that the purpose of her response was to force this student to recognize her talk as disrespectful. She was also critiquing the inaction on the part of the professor. At the end of her comments, it appeared Shonte adopted this term of *attacking* for what happened in this instance and revealed it as a strategy to combat race and class oppression. She claimed that this cultural clash she believed to be racist and class based created a situation where she *had* to attack, in other words, where she had to speak out against the oppression.

Nicole explained how the strength she claimed as a black woman led to a cultural clash, and to her being stereotyped as angry, attacking, and having an attitude:

Nicole: With one particular teacher, I definitely felt that [I was being stereotyped by someone]. She was a white teacher, and she tried to stress that she was for diversity or whatever. But I don't think she really understood what that meant, and she didn't know how to relate to myself and other, you know, blacks, students in the class(pause). I don't think she really understood where we were coming from. I confronted her a couple of times on different issues that I had with her, and she always took it as me *attacking* her. (emphasis hers) I guess she didn't understand that where I'm from, the way, if you have a problem—whether I'm talking to someone who is above me authority-wise—I'm still going to confront you if I have an issue, and she looked at it as if I was attacking her. She even wrote an email to the whole class saying, "I don't appreciate what happened. I was being attacked and some students"— and I know she was talking about me—"had issues and gave attitude." But I think she just took my concern and wanting to resolve an issue as having attitude, and I think it's more or less about culture you know, as far as me being a black woman having a strong sense of pride for myself. It wasn't that I was trying to give attitude. I'm just a very strong person, and I guess maybe sometimes that comes off wrong or she saw that differently.

Interviewer: Can you give me an example of the issues that come up that you respond to?

Nicole: One of the things that had happened is one of the students in the class—we were having kind of circle time and just people talking about anything, and one of the students kind of broke down crying in class saying how she wasn't sure if she wanted to teach, and she felt bad because she thought she was the only one in the class who felt that way, and I kind of raised my hand and was just like, "This is a problem." I said to [named teacher], "This is a problem where, you know, we need to talk about this as a class. There are a lot of people, myself included, who aren't sure if they want to teach. It shouldn't be that this woman is crying 'cause she really thought she was the only one and everyone else is excited about teaching. We always talk about how the placement's going, but we never talk about how Block 1 is going." I was like, "That's the real issue we need to talk about. You have students who think it's a problem that they don't want to teach, and you're not consoling them and being like, 'It's okay.' or 'There's others like you.' or 'Let's have a discussion about that.'" She always wanted to have, you know, we come into class, [and she says,] "Tell me something good that's going on with you." But it was never, "Let's talk about the bad." So that's what I confronted her on, and she thought I was attacking her teaching and trying to tell her how to teach. But, in all reality, I'm just saying, "Here you have a student crying; let's do something about it." But I guess she didn't see it my way. (laugh)

Interviewer: What was the resolution of that situation?

Nicole: There wasn't any. She wrote a letter to the class, an email, which I felt she sent it to the whole class but she might as well have just sent to me because she reiterated comments that were made in class, saying some students said this, which they were all the comments I had said. I actually met with her to discuss how I was very upset with the letter she wrote. And it was just, I got frustrated and ended up just leaving because I'm saying one thing and she's trying to get me to understand where she's coming from, which is fine. But, she didn't want to understand where I was coming from, and I get frustrated if someone trying not to see my way, and I just give up and just, and that's kind of what happened, and it was never discussed again with her and even in class. Like, I thought definitely the next day we had class she was going to be like, "Okay, I just want to talk about what happened the other day in class." She didn't mention it once. It was kind of like it never happened.

Interviewer: Okay. How did other students react to the email?

Nicole: It's funny because a lot of the students who I knew had some of the same issues with me and [named teacher], they voiced it to me, but then when it came to saying something to her, nothing was said. Like people who complained to *me* went up to *her* and were like, "I'm so sorry about what happened in class." The thing was that people were very afraid of her and afraid for their grades, which in all reality, I feel that they shouldn't have been. Because I really believe I received a lower grade from her than I should have received. And I think that was the biggest fear with the students in the classes, no one was willing to stand up to her for fear that they would get a low grade in the class.

Interviewer: What happened with the student that was crying?

Nicole: Nothing really, like it wasn't. It's surprising; you would think that [named teacher] would see that and just try to talk to her maybe after class; like, as far as I am aware, nothing was said to her. I know me and a couple of other students, tried to go up to her and be like, "Listen, we don't know if we want to teach either. It's okay, if you're going through this." and try to explain that to her; but as far as like, you know, [named teacher] doing it—or any of the other teachers— nothing was said to her. As far as I know, I think she's still in the program, and she's more like, "Okay, maybe this is something I want to do."(Interview, spring 2004)

In this example, Nicole opened the discussion of negotiating the stereotype of the *angry black bitch* in her education class with the admission that she did not trust her white teacher who appeared to be supportive about issues of diversity but who, in Nicole's perspective, alienated black students in the class. Nicole felt that a cultural disconnect, between the teacher and her as a black student, created a situation where, from her standpoint, confrontations that, in her world, were meant to resolve issues were read as attacks by the teacher.

Nicole said that her self-described strength and her attempts to speak up on behalf of another student in the class who was crying led to accusations from her teacher of "giving attitude." She connected this idea of "giving attitude" to race. As mentioned, Nicole claimed earlier that the teacher did not seem to "understand where black students were coming from" when she discussed her mistrust of the teacher's commitment to diversity. Nicole used this same language to explain why her teacher felt she was giving her attitude. Her words, "she didn't want to understand where I was coming from," brought this perspective back to that earlier conversation and back to the racial and cultural disconnect Nicole saw as the root of the problem. For Nicole, even though race was not mentioned in the interactions, certain words like *giving attitude* and *attacking* acted as codes for race.

Nicole felt her class needed to discuss the type of issues the student crying in the class raised in order to be authentic. This is indicated by her calling this issue "real" when compared with talks about "what good happened to you." Nicole felt punished for speaking up, and her meeting with the teacher about the content of the email sent to the class ended with no resolution.

Nicole believed the email her teacher sent to the whole class presented them with the message that she was not in the good graces of her teacher. Students who privately complained to Nicole, indicating an alliance, turned around and presented a different face to the teacher. She believed they did this to protect their grades. Nicole felt her grade in the class reflected this teacher's feelings about her "speaking up." Adding another layer to the discussion, Nicole discussed how the white students in her class attempted to use her strength and speaking up for their own gain:

> Nicole: I would definitely say they [members of her class] saw me as kind of—I mean it was never stated of course—but they saw me as kind of the black girl who always had something to say because I did always have something to say. I was always standing up for myself and standing up for them. And I was always the one to give my opinion, and whenever they had problems, they would come to me and say, "Nicole, why don't you tell her this, or tell her we don't want to do that?" you know.
>
> Interviewer: You mean the white students?
>
> Nicole: Yeah. And you know it was always—they looked at me as kind of that angry black girl who would say anything, you know. I was like, "Why don't you guys go and say it? Why are you so afraid?" and they're just like, "Well, you always say it so." It didn't really bother me. I understood the fear they had in saying stuff, but I really didn't care. I was going to sacrifice my grade if that's what standing up for myself and what I believe in meant. So, it kind of bothered me that they didn't say anything, but I didn't care because I had the same opinions they did, and I was more or less voicing it for myself. (Interview, spring 2004)

Nicole faced a cultural clash she had to traverse. Like Kimberly, Nicole was adamant about speaking up for herself and for her classmates when matters she felt strongly about came up in class. What was challenging for Nicole was negotiating the consequences she believed were the result of taking action. She believed her strength and convictions about speaking up were read as *attitude*, *angry*, and "always having something to say" by her teacher; she also had to cope with the way the students in her class attempted to use for their own gain her ability to articulate issues and her willingness to take a risk and speak out. In Nicole's perspective, additional consequences included receiving a "lower grade than I felt I deserved," having an email that showed the teacher's displeasure about her sent to the entire class, and classmates who pretended to be on her side outside of the classroom but showed no support for her in front of the teacher.

At first, Nicole said that students who tried to use her strength for their own means (by getting her to say the things they didn't want to say themselves) "didn't bother me because I understood their fear in speaking up." She later admitted it did trouble her, but since she shared their opinions, she looked at speaking up as voicing things for herself. This also is a strategy of negotiation. Nicole resisted being used by students but still voiced her concerns. She would not do it just because they wanted her to but did not hold her tongue when her concerns overlapped with theirs.

Nicole's cultural capital, namely, her sense of confidence in her beliefs, her right to speak up, and her acceptance of the responsibility to do so, helped her negotiate the stereotype of the *angry black woman*. Nicole converted the conversation of this stereotype into one about her strength as a black woman and her convictions as a student. This strength was necessary considering the additional burden of work negotiating this stereotype required of Nicole. She utilized these strategies as tools to combat what she saw as injustice in her class.

The black women undergraduates in this study pointedly discussed the impact of the stereotype of the *angry black woman* (or *angry black bitch*) in their schooling lives. This stereotype is *raced* and gendered. The word *bitch* is a derogatory reference for women and men but there is a difference in the way it is used. When hurled at a black man, for instance, the word *bitch* implies that he is carrying on in a way that is stereotypically feminine and could include crying and other forms of perceived weakness. Also, the anger of black men is most often read as violence in U.S. society. The black women in this study described the term *angry black bitch* as an attack on their strength and their vocal and forceful response to racism and injustice in school settings.

In the experiences of these students, the *angry black woman* stereotype took varied and complex forms. It was a type of attack. It was a strategy to combat racism, classism, and other injustice, and it was a strategy to draw upon to speak one's mind. For the women in this study, negotiating this stereotype required, "knowing oneself," "drawing upon a discourse of strength to describe encounters where they are accused of being angry and having an attitude," and "maintaining cultural convictions." Each of these approaches helped the women not be defined by stereotypes or be bogged down in frustration. These strategies are forms of cultural capital that help black undergraduate women find success in higher education.

Conclusions

The black women undergraduates in this study outlined a number of cultural clashes that occur, making it necessary for women to navigate oppressions in higher education. The women gave details that indicated this navigation is connected to their experience as raced and gendered beings in a society that does not privilege their social locations. For black women undergraduates, the decision to *speak up and be heard* is a complicated one. By making the choice to *speak up and be heard*, the black women undergraduates in this study put their schooling lives at risk. The risks they indicated included "being stereotyped as an *angry black bitch* with attitude," "alienating teachers and possibly getting lower grades," and "being [virtually] silenced in the classroom as one who only speaks on issues related to race and class." The black women undergraduates in this study claimed "knowing who they are," "the strength of their convictions," and the "desire to carve out a path for students who come after them" as some of the reasons they accepted these risks.

In this chapter, the black women undergraduates made it clear that in their lives at school, navigating oppressions is a complex and dynamic process. For black women undergraduates like RGB, this process changes and grows with experiences the women encounter in higher education. Critiquing systems like multiculturalism and diversity policies was a process of negotiation most evident in the conversations with black women who were not first year students and who attended predominately white Central University. Their critique of the systems allowed them to look beyond intent and challenge their schools to address the issues of race and difference in a more authentic way, specifically one that examines the ways these events inform their everyday lives at school. This process of navigating oppressions and the growth associated with challenging cultural clashes are forms of cultural capital that the black women undergraduates identified as necessary for their success in higher education as they navigate relationships, maintain cultural convictions, and challenge oppression in their schooling lives.

CHAPTER FIVE

Black Women Undergraduates Navigate Complex Alliances

Nicole: I think having a mentor like Larry is really good because he pushes me. He tells me the things I need to do to get to where I am; the kind of people I need to intern with or the people I need to get in good with to have like as references for my résumé or something like that. So I think having him is a plus. (Interview, spring 2004)

When asked what things she had in place to help her reach her academic and future goals, Nicole explained that she had a mentor at her school who supported her and her work in higher education. She referred to his presence as "a plus" and explained that this mentor gave her information that she believed would help her succeed. Academic literature emphasizes the important role of mentors in the success of black students. (Edelman, 1999; Gallien & Peterson, 2005). A mentor is most often described as one who is an adviser, trainer, counselor, guide, tutor, teacher, and guru, indicating that this person has knowledge to import to one less knowledgeable (Hill & Ragland, 1995; see also Abate, 1997). For black undergraduate women, relationships with mentors can be important in getting into school, staying in school, and being academically and socially successful while in school. Mentors in higher education often provide access to information and services not known to the general school population or incoming students. While mentoring relationships are often celebrated as necessary and useful to college success, the literature on these relationships falls short in several areas. First, rarely do we hear black undergraduate women talk about the ways these relationships support academic success in their own words. Second, while there is talk of the importance of mentors, the complexities of these relationships as related to race, class, and gender are not usually presented for an intersectional analysis. Finally, there is little detailed talk of how the roles assigned in the relationships are not simple and fixed but rather are dynamic and, at times, convoluted.

Black undergraduate women find the traditional view of mentorship in higher education useful but limited. For black women undergraduates, this partial view does not capture the intricacies of the relationships in higher education that they seek to establish or are forced into while navigating a terrain of intersecting identities. This chapter will show that some black undergraduate women, like Nicole, recognize the benefits of guidance from mentors and that these mentors exist both inside and outside of the academy. This chapter will further show that black women undergraduates also acknowledge the challenges and limitations associated with these relationships due to their intersectional lives. I contend that in addition to finding mentors, black undergraduate women, in order to be successful in college, must identify allies (who, in this text, are defined as friends, helpers, supporters, negotiators, assistants, and partners—people who understand and participate in their struggle as students and as raced, classed, and gendered beings and often have the power to make change). The process of negotiating these mentor or ally relationships is a form of cultural capital.

High School Guidance Counselors

Finding someone to advise them about higher education begins for black women undergraduates before they get to college. In school systems in the United States, one role of the guidance counselor is to provide suggestions and directions to high school students in a number of ways, including the process of selecting and applying to a college or university. The black undergraduate women I interviewed identified this relationship as one that was useful in getting to college:

> Amari: My guidance counselor was the best guidance counselor I could ever have in my life. She was always there. She was like my second mom. She was there when I was going through it for my mom. [Amari's mother became sick and passed away when she was in high school.] She would just give me her office, and I could sit on the phone with my sister for a whole school period, and she would tell people to excuse me from my work. She helped me pick all my classes. She helped me get into [named University]. She helped me get a scholarship. She just helped with everything. (Interview, spring 2004)

> Nicole : We had a really good college counseling office, and the woman who was my college counselor had received numerous awards for being kind of the best college counselor in the nation or whatever. So, we had very strong guidance, and I credit a lot of my success in being here in college to the college counseling office at my school.
>
> Interviewer: Okay. What kinds of things did they do for you?
>
> Nicole: We met kind of once a week discussing colleges. They gave us a list of schools that they thought would be good for me as far as, you know, as far as my background, being black, also grades and what I was interested in as far as education. They helped me look into financial aid and going on to college. (Interview, spring 2004)

Nicole and Amari both credited the support they got from guidance counselors with helping them get to college. Nicole described the counseling experiences as "very strong" in helping her choose which to colleges she should apply. She described the counselor's support in raced talk when she explained that the counselor was helping her identify schools that would be supportive of her as a black student, first. She then mentioned her grades and her desire to go into the field of education.

In this study, the practical help needed to get to college given by guidance counselors was most visible as classed talk when the women described the importance of fee waivers in the application process. For most of the women, knowledge about the existence of fee waivers and how to get the appropriate form came from the guidance counselors:

> Blue: My school gave fee waivers for students who needed them. So, I got fee waivers for every school that I applied to. My guidance counselor, she was really good, so, she just helped me throughout everything. I did the essays that I had to do. She read through them. I brought it to a writing consultant. So, it was really smooth. (Interview, spring 2004)

> Leviticus: Oh, I didn't pay for it. That's another thing (laugh); I lived right across the street from my guidance counselor. And that's actually how I met her first 'cuz I found out she's my neighbor and then second that she's my guidance counselor. So when it came time to apply, she hooked me up. Same thing for SATs; I didn't have to pay for any of that because she gave me the necessary waivers, and since I was only applying to one school, anyway, it was like, "I'm not fond of a $50 fee to look at my application." So, they waived my application fee. (Interview, spring 2004)

> Alana: The fee waivers were basically, since again, like I said, I went to a school that had the money. It wasn't as rich as other places like, Walt Whitman High School, which was like known for its crystal staircase. But my school was pretty nice. But anyway, yeah, so, the fee waivers worked out. You just kind of asked for them based on need. If you need it, we can give it to you, you know what I mean? But you just had to seek it out, and a lot of students didn't know how to do that. (Interview, spring 2004)

Fee waivers enabled Leviticus, Alana, and Blue to complete their college applications without cost. The women recognized that their socioeconomic status meant they had to seek out an alternative to paying the fees and that the substitute was "based on need." They saw the counselor as an ally who had the power to help them overcome this obstacle and provide a way around this potential economic roadblock. Alana indicated that some students did not know how to get the waiver. Both Blue and Leviticus pointed out that having a good guidance counselor and one that knows you are keys to obtaining this knowledge and getting the necessary forms.

Guidance Counselors as Gatekeepers

Many of the women interviewed explained that while providing practical help and support (e.g., fee waivers), the guidance system and its counselor representatives often acted as gatekeepers when it came to black women and higher education. Stereotypes and myths connected to race, class, and gender influenced the advice students received regarding access to community colleges and four-year colleges and universities. This contradiction complicated relationships with guidance counselors. These complexities showed up repeatedly in the stories of the black women undergraduates who attended Central University. In Alana's case, her guidance counselor became her challenger:

> Alana: I learned how to politick kind of early.
> Interviewer: Okay. How did you learn how to do that?
> Alana: I just—I knew that I had to get it [the fee waiver]. So, I knew I had to find out who I needed to talk [with] to get it, so
> Interviewer: Okay, and who was it that you talked to?
> Alana: This lady who said I actually wasn't gonna get into Central—and I did.
> Interviewer: Oh, why did she say that?
> Alana: She was just some old hag who didn't have nothin' else to do.
> Interviewer: So, what did she say to you?
> Alana: She was just basically kind of like, "Oh, yeah, I'll doubt you'll get in, you know. Your grades are kind of low. SATs scores are kind of high, but we'll figure it out." And I was just like, "Write the waiver; I don't need all the rest of it." You know, at that time in my life, I didn't let those types of things get to me because I was concentrating. I had this goal; I was gonna get it, and I didn't care how I was gonna do it. I was gonna get it.
> Interviewer: Does she know that you got accepted?
> Alana: Yeah, she does. I made sure she knew. She tried to hug me after that; I was like, "uh, ah." [Alana gestures as if she were pushing someone away.] And ironically enough, she was a white woman, and so I just realized that she was not helping me. (Interview, spring 2004)

Alana was able to identify her counselor as the person who held the essential form and to communicate her need. She described this as *politicking*. Alana talked about this diplomatic work as part of a strategy she learned early in order to get what she needed from her counselor. This idea of *politicking* as a compulsory practice gives insight into the additional work Alana and other black women undergraduates from lower socioeconomic status must engage in order to get to college. For some of the women, the process of completing an application for college is not straightforward, and asking for assistance goes beyond getting help with things like directions and mailing. For Alana and others like her, it means making your social-class status visible, opening oneself up to being read in a way that perpetuated raced and classed stereotypes. Alana's understanding of the need for *politicking* also showed that she did not have the expectation that the processes involved in her work toward higher education were free from op-pressive societal ideas about her race and class, so she developed a strategy early to combat the effects.

Alana explained that her counselor discouraged her college choice. At that moment, in Alana's mind, her ally with the fee waiver became an "old hag" who was placing an obstacle in her path at the same time she was removing one. Alana's resistance to being told she would not get accepted at Central University was to dismiss this admonition as an irrelevant bump in her determined road to success. The long-term effects of this encounter on Alana are evident in both her need to "make sure" the counselor knew she was accepted to Central and her refusal to accept a hug from the counselor during that conversation.

While it may appear that Alana's counselor was just giving advice on college admissions based on traditional markers (e.g., grades, SAT scores), from Alana's perspective, this advice was connected to her race. This standpoint was evident when she described the counselor as "a white woman that just wasn't helping me." Implicit in this response is the idea that the guidance counselor could pro-vide the fee waiver, but her views on Alana's successful acceptance to Central, which Alana connected to her guidance counselor's whiteness and her own blackness, stopped her from being an ally. The guidance counselor did not un-derstand, chose to ignore, or was blinded by white privilege to the impact of what Alana called "those types of things." Those types of things included making discouraging remarks about acceptance to college to Alana as a nonprivileged, raced, classed, and gendered student. It is true that another counselor, who was a white woman may have helped Alana and could have been encouraging. It is also true that many white students may have also gotten the admonition from Alana's counselor not to apply to certain schools. What is important in this discussion is that Alana's lived experiences informed her read on this encounter as connected to whiteness and the larger social demon, racism. This connection informed her reaction to the encounter and the subsequent strategic *politicking* she adopted as a way to contest it.

The link between this type of advice and race and class was also evident when RGB described an experience with a guidance counselor. She spoke in terms of race and class while discussing perceptions about her ability to succeed in college:

> RGB: Another thing that I found to be interesting was I had a guidance counselor that was very good at helping me find scholarships and things like that, but when it came to my school choices, she was very discouraging. You know it's like, "NYU? You're not going to get in there, or if you do get in there, they're not going to give you any money, so you may as well go for other schools that you know are going to give you money and you know that you can use when you get into them, and blah, blah, blah." And she was like, "Central? Oh no. They're probably not going to let

you in there. Oh, come on." So I'm not one to really listen to people like that, especially when they say I can't do something that a lot of people have done. So I was
like, "yeah, okay," and I applied anyway and I got in.

   Interviewer: Did you tell her?

   RGB: Yeah! She was very surprised, and I remember my sophomore year, I
went back to [my] high school, and that same guidance counselor was there, and I
told her, I said "You know, I made a 4.0 this semester." It was sophomore year, first
semester, and she was like, "What?! 4.0?" She said, "How many classes are you taking?" I was like, "I was taking four classes. And, you know, two of them were four
credits." And she was like, "And you got all As in all of them?" Like, I was like, (in-
credulously) "What did I do when I was here?!" Like, "I was a good student here,"
you know? It was as if she (pause)—she either didn't believe in me when I was at
school because I went to a mostly black school—she had that kind of mentality of
that, "Oh, teachers are just being easy on her."—or she just really didn't think I was
that smart, you know. I was just really taken aback by her reaction to it. Whereas,
you know, people like my principal and my attendance counselor there were like,
"You know, we're not surprised because you were always a good student."—and
things like that. And she was the only one that was flabbergasted. She was black,
but you could tell that she was very, you know, high falutin'. You know, "Because I
live in Virginia, I'm a higher class of Negro." or something. (Interview, spring 2004)

The shared social locations of *black* and *woman* did not automatically make
RGB's guidance counselor her ally. The practical information about scholarships
she provided as a mentor was not enough to make her an ally. RGB understood
that the advice she was getting regarding school choice was connected to race
and class. Since RGB had to make her socioeconomic status visible in her applications for college and ask for scholarship applications, the guidance counselor
was able to use RGB's socioeconomic status as one reason to tell her to consider
less-prestigious schools and programs of study. Her threat was that Central
"wouldn't give her any money" even if RGB was accepted.

   RGB read the behavior of this guidance counselor in a specific raced and
classed way. In RGB's eyes, this black woman counselor was in a socioeconomic
situation that allowed her to be a "different class of Negro." This type of black
woman, from RGB's standpoint, could be skeptical about the abilities of blacks
less financially fortunate than she was and blacks, like RGB, who had "attended
all-black high schools." Being a "different class of Negro" allowed her to act as a
gatekeeper. The counselor had practical information and in her role dispensed
practical support like scholarship applications. But according to RGB, being
"high falutin'" and subscribing to societal ideas about blacks and education that
render some unworthy of admittance stopped her from seeing the counselor as
an ally.

   Both RGB and Alana showed how difficult it is for black women undergraduates, from lower socioeconomic backgrounds to negotiate relationships and
find allies in school systems that are steeped in racist and classist ideologies.

Each woman recognized, appreciated, and took advantage of the fact that their counselors could supply them with the necessary forms and information that helped them negotiate the obstacle of cost in applying to college. Yet, both were frustrated by the fact that their guidance counselors had no expectation that the women could succeed in getting accepted to Central University. This frustration led to the development of strategies to deal with the discouraging remarks. Both women chose to dismiss this read on their ability to get into and succeed at Central University and viewed the counselor's perspective as an obstacle to overcome. Neither woman allowed this advice to stop them from applying to Central, and both gained admittance. As RGB said, "I applied anyway and got in."

The far-reaching effect of racism as played out in the encounter with her guidance counselor was evident when RGB, like Alana, returned to her high school after an academically successful semester at Central. Upon sharing the news of her 4.0 GPA with the counselor, RGB was met with disbelief about her performance and the authenticity of her grade point average. She was "taken aback" by this response and felt the need to identify the source of the counselor's disbelief. She believed that for this counselor, her performance in high school, her acceptance to Central, and her academic performance there were still not enough to combat the typecast and limiting, raced and classed beliefs RGB felt this counselor held about her ability to succeed.

For black women undergraduates, negotiating their relationships often involves work to dispel racist and classist viewpoints about their inability to thrive in college. These beliefs are so entrenched in societal discourses about race and education that even sharing their successes becomes burdensome when the responses are distrust and disbelief. This, in turn, requires another negotiation, a way to deal with additional rejection. For RGB, this included the discourse of the "high falutin' Negro," one who has class privilege, as the explanation for the behavior and perspective. For Alana, it was the refusal of the hug. She would not give in or make her counselor's words and attitude acceptable by sharing a hug on her return visit.

Kimberly told a similar story about the guidance counseling system at her predominately black and Hispanic high school, where she attended "specialized classes":

> Kimberly: We had one college counselor for a school of 3,000 people, and the way we met with our college counselor was based on our GPA; so if you didn't have a high GPA... (shrug) The people in the Center for the Intellectually Gifted [CIG] program got to meet with the counselor first because, of course, we had the highest GPAs, but by the time you reached the other students in like the 70s or low 80s whatever, they were getting, and 60s or whatever. They were not meeting with their college counselor till the summer time and that's when all the college applications are in. So, it's just like something's crawling on my skin just thinking about it be-

cause so many of my peers, I thought, were cheated out of a chance. The school is predominately black and Hispanic, but yet the CIG program was filled predominately with Caucasians and Asians, and my college counselor was in the position of authority to decide whether or not she thought they should be granted an education instead of them deciding it for themselves. (Interview, spring 2004)

The process of seeing the counselor in Kimberly's school was a form of institutional racism that was inherently limiting and discriminatory. There was only one counselor for 3,000 students, and the counselor saw students involved in the CIG program first. To Kimberly, this process was unfair and racially discriminating since the students in CIG were not her peers, in this case, meaning they were not black students, but rather were Asian American and white students, even though her school was predominately black and Hispanic. High GPAs rendered these students worthy of meeting with a counselor before college applications were due and, by extension, deserving of college admission. Kimberly goes on to explain how this counselor's position of authority informed her own school choice:

> Kimberly: I will always remember because I felt like she was very limiting to us, like she told me, "Don't apply to Central University; you'll never get in." Do you know what I mean? Like, stuff like that and I just—after that I was like, "You know, you're just an advisor. I don't know if you understand, but that means that you give advice; I don't have to take it." Do you know what I mean? 'Cuz like, she wouldn't want to write you recommendations or sign your things if you didn't go along with what she was saying, and I'm just like, "You know, I'm not going to let you define me; it's really not going to work out." So, it's just really pathetic if you think about our school system, and for people to even fathom the thought that we're equal is ridiculous. (Interview, fall 2004)

Kimberly's membership in the Center for the Intellectually Gifted (CIG) program did not protect her from the guidance counselor's attempts to discourage her from applying to Central University. She was told she would "never get in." Her work in this relationship with her counselor involved limiting the interactions to "just advising." It is important to note that Kimberly had a response to the counselor's discouraging words. Yet this response, "I'm not going to let you define me." was not verbal. Awareness of the inequities that already existed in the counseling system at her school and the power dynamics between counselors and students that fueled them forced Kimberly's resistance to remain hidden in her own thoughts. This skill of navigating racist systems, specifically knowing when to speak out and when to resist internally, is a form of cultural capital black women undergraduates like Kimberly must employ. It allows them to get what they need (e.g., written recommendations) and still not succumb to discouraging advice about their school choices.

Kimberly saw the counselor as one who could give advice—that she did not have to take—but not as an ally who understood her raced, classed, and gendered struggles. This is evident in her words, "I'm not going to let you define me." For Kimberly, this guidance counselor and the system at her high school reinforced social ideals that deemed black students as "less than." She said, for anyone to "even fathom that all students are equal is ridiculous." Unlike Alana and RGB, Kimberly did not go back to her high school after acceptance and success at Central University, but she did describe what she would have said if she had gone back to the school with a friend who did visit the counselor:

> Interviewer: How did you tell [your guidance counselor] that you're at Central?
>
> Kimberly: Well, she knows that I went to Central but, I mean, I have accomplished so much here at Central, and my friend, Olivia, she is in college, another black woman, she actually had to go back to [the high school], and she was speaking to her or whatever, and it was just like I wanted to be there with her because I was like, "You wanted to limit me, and if I didn't stand up for myself, I probably would not have done what I wanted to do." I came to Central and I've never gotten below a 3.5, you know what I mean? I've accomplished every goal that I've set for myself. So, I just wish that she could see that you just have to give people a chance. You have to give them a chance to... (pause) I mean, sometimes people will disappoint you when you put your trust in them. But, that's not always the case, you know. (Interview, fall 2004)

Kimberly felt it was important for her guidance counselor to recognize her academic success and that of her friend who she described as "another black woman in college." She wanted to tell the counselor that, had she listened to the counselor's "limiting advice," she would not have accomplished her goals and that other students deserve "a chance." Kimberly talked about this relationship between student and counselor as one that must be based on trust. It is this trust that Kimberly felt was lacking in her experience with the counselor, and the lack of trust was why her guidance counselor was not, in Kimberly's eyes, an ally. She explained further:

> Kimberly: You know what she told my friend Olivia? She told—'cuz my friend Olivia was having a conversation with her and the director of the CIG program about this idea of pigeonholing students who could have [gone to college]. And she said, "You guys are different. You guys are not like the other students." And Olivia's [response] was like, "Explain to me, what do you mean we're different? What does that mean?" "You guys have something. You know how to talk, you're not—" "*What does that mean? What are you talking about?* (emphasis hers) Say what you mean." You know what I mean?
>
> Interviewer: What was her race?
>
> Kimberly: She was white. (Interview, fall 2004)

This conversation that Kimberly and her friend were "different," "had something," and "knew how to talk" reflected the counselor's raced ideas about black students and academic success. Kimberly later explained that she believed this coded talk from the counselor was "separating her out and putting down other black students." The counselor's subscription to the beliefs that students who deserved college and were capable of academic success look and talk a particular way limited her ability to be an ally for students who did not fit her description. In Kimberly's high school, both the way the counseling system was organized, that is, the large number of students assigned to one counselor, and the buy-in of her counselor to prejudices and stereotypes about black student success, made this a mentoring situation but not an alliance.

High school guidance counselors can be helpful mentors to black undergraduate women. In their search for allies, black women undergraduates often name these relationships as important and complex. Practical help, like fee waivers can lift financial hardships during the application process, yet this type of practical help is not insurance that guidance counselors can act as allies for black undergraduate women. There is a need for counselors to examine their ideas around race, class, gender, admissions, and academic success and then actively work to challenge stereotypes and work to keep them out of their encounters with students. This active work is necessary to stop discouraging black women undergraduates and others from applying to colleges based simply on these ideas. Challenging their own raced and classed assumptions will also help counselors support students who return to their high schools to discuss their success. As the women revealed, trust and believing that all students can succeed are qualities that a counselor who is an ally must possess. The women in this discussion explained that they turned the obstacles presented by counselors into a way to succeed. These strategies reflected a powerful drive to succeed and supported the ability to "take what you need and dismiss the rest" and "not let anyone limit you." This strategic plan is a form of cultural capital that fosters their continued academic success.

Family Relationships and College Success

Parents: Coaches on the Sidelines

Educational literature stresses the importance of parental and family involvement in the schooling lives of children from kindergarten to college (Banks, 2004b; Freeman, 2005). This involvement looks different at different levels of schooling. Parents with a college education can provide particular support to black undergraduate women. Nadia, whose mother has a master's degree and whose father has a doctorate, both from prestigious private universities, acknowledged the ways she benefited from the level of education her parents attained:

> Nadia: Education is promoted so much in my family just because both my mother and my father have always been in the academic arena. But they striven, strived? (laugh) for a long time to get where they have and that's only because they've been

in school. My father stays [is always] comparing people that have not gone to college to people that do just because that's just a great leap—which I sense, too—in maturity that prepares you for life.

Interviewer: What does he say?

Nadia: Like, he'll say to me—let's say he sees somebody on the corner or like somebody got shot and he'll say, "I bet you he didn't go to school." You know what I'm saying? But it's just because he feels that when you're in college, you're being exposed to so many different things that you look forward to doing other things, you know. But if you don't go to school, you don't get exposed to all of that. Like let's say if you just stay around here and you just go to high school, you're always around the same people, the same environment. You have nothing to look forward to 'cuz you haven't been exposed to anything that's any different. So, I think that has a lot to do with it. But also, my parents told me that if you stay in school and you do what you have to do, you're going to achieve something. So if you just kind of work down that road, eventually it will pay off. (Interview, winter 2004)

Nadia had both the example and the admonition from college-educated parents to help her develop an understanding of the importance of higher education and the privileges that come as a result of going to college. Her father pointed out examples of lifestyles he found less desirable, like "standing on street corners and living with violence" as the consequences of a lack of education. In his eyes, according to Nadia, "education exposes you to other things to do." Nadia explained that she, too, "senses college as a measurement of how prepared you are for life." This sense, informed by her parent's educational example and value system, is cultural capital that fuels Nadia's success in school as she "works down the road to achievement." Nadia was able to clearly outline the practical benefits she received as a student, since her father works as a dean at Central University:

Interviewer: So, have the resources that your father has had been useful to you?

Nadia: They were very useful, very useful.

Interviewer: Can you tell me in what ways?

Nadia: I mean its minor ways when it comes down to it. I know I can always get books. I'm very close to everybody in his office, and he happens to have an office that's connected to every source of undergraduate preparation or anything that you do, that you take part in. Like, I participate in the [academic] program, I'm not necessarily in it, you know what I'm saying. But certain things like that have helped me with, like, my GREs. There are a lot of people my dad knows now that I didn't realize and appreciate, now that I'm trying to get into grad school, that I'm hoping are really going to help me out. I've met faculty that I'm a lot closer with and I'm comfortable with now. You know, through him and just saying, "Well, you know, that's my dad." Um, I think that's about it. (Interview, winter 2004)

Nadia expressed appreciation for her father's position and his connections at Central University. These privileges scaffold her work in higher education. Nadia recognized that this was capital that allowed her to "benefit from programs she is not officially enrolled in and meet and feel comfortable with faculty on her campus and at other schools" who may be able to help her with graduate school applications and offer guidance and direction once she is accepted. While Nadia valued and utilized the cultural capital she has from her father's position, she also understood that this cultural capital is not all she needed to do well. For Nadia, more was involved in her academic accomplishment than the benefits that came from her parents' education and her father's position at Central. She explained:

> Nadia: I kind of appreciate in myself that I've never wanted to use him as an excuse, but just like a resource, you know. I don't really even tell people, unless people know, unless they're saying something, unless it's necessary. Just 'cuz I don't ever want to be like, well, "My daddy works here." 'cause it's not even about that. He can't work miracles. (laugh) He can't get me an A in a class. (Interview, winter 2004)

Nadia understood that her success in school, which she described as "getting an A in a class," depended on *her* work. She is proud of the way she uses the cultural capital she is privileged to have. She doesn't use it as an excuse not to work hard, nor does she flaunt it. She just uses it as a resource.

Roe's mother is college educated and gave very specific support to Roe since she is a graduate of the program that Roe is now majoring in at Central University:

> Interviewer: Is there anyone else that you look to for support?
> Roe: Nope. Just my mother and I think so because I'm going through the same program that she went through. Like, she can help me deal with professors that, like she's like, "Okay, don't take him yet," you know; so, we were discussing stats, and I was telling her they really want me to take stats now, and she said, "Take my suggestion." (laugh) And she doesn't make a lot of suggestions, so she was like, "Please take this one." She's very informative, and although she doesn't think I take everything that she says and receive and process and use it, I really do, just because she understands where I am right now and she's been through it and it help[s] me realize that I can go through it and complete it and be where she is right now. (Interview, summer 2004)

Roe's mother's college education and the suggestions she gave to Roe to aid her success are traditional forms of cultural capital. Roe recognized and valued the advice from her mother over that of others connected to her education. She claimed that she "received, processed, and used" her mother's advice even when her mother doesn't think that is occurring. This familial alliance was important to Roe since she could see her mother's accomplishments and duplicate the steps her mother used to make them.

Roe's mother is her academic and social ally in her quest for a college degree. Roe acknowledged that this alliance was important and informed by race, class, and gender. She explained that her mother's behavior, as a college-educated black woman in a certain academic settings, set an example for behavior that she identified as necessary for her college success as a black woman undergraduate:

> Roe: I've definitely learned to work in different circles around these issues [race, class and gender]. Actually my mother helped me with that. When she was [a] student here, she would always bring me to different functions. So I learned how to act and participate in different situations by observing her, like we did a lot of alumni dinners and functions and things like that.
>
> Interviewer: Okay, and so what did you learn?
>
> Roe: Like one of the dinners that we had attended, there was a certain way that you had to dress. There was a certain way that you had to speak. And just by watching the interaction, even watching my mother, I thought she was white for a minute. (laugh) I have to be honest because I had never seen her in, in that environment where she had to be this whole different person. And I learned that you have to, (pause) I don't know how to put this, how to describe this. There is just, just this code thing, you know. You have to know how to act in different situations. When she was in the environment when she was surrounded by a bunch of, um, ah, white individuals or educated individuals or people in position of, you know, power and privilege and all of that. She knew how to maneuver in that situation and how to address certain issues that may have arrived. Even in her work environment, watching her in her work environment how she dealt with, basically white individuals who are over her or even under her. It's amazing, and so I learned to pick up on all of these qualities, learned how to dress, learned how to speak, to be polite, to use correct English, um, how to eat with a fork. I mean even in, even up to sitting at a table there's a way, there's different etiquettes that come into play. And I learned it all. It's funny because as I watched that whole dinner table session, it was interesting because as I watched the white individuals at the table, it was like they didn't really particularly care about how they were eating or how they were drinking or speaking with their mouth full or just you know, belching at the table where they were at. It just was not an issue for them. But *I knew*, for me, that was something that I haven't had done that everyone at the table would have noticed, and it would have been an issue. (emphasis hers) It's those things that I learned, to talk, to observe, and take notice and make sure that, you know, I was always the other person, I guess you could say. You definitely have to change modes in that environment, and then be yourself around those individuals that you can be yourself around. (Interview, summer 2004)

This conversation revealed that Roe buys into the idea that certain behaviors necessary for social success are considered inherent attributes of whiteness. These behaviors included ways of speaking, dressing, and sitting at a table that are considered proper. Roe observed her mother and "thought she was white for a moment." This observation made visible one way the supremacy of whiteness, as a concept and as a descriptor of appropriate social behavior is so deeply rooted in U.S. society that it is perpetuated, often unknowingly, by those most oppressed by it.

Roe's observation also laid bare her understanding that the socially constructed expectations or "codes" connected to whiteness were a catalyst for very real consequences for those who do not follow them, particularly if they do not have white privilege (Rothenberg, 2002). Roe knew that belching at the dinner table, in this setting, was not considered proper behavior. She also believed that her white tablemate could belch freely, without the repercussions she would face as a black woman if she engaged in the same behavior. This reality of whether or not her white tablemate would be judged negatively for belching out loud was not in question. It can be argued that anyone belching at the dinner table may get a negative reaction from those sharing the meal. What is crucial to understand is that from Roe's perspective, as a black woman surrounded by white people at a school function, her engaging in socially inappropriate dinner behavior, like chewing with her mouth open or belching, would be read in a racialized way. Roe believed both she and her mother would have stood out and been noticed in negative ways.

Roe observed her mother's behavior and recognized the adaptations she made to adhere to the codes she deemed necessary to avoid social stigma. Jones and Shorter-Gooden (2003) describe this phenomenon as "*shifting*," a process black women adopt to combat racialized and gendered stereotypes that inform their lives in work, school, and home and almost every other setting (p. 7). These authors expanded on this topic as follows:

> Our research shows that in response to this relentless oppression, black women in our country have had to perfect what we call *shifting*, a sort of subterfuge that African Americans have long practiced to ensure their survival in our society. Perhaps more than any other group of Americans, black women are relentlessly pushed to serve and satisfy others and made to hide their true selves to placate white colleagues, black men, and other segments of the community. They shift to accommodate differences in class as well as gender and ethnicity. From one moment to the next, they change their outward behavior, attitude, or tone, shifting *white* then shifting *black* again, shifting *corporate*, shifting *cool*. And shifting has become such an integral part of black women's behavior that some adopt an alternate pose or voice as easily as they blink their eyes or draw a breath. (pp. 6–7)

Roe's mother showed her by example and gave her the insight that she will have to *shift* in certain academic circles. Roe accepted this knowledge and ability and used it to negotiate her way in these settings. This work that Roe learned from her mother and then took on is additional evidence of the labor black women undergraduates must perform while at college. Raced and classed expectations that inform social life, namely the idea that Roe, a black woman, would not frequent formal dinners and thus did not know how to conduct herself, meant that Roe could not just spend her time at the dinner engaging in conversation or enjoying the atmosphere. Her understanding of how raced bodies are watched and evaluated, forced her to focus on her every move and how each move could be interpreted by the gaze of her dinner company. Roe felt that this type of knowledge would benefit her in higher education as she presented herself in various situations:

> Interviewer: What is it that acquiring those skills to be in different modes, what do you think it gets you?
>
> Roe: Well, um, (pause) I think it provides you with opportunities that if you were not, if you don't present yourself as educated, knowledgeable, respectful, you know, a very good communicator, you, you're just, you wouldn't achieve very much. Most people would deem you to be ignorant 'cuz you don't know how to work in both the circles or how adapt to different situations. I mean, you would gain a reputation. It will be greatly increased. People would notice you for who you are and say, "That young lady is—she's on top of things. She's knows how to deal in certain situations as they arrive." So you gain a sense of just—I don't know the right word to use. Just that, you know, just like an increase to a higher level of who you are in other people's eyes and you gain others' respect. And I believe I have done that in so many different aspects, just in my educational career and life. (Interview, summer 2004)

Roe is clear that "changing modes" is necessary in higher education and that "being yourself," as a black woman undergraduate, should be saved for "individuals you can be yourself around." Implicit in this idea is that there are allies with whom you *can* be yourself. Roe believed that her performance could undo the impact of racist and class-based stereotypes, inform how others see her, and help her gain respect. Roe was also clear that her achievement, in part, hinges on her ability to prove to others that she is "on top of things and can adapt her behavior" in higher educational settings to reflect what they and she deem as proper, as informed by societal expectations steeped in white, upper-class privilege.

In Roe and Nadia's cases, the cultural capital and academic currency their parents possess has supported their academic and social success in school. Both women realized that this cultural capital did not relieve them of the responsibilities they have to make decisions and perform well. This capital alone is not all that it takes to succeed. Nadia defined success as getting "an A in class" and knew that her father could not get the grade for her despite his level of education and his status on her campus. Roe appreciated that listening to her mother could help her "not lose anything" if she scheduled her course work properly. Roe also decided when to use advice from her mother and when to take a different path. Roe understood that, like most people, she had to navigate social settings. She also recognized that her negotiating social events like academic dinners was a specific process that involved her social locations and the ways they are read in society. Seeing her mother *shifting* (Jones & Shorter-Gooden, 2003) in those settings was a useful lesson to her as a black woman in higher education. It gave her a model to follow and strategies to incorporate that are a form of cultural capital that will aid her success.

Parents with college degrees can provide an abundance of support and impart critical knowledge that can smooth the educational path of black women undergraduates. The question then arises, what happens to black women undergraduates with parents who have no college education? Fortunately, the women I interviewed addressed this topic vigorously.

First-Generation Black Women Undergraduates

First-generation students have often been deemed less prepared for college based on the lack of college education and thus lack of knowledge about college held by their parents. The term *first generation* can be defined in many ways. For example in her study of first-generation students who lead activist lives, Rodriguez (2001) defined *first generation* as those who are first in their immediate or primary family to have any college- going experience (p. 10). In this text, I am using the term to describe the experiences related by black women undergraduates whose parents did not attend any college in the United States. I chose this definition because some of the women had siblings and parents who were presently college students but not college graduates. The black women undergraduates represented in this part of the discussion may have siblings who were attending or have attended college, and they have parents who have not obtained any level of college education.

Several black women undergraduates made clear that garnering parental support was challenging when parents have not had any college-related experiences. Kimberly, whose parents completed high school in Guyana explained that this situation affected her schooling life in both high school and college. She stated:

> Kimberly: My parents, because of like, I feel, the immigrating experience, were very disconnected because it's not something, it's not like they went to high school in America. You know what I mean? It was always like they checked my report card you know, the things that they could relate to. Like, "You should get an A." because they know what that signifies. But, like other things, I couldn't come home to talk to them about because it was a total different experience. They always went to parent–teacher night and stuff like that, as well. Even here at school, my parents don't understand what it is to be like at a University. And they'll be like, "Oh, you have As." That's what they can relate to. But other issues, like how I felt when I was a freshman and I realized that I was the only black girl in my class, they can't really deal with that because, for the most part, everyone that they're around are all black. You know what I mean? So, like, they don't have to deal with that displacement kind of feeling. (Interview, fall 2004)

Kimberly discussed how the intersection of her parents' immigrant experience and their lack of understanding of how school works in America limited the help they could give her as a student. Still in high school, they encouraged her to get good grades and went to parent-teacher conferences, evidence of their desire to see her thrive in school. Kimberly's parents understood the codes in U.S. society that deem education, particularly good grades, as a predecessor to success. However as Kimberly explained, the social challenges she had to deal with in college were beyond their realm of understanding. Her parents do not know what it is to be the "only black girl in class" because their social circles revolve around other black people. Kimberly stated that she felt "displaced" and, in her mind, her parents could not help her, since they had not had the experience. Kimberly's feeling of displacement may stem from a belief that black students with college-educated parents garner support around race and class issues in ways she does not. She sees this ideal of being college educated as the normative precursor to parental understanding and support, an assumption that may or may not be accurate but mirrors a privileged ideology that often leads to parents without a college education being devalued in the institution.

The alliances around schooling for black undergraduate women and parents who have not gone to college are complex. Some black women undergraduates found themselves and their parents learning about the process at the same time. Consider the experience Nicole described when choosing a college:

> Nicole: Honestly, like my mother wasn't really involved in the college process. It was more my father, and the only thing, like, he really said to me as far as schools is that you're going to go where they give you the most money. But besides that, it was up to me, you know, I told him I wanted to get away from home. I didn't know I was going to be this far away, but it was mainly up to me, I wouldn't say they were really into, you know, my father took me to visit schools. But it was the schools I wanted to go to. He never really put in his opinion of where he wanted me to go. I think also because he wasn't familiar with the college process, you know, because he hadn't gone through it himself. So, it was like he was learning along with me. (Interview, spring 2004)

Shonte talked about being her mother's teacher, since she wanted to attain a college degree:

> Interviewer: Okay, how involved is your family now in your college experience?
> Shonte: Not very, like, they really didn't help me through; a lot of what I've been doing is on my own. But I keep them abreast of what's going on, and they're more interested than before. My mother, she's interested in it because she wants to take college courses, so I kind of teach her. She's interested in the books that I read in certain classes and things like that. (Interview, spring 2004)

Both Nicole and Shonte described the independent work they must do because their parental involvement in aspects like choosing schools and the college experience is limited. This work includes taking on the role of teacher and participating in simultaneous learning. The strategies and skills involved in taking on these roles and seeing them through, that is, learning how to choose a college, getting into the college, and simultaneously teaching their parents all that is involved in the process is a form of cultural capital that supports academic success.

First-generation black women undergraduates were clear about the ways their parents who have no college education could act as allies and provide cultural capital they deem necessary for college success:

> Kayla: My mother didn't go to college, and my adopted mother didn't go to college, and my father, I don't think he went to college, either. He grew up in the South, and he came to New York. I think he was 19. He's retired now, and he started from the ground up, and somehow they got together. I don't know when that happened. (laugh) And they helped each other through everything. They've been married, um, don't tell my mom's age, but, they been married last year, last month, I think 35 years.
> Interviewer: Oh, wow.
> Kayla: So, they've been together for a long time. They didn't go to school, but they knew, they know, hard work. They know what it means to work hard, and I felt she deserved to see somebody go forth and do something with, with their lives. So, I'm doing it for me, but I'm doing it for her, too. So as far as school is concerned, they didn't push me, but we all know, your parents want to see you succeed. Any loving parent wants to see their child succeed. So, it wasn't a push, it was a want. (Interview, spring 2004)

> Nicole: My father he tells me all the time, actually the other day, he called me and left me a message, and I almost started crying. But told me, you know, that he was very proud of me and, you know, he's happy about the things that I'm doing in school, you know. 'Cause I've been like milking this school for money, and so I was getting funding for all these different things, and he just tells me that he's very proud of me. (Interview, spring 2004)

> Interviewer: Okay, you said your parents didn't go to college, but what is it, what do you think they've given you that helps you in college?
> Blue: I think that they've given me, like, a drive; whereas they, you know, push me in order to do better, to do better. Not to just stay in one place, always want to do more.
> Interviewer: And how do they do that?
> Blue: I don't know how they do that. They're so tricky. Tricky, you know, it's just drilled into me, it's just like, "You sure you just want that social work degree? I think you should, you know, maybe try something else." I don't know. They just, they plant seeds in me, and then they just grow. (Interview, fall 2004)

Blue, Kayla and Nicole explained that motivation to do well came from seeing their parents work hard and hearing their words of encouragement and pride. These women believed their parents to be allies that used "tricks to plant seeds that grow" and provided a drive to do better that facilitates their work.

Kimberly described the strong sense of identity instilled in her by her parents:

Interviewer: Okay. If you wanted to think about the types of things your family gave you that have helped you be successful in college, what kinds of things would you talk about?

Kimberly: Just, I would say, a definition of myself that is not related to anyone else. So, I'm Kimberly Noel, I have what it takes, like, I've always been taught to be proud of me, proud of my heritage. Never to feel less than anyone, so that really helped me. I feel like for the majority of students of color, what really traps us up? It's not the academic aspect. It is the social aspect and getting your mind psychologically ready for this. 'Cuz *this is like warfare*, you know what I mean? (emphasis hers) And, if like, I didn't have a strong sense of self, I would have questioned myself. I would have felt like inferior to my peers because they're coming from different backgrounds. Especially like in the majors that I'm in.

Interviewer: And just real quick back to what you said about the counselor [telling Kimberly not to apply because she would not get in], so how did you finally get to Central?

Kimberly: I made an appointment for an interview because I knew that my, that I wasn't like an outstanding student, but I knew I wasn't like a garbage student. I was like in between, so there's strength to my application. (Interview, fall 2004)

A strong sense of self implanted by her parents who had no college education enabled Kimberly to utilize the strategy of an interview to increase her chances of acceptance at Central University. She knew that whatever her traditional report may have appeared to be lacking and no matter how little faith her counselor had in her abilities, she was a strong candidate. Kimberly took it upon herself to show the university her strength in person. In Kimberly's eyes, the sense of self given to her by her parents, who I contend were useful allies in this experience, gave her the capital she needed to engage in "academic warfare, remain psychologically strong, and not feel inferior to her peers." This capital facilitated her academic success by reinforcing her sense of belonging at Central University. She continued: "I never once question myself and my ability or my integrity or my reason for being here. I'm supposed to be here. I deserve to be here. No one's doing me any favor" (interview, fall 2004).

In the lives of Kimberly, Kayla, Nicole, and Blue, parental support, including support from parents with no college education, was a factor these black women undergraduates and I examined and appreciated for the cultural capital the alliance provided. As these "coaches from the sidelines plant seeds that grow" they provide currency that scaffolds the academic and social accomplishments of their daughters in college. All these women, except Kayla, were residential students at Central University; Kayla commuted daily to International Community College. One aspect of this discussion to explore in the future is how support is similar and different in these diverse school settings.

Mothers and Daughters

In this discussion of parental support, one relationship that continually and consistently stood out as crucial for academic success was the relationship some of the black undergraduate women had with their mothers. Black families are historically matriarchal. In my study, 8 out of 19 women came from single-parent homes where the mother was the head of the household. Of the women from single-parent homes, 3 had limited contact with their fathers, and 5 had no contact with their fathers at all. In all 8 cases, the mother was the main financial provider. When black undergraduate women whose parents were not married or not raising them together were asked to describe their socioeconomic status, most of the women identified their single mothers as their main financial support in college, even when their fathers were involved in their lives, had more income, or contributed money toward education. Examples of their comments follow:

> Leviticus: Well, we're not poor and we're not rich. My mother has a good job and she gets the things that she wants in life, like materially. I mean there's always been a distinction between my mother's money and my money. I know I'm po' and I don't have any money, but at the same time, I know that I have my mother, who isn't poor, to back me up in any situation. (Interview, spring 2004)

> Teena: I don't know anything about him [my father], so it's a struggle. Everything is from my mom only, and like, she's paying for, like, I didn't realize before I got here that a lot of parents say, you know, "Once you get to college, you got to deal with that on your own." But she's paying for everything for me, as well, so. (Interview, spring 2004)

> Alex: My mother, she's constantly sending me money. [Alex lives with her father.] She opened an account in Philly [where her mother lives] so she can put money in there, and I can have my debit card. She makes sure there's money in there whether its $20 or whatever, she makes sure there's money. (Interview, summer 2004)

> Nadia: To be honest, I look at everybody's money differently. Like, I think when my father was living in the house, it was a little different, you know. I would never describe myself as high class now just with my mother's earnings, you know. So I think we're comfortable, we're still middle class, but I understand that his money is his money. My mother's money is my money and my sister's money; you know what I'm saying? Like, he supports me, but she will support me till the end, you know, and I live with her, I don't live with my dad. But it's just that fact that I don't live with him, so it's not my first choice, my first step when I need something, it's my mom. (Interview, winter 2004)

In this gendered talk, these students acknowledged the socioeconomic status of their mothers and the financial work their mothers do to support their schooling. The women felt connected to their mothers' status in this social location. This is indicated by their identification and claim that their mothers' status was also their own. Single black mothers are disparaged in American society in almost every arena including media, popular culture, social policy, social settings, politics, and religion. They are accused of being a financial drain on the U.S. economy (Giddings, 1984; Yoo, 1999). The above "class talk" challenged that negative stereotype as the women identified and respected their mothers' work to support them financially.

Black women undergraduates also challenged this societal scorn by paying tribute to their black single mothers' part in their academic success. This tribute included descriptions and metaphors that described their feelings about their mothers. In each example, the emphasis has been added:

Roe: She's my *backbone*, she keeps me going, um, and then when I need help, I seek help. (Interview, summer 2004)

Malikah: She never actually finished her college education, but *she's one of the smartest women I know*. (Interview, fall 2004)

Kimberly: She has, like, a hair salon, like, a nail salon; and she's just the epitome of the American Dream coming true. Because someone that never was able to go to school was able to open her own business, run a successful business, and have other business people coming to her for advice. Like *she is definitely, like a phenomenal woman*. (Interview, fall 2004)

Leviticus: My mom is my mom. *She's a strong black woman*. She's one of those women that people call a jack-of-all-trades. So anything you need, if she can't do it herself, she has references and contacts of who can do it. (Interview, spring 2004)

Teena: So, basically my mom is the *glue that holds us together*. (Interview, spring 2004)

Malikah: 'Cuz my mother has been like, you know, *this spine in my back*, you know, keeping me up. (Interview, fall 2004)

Teena: Junior college (in Belize) is like our high school so she never—she didn't go back. But it's so funny, because I just, I think she is just *brilliant*. I just think, like, in terms of, like, maybe in terms of that schooling and stuff, she was limited in that way, but in terms of the other stuff, I think *she's really rich, really rich*. (Interview, fall 2004)

Much of this respect and drive for education comes from the way the intersections of race, class, and gender informed the financial sacrifices their mothers made for them to have an education:

Malikah: I think it's because, like I said, my mom gave up; she had a very, very good job in Jamaica, she was a detective, and I knew she was getting paid well, but the fact that she gave up a beautiful lifestyle just to come here, has been my key motivation. That had been her goal to come here, and I feel like since that's a goal, then we're here to do just that, and that's been my motivation. Being because we're coming from a poor family, education was a priority in our family because education was, um, the escape that we saw for poverty, and that was the main reason why my mother migrated from the Caribbean to come here because she felt that all her kids would have an opportunity to have an education, without her having to worry about how to send them through college. Because then in the Caribbean was so expensive to send all three kids. So, that was the main reason why she migrated to this country, so all her kids would be very successful and, um, have an education. So, education is, like, very important in our family. My mom started school. She wanted to complete her RN [registered nurse training]. She got her credits, and she dropped out. She said she was being overworked because she had to do two jobs just so she could take care of us and go to school, and it was very hard so she dropped out. And that's always… Well, now she's saying as long I finish, it doesn't matter whether she finished or not. (Interview, fall 2004)

Malikah's mother sacrificed a "good job" in the Caribbean to come to the United States so that her children could go to college. Once in the States, her mother sacrificed her own education, worked two jobs, and took care of her children. Malikah recognized this sacrifice and the way it transformed her family's economic status and lifestyle. In Jamaica, Malikah's mother had a middle-class income but feared she could not afford to educate all her children. In the United States, Malikah and her family were poor and were focused on educational attainment. Malikah understood that this classed dilemma required strategies to negotiate as well as sacrifices on the part of her mother. Malikah too, must strategize. She uses her respect for her mother's sacrifices to boost her ambition and desire to do well in school and "finish."

Malikah told me that she wanted her mother to finish the nursing program she started and gave up. Her plan was to complete school, find a job, and then financially support her mother while she goes to school. Thus, Malikah has an added drive to be successful in college, fueled by the responsibility she has taken on to give back to her mother what she has received. All these examples showed that black mothers are an integral part of their daughters' motivation. These single black mothers set specific examples that challenged the stereotypes about them and that helped their daughters succeed as raced, classed, and gendered beings in higher education. These examples included making financial sacrifices so their daughters could attend college, offering motivation and encouragement, and looking for ways to get their own education.

Professors

Like guidance counselors in high schools, college and university professors are a foundational fixture in colleges and universities. Black women undergraduates must navigate and negotiate relationships with professors both inside and outside of the classroom. This relationship was a subject of conversation for the black women undergraduates I interviewed; they valued the relationships they had with black professors. They outlined the ways black professors bolstered their college success:

Interviewer: Talk about your interactions with black professors.

RGB: They've been more like mentors than professors. I know in the African American Studies Department, I feel very close to that department. They care about my future. They care about our organizations.

Interviewer: How do they show you that they care?

RGB: They come to a lot of our events, a lot of them. Whenever I go there, no matter how busy they are, they'll sit right down and talk to me about my academics. They talk to me about my family life. They talk to me just about issues that are going on in the world. They invite us to their houses and listen to us when we have personal problems or we're trying to get money or something like that. They are there to help us with constructing our game plan and getting what we need to get out of this university, and I just feel like that going above and beyond what a professor is traditionally supposed to do. And whenever there's new books out that they think would be of interest and things like that. Like Professor Johnson, there was a book called *Ready for Revolution*,[1] and she bought it for me. Like, you know, that's something that's really above the call of duty for a professor to do. (Interview, spring 2004)

Interviewer: Talk about your interactions with black professors.

Shonte: I love them all—love them all because they're not professors who are like, "This is just my job." There are black professors who care about black students on this campus—like, they go above and beyond for their black students. But they don't do things like, "I'm going to pass you because you're black." They want to see you do better. So they give you the grade they feel you deserve, and I really respect pretty much all of the black professors who I come in contact with—*all* of them. (emphasis hers) (Interview, spring 2004)

Teena: My best professors are always black, you know. Because they are just extra. They are really good.

Interviewer: What do you mean by that, "They're extra?"

Teena: Well, first of all, in the African American Studies Department, they are like a family. So I just feel like any class I take in that department, they just take me in, too. I feel like I'm with people who care about me. (Interview, spring 2004)

For Teena, RGB, and Shonte, black professors at Central University have been like family. This feeling was cultivated as the professors took interest in their lives, supported their academic work, and pushed them to "do better." Teena explained that the family-like care goes "above and beyond" what she sees as a role of a professor.

These women recognized that the professors themselves faced issues in their place in higher education that are related to race. This knowledge informed the alliances between black professors and the black women undergraduates:

Shonte: I know any professor has a hard time getting tenure, but it has to be especially hard for a black professor.

Interviewer: Why do you say that?

Shonte: Because, I don't care how progressive this campus tries to get, I just think that if there are two people who have their PhD's who are working in the department, I really feel like the white person—and they're both qualified for the same position—I really have a feeling a white person will get it before [a black person]. You know, they are the face of this university whereas the black professor isn't. (Interview, spring 2004)

Teena: Now the black professors I've had in [my department], I've had two and they were just phenomenal. But then you have to sit down and think about this, one of these professors, he is just amazing. He had so much experience in broadcast[ing] before he came, and every student, black or white, they love him. Now the thing with him is that he is—when I say he is extra, I feel like he has to be, he has to probably be 10 times better than any other person on the staff. (Interview, spring 2004)

Shonte and Tina understood the racism that some black professors have to face in higher education. This basic assumption is one of the ways they made sense of their relationships with black professors on campus. They saw themselves as allies who acknowledged this particular struggle for black professors and who championed the work the professors were doing to support them in school. Understanding the complexities of this alliance is a form of cultural capital that black women undergraduates cultivate as they evaluate these relationships around intricate racial concerns.

Teena moves on to talk about her interactions with white professors:

Teena: The white professors I've had, some have been less memorable. You know, they're okay. Nothing special and I don't know if that's because I'm black and gravitate towards? You know what, I mean? I would gravitate towards that, but even now, one of my black professors, like, I still love him, but I'm not sure where he stands in terms of his blackness and how he identifies himself. He doesn't strike me as the type of person who wears their blackness on his sleeve or is always talking or specifically reaching out to black students, and he doesn't strike me as that, but he's still amazing. (Interview, spring 2004)

For Teena, blackness was not just one identity. Teena realized that she may have sought out black professors, but she did not assume that the color of her professor's skin immediately branded him as an ally, nor did she expect every black professor to be exactly the same. Teena decided that, for her, this one black professor could be remarkable even if he wasn't wearing that blackness on his sleeve. She identified what made him outstanding in her eyes, namely, "his experience in broadcasting" and how he relates to students.

Kimberly explained that the "wearing of blackness" on one's sleeve on the part of a black professor wasn't necessarily a good predictor of a successful alliance:

Kimberly: So, I had [a black professor] from the African American [Studies] Department. That was interesting because I enjoyed him. But yet, I felt like he kind of put a lot of pressure on me to be what he thought I should be, and sometimes I feel like with the black professors, in an attempt to like mold us into, you know, people that are conscious, they don't want us to be like passive consumers of the society and act like everything's okay. Yet, I feel like they want us to be extremists sometimes, and sometimes I feel like that's a problem 'cuz they don't let you get to that point for yourself.

Interviewer: So how did he let you know that that's what he wanted to do?

Kimberly: Just the ways he speaks to me, "You don't know what you're talking about; like, you're not deep enough; you're not—you're not soul sister enough." And I was just like, "Whatever, [named professor], forgive me 'cuz I don't want to go burn a building down." (laugh) And I don't feel like all of the [black professors] are like that. He always told me I wanted to be a part of the black bourgeoisie, and he feels like a lot of black professors are kind of a part of the black bourgeoisie. I was just like, "Okay, whatever, and what car do you drive?" (laugh) (Interview, fall 2004)

Kimberly's relationship with this black professor was complex. Like Teena, she saw blackness as multifaceted and resisted attempts to mold her into what she called an *extremist*. This call of Kimberly to radicalism on the part of the professor was an engendered discussion. As discussed in Chapter Four, assertiveness on the part of black women is read in stereotypical ways that can make their schooling lives oppressive. Kimberly knew that, even though both she and her professor were black, she did not have to be who he wanted her to be. Kimberly did not agree with the professor's assessment of how she should behave as a black woman. She was able to take in his opinion, critique it, and make her own decision about what it meant for her to be black. Utilizing this strategy helped Kimberly negotiate this alliance. Even with the knowledge that she and the professor looked at *blackness* very differently—that is, she perceived his view as more militant than hers and resisted his attempts to change her—Kimberly said that she was still able to "enjoy him."

Leviticus described a different outcome after one encounter with a particular black professor:

Leviticus: I'm more likely to interact with them [black professors] 'cuz I see them more often and they're more, like, you just have that camaraderie. You just automatically feel a little bit more of a stronger bond with them, but at the same time, that doesn't automatically mean, like, every professor is your friend. And you learn very quickly that every black professor isn't gonna care, and a lot of them are doing their own thing and just trying to get their tenure. Actually, the *only* black professor I've had [in my department], I had last semester. And I had asked her some questions like what it's like to be the only black professor over there, but the answers I received were not satisfactory as far as where black culture should be.

Interviewer: What were her answers?

Leviticus: It was one of those, "Oh, I don't focus on it. I just do my job, and everyone sees me for the job I do." And I was like, "Oh, okay." (laugh) "Conversation over. Yeah. Have a nice day." You know, that kind of thing. So I really don't, like I said, when I graduate, there's gonna be certain professors that I have spoken to and have seen that have nurtured me and seen me grow and have encouraged me to keep striving. Those are the professors I'll remember. (Interview, spring 2004)

The black professor Leviticus described in this encounter did not fit her ideal of what a black professor should be. Leviticus, seeking an alliance, raised a question she thought would give her insight into the ways race informed the life of the only black professor in her department. Leviticus interpreted the black professor's response as one indicating that race was not an issue in her position at the school. For Leviticus, this denial was a conversation stopper. She indicated that this professor would not be "memorable" in her higher education experience, since this professor could not, in Leviticus's eyes, "nurture her and see her grow."

Leviticus had a specific discourse she wanted this black professor to engage. Leviticus appeared to have little understanding that, as the only black faculty member in the department, this professor may have felt that the strategy of denying that race informs her job in a challenging way was an approach to prevent or combat obstacles. She did not know Leviticus well and could have chosen to give this less-combative response because she was not sure she could trust that her words would not be repeated and heard by those in a position to create difficulty for her at work. This example presented another complexity for black women undergraduates and black professors in choosing and evaluating relationships. Leviticus, by only creating space for one discourse around race and school and by making the hasty decision not to consider this woman as a resource, may have lost the opportunity to form an alliance with the only black woman professor in her department. Recognizing the need to make space for blackness as a multifaceted identity and then negotiating relationships with this realization is a form of cultural capital that can help black women undergraduates form alliances that foster success.

Black professors can act as mentors and allies to black students, even when the relationships are complex and expectations differ. The depth of these relationships can be seen as Shonte described how the death of a black faculty member informed her drive for success:

> Shonte: Getting through the loss of one of the best professors I could say I ever, ever, ever had, you know, he was. To know that there was a black professor in his position was amazing, and then to have him taken away the day after our last class was so hard. I really went through it with that, and I can say it only made me want to do better. Knowing that his legacy, he did what I wanted to do and to know that now I have to live out his legacy, even though I'm not his child, I'm not even related to him, I feel this extra closeness. (Interview, fall 2004)

For Shonte, he was an inspiring teacher and professor, and the presence and then absence of this mentor and ally motivated her to excel. She wanted to carry out a legacy of educational distinction. Her cultural capital was the recognition that there is a need for this important kind of support, that is, nurturing, mentoring, and affirmation from black professors.

Conclusions

The discussion of alliances in this chapter is by no means exhaustive, nor does it describe every relationship black women undergraduates deem necessary to succeed in school. This conversation does show that for college students, including black women undergraduates, there are relationships that facilitate that success. Some of these relationships are built into school structures, like that of the high school guidance counselor and that of the college professor. In both these relationships, black undergraduate women must negotiate when to take advice and when to forge ahead with their own ideas and goals. Black undergraduate women in this study recognized the importance of alliances as they sought out practical advice, financial support, and other forms of mentoring and nurturing to help them get through school. These women also had to evaluate these relationships around race and class. This often made visible the complexities of their relationships with black professors which included the need to be open to discourses about race that may have been different from their own expectations and experiences about blackness and schooling.

The black women undergraduates I interviewed insisted that their allies must understand that they are raced and classed beings and that this informs each aspect of their schooling lives. They did not all have the exact same needs or expectations from their alliances, but they did recognize the need to have this support. For black women undergraduates, negotiating these relationships is both complicated and crucial. The strategies they described that they used to do so were a form of cultural capital that has often been overlooked in traditional ideas of mentoring in higher education.

Family alliances can also be complex for black women undergraduates. Parents with college degrees can provide a wealth of information to support their daughters' educational success since they have had the experiences and often have the resources—both monetary resources and access to people, as in Nadia's case—that can make the path smoother than for students who do not have these specific resources. Parents without college degrees, particularly single mothers, also send their daughters to school with capital that the black women undergraduates named as invaluable to their success. For these women, this capital included financial support, motivation, and a strong sense of identity. The black undergraduate women I interviewed challenged the public scorn (informed by race, class, and gender oppression) that is often heaped upon single black mothers and parents without college educations. They did so by clearly identifying the role these alliances played in their academic success including the shared learning that occurred. This shared learning placed the women in many positions simultaneously; they acted as teacher, student, mentor, and mentee. They were dependent and independent, leaders and followers. They were allies.

The black undergraduate women gave glorifying shout-outs to their mothers, whose lives also reflected the material consequences of being raced, classed, and gendered beings. This acknowledgment praised the mothers for all they had done to help their daughters reach their goal of obtaining a college degree. The black women undergraduates praised black professors who dealt with racism in their colleges and universities and still found time to support and nurture them as students. The existence of these alliances and the processes and skills connected to establishing, maintaining, and negotiating them are cultural capital that these black women undergraduates told us they used to cultivate, navigate, learn, and grow in their colleges and universities.

CHAPTER SIX

Black Women Undergraduates Shape Campus Policy and Practice

The black women undergraduates in this study engaged in theory work as they made meaning of their schooling experiences. As theorists, they outlined the cultural capital that they bring, utilize, and gain in college. They critically analyzed the place that cultural capital has in academic discourses and in their respective institutions and recounted some of the real-life outcomes and practicalities that informed their thinking and behavior. The capacity to marry the theoretical and the practical and to use this union to suggest campus policy, procedure, ethos, and habit is evidence of high-level learning and intellect. It is a form of cultural capital that is crucial to the mission of equitable and just education. This skill is a must for black undergraduate women who strategize their way through schooling oppressions.

Colleges and universities that claim a commitment to equity and social justice are required by this assertion to institute policies and practices that mitigate the dominance black undergraduate women face based on their race, class, gender, and other non-dominant social locations they may embody. To that end, this chapter utilizes the comments the women provided to explore practical ways educators and institutions can meet the needs of black women undergraduates. It outlines the ways colleges and universities can, as they learn to recognize and value the cultural capital of black women undergraduates, turn this knowledge into active practice that challenges race, class, and gender oppressions. Schools that take on this task and succeed will create an environment that benefits all students, faculty, and staff.

When I was asked to add a chapter that addresses the practical application of the theoretical material in this book, I was temporarily bemused. In my head, this book was done. I was already working on other writing projects and it took time to reconnect with this endeavor. I also grappled with how to get around the tendency of some texts about educational equity to create toolboxes and checklists that educators and institutions can use as manuals when interacting with and educating undergraduates. One of the underpinnings of this text and the women's conversations is that the consequences of the intersections of race, class, and gender that inform their schooling experiences make it difficult to create a how-to handbook that applies, at all times, to all of them.

The toolbox and checklist strategies can, at times, guide educators and institutions as they work to challenge oppressive policy and practice and these attempts do have a place in academic discussions. It is wise to use such strategies cautiously, since these approaches often reinforce stereotypes about black student learning and facilitate deficit models about ability and intellect. When all the checkmarks have been made and all the tools have been employed but the struggles around educational oppressions continue, practitioners and institutions revert back to these oppressive stereotypes and deficits arguing that the needs of "these students" cannot be met and that the flaws must be individual. Checklists and toolboxes, followed rigidly, do not allow for the changes in contexts that occur during the tenure of any black undergraduate women at colleges and universities, since our schooling institutions, as social spaces, do not exist outside of dynamic social, economic, and political systems. Changing contexts, such as the public dialogue resulting from the Don Imus controversy or the current economic crisis in the United States, inform the lives of black women undergraduates in ways that require ongoing and varied evaluation and action.

So, this chapter is not a checklist, a toolbox, or a manual. It is a discussion of good teaching and institutional practices that highlight the cultural capital of black women undergraduates and that provide support for their success. During my preparation for this chapter, I have come to realize that for many institutions and educators this is not an ongoing dialogue. It still, most often, sits at the margins of other classroom or institutional business, if it happens at all. For example, most instructional time in college is spent on the content knowledge students need to understand various academic disciplines. Some disciplines lend themselves more easily to discussions and scholarship about identity, inclusion, diversity, difference, and acknowledging all kinds of cultural capital. Other disciplines must work harder to incorporate these ideals. Often, professors who are committed to these standards are not adequately prepared to address them in the colleges and universities in which they work. First, not all graduate programs incorporate pedagogy aimed at addressing and incorporating differences in the classroom. Second, there is often only limited time and few opportunities for academics to spend on "how we teach" after obtaining a faculty position at a college or university. One of my colleagues, Kristy Kenyon, recently explained that while being trained as a biologist in graduate school, she received neither direct nor indirect instruction regarding teaching and pedagogy, culture and identity relevant or otherwise. She has taken advantage of opportunities to learn this piece of her pedagogy through faculty development offered on our campus, through scholarship from this field, and in dialogue with other colleagues who do this work.

When educators and institutions have not prepared to deal with the classroom interactions and campus issues that arise that are connected to race, class, and gender or to create academic and social experiences that are in tune with students' necessary identity work, they will most often draw upon their own historical, biographical, and social understandings, which are often drastically different from those of black women undergraduates, to decide how to act and be (Villegas & Lucas, 2007, p. 30). The tenets of good teaching that support identity work and educational equity must be at the center of:

- faculty and staff hiring, training, and evaluation

- campus-wide communications and assessments

- strategic planning and budgeting

- regular campus climate checks and measures of accountability

When these tenets are not central, colleges and universities continue to facilitate oppressive schooling environments even while they are expending energy and resources aimed at combating such obstacles (e.g., practices associated with multicultural weekends). For black undergraduate women, the results are reinforced oppression and an increase in the work they have to do to negotiate their way to college success.

My colleague Kristy, mentioned earlier, is an educator deeply committed to equity and excellence in teaching. She looks for ways to address inequities related to race, class, and gender with a goal of helping all students learn and also looks for ways these ideas inform science content and pedagogy. As I was discussing this chapter with her and fearing I was simply stating what was already evident in earlier chapters, she said, "I don't know the things that may be obvious to you. I need someone to tell me how to translate what these women have said into practice." Her honesty reminded me again that strategies and policy that facilitate equity, that value a wide range of experience, and that recognize the cultural capital of all students are not at the center of pedagogical or policy discourse in higher education. Kristy helped me remember that implementation of strategy and policy that promotes and promulgates equity requires bringing the need for it to a high level of consciousness. It requires acquiring knowledge about how oppression works and how to combat it as well as advanced thought, careful preparation, deliberate action, and constant evaluation.

What follows is a discussion of how this ideology can become practice on campuses and in classrooms. Utilizing the conversations black women undergraduates provided earlier, this chapter will explore, using suggestions and questions, how this practice supports alliance building. It will help educators and institutions gauge their commitment to helping all students learn in an environment that is safe and to doing the constant work of challenging oppression.

Classroom Practice

Black women undergraduates referenced specific classroom interactions that shaped how they made meaning of their schooling experiences. Like most students, black undergraduate women recognized that what happens in the classroom is a primary way their value is assessed. To that end, the women described encounters that were helpful and those that created obstacles. Analysis of these discussions lays bare ideas about classroom practice that educators who are committed to equity must consider. For some, these ideas are not new, since they have been reviewed in scholarship about good teaching. However, discussion of the practical application of these ideas in *college* is a missing link in the academic literature.

Know Who Your Students Are

Getting to know students is not hard. It does not require an exorbitant time commitment or a major reduction in content teaching time. It does require that professors ask questions and this asking can take many forms. My colleagues Jonathan Iuzzini, a social psychologist, and Jennifer Roche, a math professor, require each student to write a short autobiography, due early in the term. They ask students to write about their personal educational journey, their histories with the discipline, and connections to course content. I have had great success using *free writes*. A free write is a one- or two-page, handwritten response to questions I pose. Free writes are completed in class and can be used any time during the term. Using this method allows me to ask students important questions about their understanding of course content and how they are experiencing the course. I use free writes to introduce difficult material and to spark dialogue when students seem reluctant to speak. Sometimes the free writes are anonymous; other times they are not, depending on the information I am seeking and whom I want to engage. Each member of the class completes every free write, even if my concern or information gathering is focused on a few students. No one person or group is ever singled out in this form of data collection, thus eliminating a common problem black women undergraduates face in college classrooms; plus, I obtain the voices of all students addressing the topic at hand.

Gathering student responses and stories and then using this knowledge to guide how and what we teach lets students know their input is important . These strategies allow students to directly disclose important information they may feel uncomfortable discussing in class or with professors they do not know well. An added bonus for professors is that there will be fewer surprises at the end of the term course evaluations since students have had input all term long. Ladson-Billings (1994) explained that culturally relevant teachers "help students make connections between their community, national, and global identities" (p. 34).

Understanding and relying on these connections are ways black women undergraduates said they navigated school oppression. Understanding what these connections are and how they inform teaching in any discipline can support that negotiation. This can only happen if we know who our students are.

Know the Many Ways Students Learn

As the black women undergraduates explained, sometimes they learn differently from the traditional ways professors are taught to teach. How then should we teach? While it is not possible to tailor every academic lesson to meet the needs of every student, we can offer a wide range of ways for students to show what they know. The various student *intelligences* and learning styles (i.e., interpersonal, intrapersonal, bodily kinesthetic, artistic, musical, mathematical) so often applied in K–12 educational settings do not go away in college (Baum, Viens, & Slatin, 2005, pp. 7–20). Yet, in college classrooms, little time is given to incorporating the strongest skill sets students have and helping them develop others. Educators, ask yourselves, do you know what your students consider their academic strengths and weaknesses? Are the assignments you give varied enough to allow students to use a range of skill sets to show what they know or does every assignment look the same? Do you offer a range of assessments and evaluations? Do you use technology and encourage students to do so? Do students get to participate, when applicable, in teaching content and assessment design? Designing a final project, sharing in the creation of grading rubrics, having choices about types of assessments, and opportunities for structured peer feedback are all ways to incorporate multiple and varied learning styles into classroom pedagogy.

The black women undergraduates in this study acknowledged that they do not always come to college prepared with the academic skills that students who attended well-resourced high schools may have. This phenomenon is not just an academic state of some black women undergraduates. Many white middle- and upper-middle-class students come with limited writing and math skills, for example. For black women undergraduates, the connection of the academic challenge to their race, class, and gender make their lack of preparation hypervisible and individualized. The stigma and discriminatory practices that result render a particular and distinct sting. Recognition that the inequitable K–12 educational system in the United States renders some students less prepared academically than others should influence and inform how professors respond to black undergraduate women living the consequences of this inequity. This recognition is also useful when undergraduate women enter disciplines that are typically male dominated. For example, as colleges and universities work to attract women, including women of color, into science and math, it is important to recognize that the race, class, and gender biases in K–12 educational settings, that is, "gender typing" that can "pigeonhole students into curriculum paths (for example, entry into science and math careers for boys and into the helping professions and language arts careers for girls) can leave undergraduate women less prepared and less secure about success in these disciplines in college (Spradlin and Parsons, 2008, p. 14).

Applying this systemic analysis changes deficit discourses, such as "these students do not belong in college" or "women cannot master this area of study," to language and action that are affirming and that help students acquire necessary skills. For example, I teach a course entitled Social Foundations of Multiculturalism. The course is an upper-level undergraduate and graduate course that examines concepts of privilege, intersectionality, dominance, and cultural capital in educational contexts. In this course, many of the students, representing a range of races, ethnicities, social classes, and schooling experiences (e.g., public, private, single sexed), know little about the multicultural history of the United States. I have found that when I allow time for students to research relevant historical information and then teach a brief lesson or two (or allow them to do so) focused on this information, students are able to engage in the regular course content in more meaningful ways, and they feel empowered to participate.

Educators often lament the limited proficiency of students as they enter college and resist helping students acquire what they need. I am not suggesting that all students can acquire every skill or master all content. At times, it is appropriate to counsel students into majors and disciplines that suit their academic interests and abilities. Advisors who counsel students in this way must ensure that their steering does not stem from bias and is not connected to race, class, and gender stereotypes about student identities and learning. Faculty need to be sure their advice is not given because it is the easy choice. Without precautions in both these aspects of counseling, marginalization and discrimination can result. Teaching adequately supports students' academic achievement when it allows students to acquire the prerequisite content and skill set and when it acknowledges and mitigates consequences of schooling inequities related to race, class, and gender oppression.

Set Clear Expectations and Be Open to Student Input

At most colleges and universities, the syllabus is a contract between faculty and students that each are expected to honor. The clearer and more detailed the contract, the stronger the possibility that students will perform well. For example, equitable education requires that students have a clear understanding of how they will be evaluated in a course. A syllabus should include the grading standards and scale. It should include a thorough description of each assignment that outlines expectations and provides a detailed grading rubric that can then be used in assessment.

Setting clear expectations equips students with the knowledge necessary to complete their assignments. It allows them to enlist the strategies and services (e.g., study groups, tutoring) they need to utilize in learning and assists them with time management. The use of a grading rubric builds trust in the academic assessment process, since students know the criteria by which their work will be judged. Faculty can pinpoint the content and skill they want students to demonstrate and provide regular, constructive feedback based on this shared understanding. Student learning is challenged when expectations, due dates, and guidelines are not clear, not communicated, or changed in major ways during the term. Students who have to work in addition to going to school may have tight schedules and less flexibility for major changes, which can create hard choices between taking care of themselves and their academic success.

Conducting student evaluations throughout the term is a way to hear what students need and how they are experiencing the course. At Hobart and William Smith Colleges, Susan Pliner, director of the Center for Teaching and Learning, conducts midterm evaluations for professors at their request. The model she uses, "Small Group Instructional Diagnosis" helps students come to consensus around constructive feedback (Angelo & Cross, 1993). Once she has gathered student feedback, Susan meets with each professor within 24 hours and gives them input and strategies to address any concerns; many of the suggested strategies are designed to be immediately incorporated into teaching. For educators, this can be vulnerable space and a wonderfully affirming place. Knowing what is working and what is not working allows for change long before the end of the term evaluations.

Manage Interactions in the Classroom: Group Work

In engaging and interactive classrooms, students work together on projects, presentations, and assignments in small groups. Group work has been identified as good practice for students of color who often learn best using this collaborative, peer-to-peer model. However, if group work is not managed, it can lead to oppressive situations. For example, it may seem reasonable to divide the few students of color in a classroom in an attempt to make each group diverse. Yet, for many, being the only student of color represented in a group can be painful and challenging because, as the black women undergraduates in this text explained, their intellect is often called into question. Black women undergraduates described being shut out of or ignored during group processes. Others have described instances where their ability was called into question. Leviticus told this story:

> Leviticus: You know, freshman year, I was in a group where all of the members of the group, all white, disregarded everything that I said. And it was really frustrating

because at that point I was a control freak when it came to groups. I had to make sure everything was getting done at a certain time, and I had to edit everything. I am really good at editing, and I know that is one of my strengths. And this one guy in the group—I was doing all of the work, and he would be like, "Let me make sure you didn't miss anything." and I *knew* I didn't *miss anything* 'cuz this is what I do, and I am good at it. (emphasis hers) And we would just butt heads because of his racist attitudes. He used to live on the Mount, so you know, it's just a segregated community of white folks up there that have money, and most of them have cars. They have money so they don't care. They live in their own little world up there. (Interview, spring 2004)

The Mount is a section of student housing at Central University. The name of this housing location is both literal and metaphoric in that it sits on a hill, and if you did not have a car, accessing the Mount required walking up many stairs, over 100, according to Leviticus. The Mount is also known as housing for students who are wealthy and white. Leviticus invoked the Mount as she connected her experience with group work to race and class. She negotiated the *gaze* of her white male group member with her insistence that she is "good at editing" and "it was her strength."

The Mount represented a group that Leviticus could not join. She was not white or wealthy and did not own a car. During group activities, as the only black student in her group and one who was being both ignored and then questioned, she felt like an outsider. For Leviticus, the fact that the white male student lived on the Mount, a place to which she had limited access, was directly connected to how she was being treated during the group process. The exclusion is an extension of how she sees her membership and value on campus and in the classroom. She felt the need to defend her role and ability in the group as evident by her insistence that she is "good at editing" and "it was her strength." She continued:

Leviticus: I mean, I never lived up there. I only had to go up there freshman year for those group meetings and I didn't mind the exercise to get up there. That's what I called it, exercise; 'cuz I knew I could leave there. It would be different if I had to live there. (Interview, spring 2004)

Student lives, particularly at residential campuses are connected. Where they live, classes they take, co-curricular activities they undertake, all have raced, classed, and gendered implications. What happens in the classroom carries over into these spaces. It is important to find creative ways to group students together for class work both inside and outside the classroom venue and to pay attention to where they congregate when they meet outside of the class time. For Leviticus, as a black women undergraduate, going up to the Mount for group work affected more than her health. Her negotiations around her identity, intellect, and group membership all became a part of her group work experience.

Black women undergraduates need opportunities to work together in small group assignments. This is a privilege that white students are granted without thought or intent, since they are still a numeric majority in most institutions of higher education. One way to find out if groups are functioning well (e.g., each student has a role, all voices are being heard, learning is happening) is to require students to evaluate the group process in writing as part of completing the assignment. Their assessment should include the details of when and where they met, how they interacted with each other, and how they evaluate their own con tribution and experience.

Manage Interactions in the Classroom: Voice

Black women undergraduates in this text discussed the complexities of being the *only* black person in their classes and other academic settings. The challenges of being an *only* have been recounted vigorously in academic texts about race and schooling (Tatum, 1997; Watson, Terrell, Wright and Associates, 2002). The challenges the women echoed included being singled out and expected to *represent* their race, *explain* a seeming cultural norm, or *expound* on particular cultural knowledge. These expectations on the part of students and educators are most often connected to stereotypes about the women's perceived raced, classed, and gendered lives. As Alana discussed earlier, these expectations can created a conundrum for black women undergraduates. She was expected to speak, but when she did, she suffered the stigma of being a "loud mouth girl who is obsessed with race." Blue told a similar story:

> Blue: Like, it would be someone taking one of our classes [in social work] and not really thinking before talking when we're talking about, you know, the context of human behavior and cultural issues and all that; and sometimes people don't think before they speak and they just say things that are so hurtful to other people, not being open to other people's cultures and the way that other people live, just thinking narrow mindedly.
> Interviewer: Can you give me an example of something that happens in class?
> Blue: Well, one example is when you're in a class with, and you're the only person who is black, and they ask you like you're the expert, "So, what would you say as a black woman?" I mean, I don't want to give an answer where they would be like, "That's *the* answer." (emphasis hers) But that's happened in classes where they have asked me, like I am an expert on what all black people do. (Interview, fall 2004)

Black women undergraduates have made it clear that being asked to *represent* all black women or all black people in classroom discussions is oppressive. This oppression also occurs when students who embody dominant social locations opt out of speaking about race, class, and gender in classroom discussions. For example, when conversations about race and class come up in the classroom, some white, upper-class students will opt out of speaking. Male students will often sit silent during conversations about gender. Students may take this stance for multiple reasons including the following: they feel the topic is not relevant to their own lives, they feel they have nothing to contribute, they fear exposure or disclosure, and they fear how others will react to their attempts to explore their dominance for the first time. This stance of silence is an exercise in privilege. Allowing this silence reinforces the misconception that inequity is a burden to be carried by students who do not have race, class, or gender privileges and permits race, class, and gender *privileges* (which exist simultaneously with race, class, and gender *oppressions*) to go unchecked (Wildman & Davis, 2002, pp. 89–95). The silence makes more visible the oppressions connected to the identity of black women while simultaneously making invisible the privileges that cause black women undergraduates to feel the need to *represent* others. These undergraduates are left to do the hard work and take the risks that students who opt out do not take. Malikah expressed the belief that the college classroom is a space where everyone can be required to communicate. In her own words, she explained:

> Malikah: People just stick to their own race, communicate with their own race. And we're not actually talking to each other, and that's why I think that if we *have* to in classes, it kind of forces us to talk. (emphasis hers) If everyone *has* to talk, then no one is singled out. (emphasis hers) (Interview, fall 2004)

In classrooms where the academic content is not about culture or identity, it is still important to pay close attention to class discussions. For example, in science and math courses, when virtually all the academic content (including the books read and the research examined) is based on the work of men, the misconceptions are reinforced that only men have made important contributions to these disciplines. In these courses, when male participation is solicited more often or occurs more vigorously than female participation, the notions are reinforced that these disciplines are for men and that women cannot succeed. Also, when the voices that appear most valued in class discussions are those of whites, the notions are strengthened that the exclusive discourses in these disciplinary spaces leave black women undergraduates' abilities and contributions open to cynicism and suspicion—even when that is not the intent.

Classroom conversations that are active and engaging and that require everyone in the class to participate help the entire class recognize the collaborative way knowledge is produced, used, and exchanged. There are creative ways to make this happen. Professors can have every student prepare a one- or two-sentence response to a reading and then spend part of a class period hearing from each student. Content can be taught through group presentations and through fishbowl or concentric-circle discussions for which the instructor chooses students to present particular subject matter. Asking a range of diverse students to lead class discussions or 5-minute reviews of material discussed in a previous class provides opportunities for all students to be presented as capable and smart; no one student is singled out; and it creates an environment of trust. Students feel safe showing what they know and asking questions about what they do not know when it is clear that the professor or instructor values the voices of all students. When that is not the class standard, students do not feel safe. Teena provided examples from her own experience:

Teena: I will be the only black person in my class, and people—especially during class discussions—people say things that—not that they are trying to offend me, but it offends me. And then the feeling that I have like, "Well, I am the only person in here. Like, there is no one who has my back." A couple of years ago we were doing a beat. We were assigned beats for one of our recording classes, and we all had to do a different beat. And I got the religion beat, and this one girl (sigh)—she was white, you know—and she got the minority beat, and she's like, "Um, I don't want to do this. Can I switch with someone?" Do you know what I mean? Just that type of thing, and it's like—it's hard every time you are in class by yourself. You can't fight everyone. You can't fight everyone all of the time, and you just feel like no one has your back. You feel like you are out there on your own. In some of the classes, sometimes issues are confronted and sometimes they're not. I remember one time, I was in a political science class, and we were talking about the issue that is always connected about us, affirmative action. Like, I literally was the only black person in the class, and the guys were always arguing—one was Indian or Middle Eastern. Like, everyone in the class was *on my back.* (emphasis hers) I was like, I left that class, I was crying. No, *not* in front of them, but when I left. (emphasis hers) I was by myself. I felt so defeated. I'm like, "Okay, nothing I could possibly say could get through to them."
Interviewer: What were they saying? What were you saying?
Teena: It was sophomore year, so I don't remember all of the specifics. But in terms of the basic argument, like, "Well, you don't need—it's been so long, we don't need people to get preferences over others. Then some people were talking about how they didn't get into school or had friends that didn't get into certain schools, um, certain colleges, and it's because of affirmative action, and a black person or whatever who was less qualified took my spot. It was that type of thing. The TA [teaching assistant] was trying a little bit to be compassionate towards me but it just wasn't working. Like my basic thing was, "Well, who benefits from affirmative action in the first place, and how could you think that a couple of decades of affirmative action could replace the 400 years when people had no access to learning or were killed or beaten for knowing how to read. It's just like I hate those—I just—I dread it. You know what I mean? If we have a class and we are going to have a discussion about something that is a part of me, I hate it because they just don't get it, no matter what. They are oblivious to everything going on. I think that when you're a black woman—ah, I guess I would say any person of color—you have to see it from the white side because that is the side that is presented to you. So, you have a better understanding of the picture because you have to see it from both sides. They don't have to see it from both sides. They only have to see it from their side—makes it a little tough. (little laugh) (Interview, spring 2004)

Teena utilized her sociological imagination and introduced a systemic analysis into a classroom conversation about affirmative action. She believed that her status as *black* and *woman* gave her an expansive understanding of this topic in that she had to both see "her side" and understand the responses of her classmates, which she called "the white side." Teena's dread about these "types of discussions" in classes was also connected to her race, class, and gender. She felt alone in arguing her stance. It is not clear that everyone in the class participated in the discussion; but Teena's perceptions about her *representative* role as the only black person in the classroom, her understanding of the affirmative-action debate as one shaped by raced and classed stereotypes about black people, and the lack of support she felt, all fueled the feeling that she was in a battle against everyone else in the class.

Teena's feeling of dread and isolation continued in "tears of defeat" after she left the classroom. She was not specific about the teaching assistant's attempts at compassion, but it was clear these attempts did little to mitigate the negative consequences Teena experienced when lending her voice and knowledge to this discussion. In this instance, the teaching assistant needed to recognize the accuracy of Teena's content knowledge and manage the classroom in a way that required all students to speak from a place of academic accuracy not just individual ideology. Altering the class discussion this way would have helped Teena know that her educator "had her back."

Institutional Practice and Inclusive Excellence

Classroom practice alone will not challenge the inequities black women undergraduates face on their college campuses. The impact of institutional practice and policy on their schooling lives was highlighted in the discussion the women had about the obstructions they face. Equity scholars who study inclusive excellence in education explain that this ethos incorporates both traditional diversity measures (e.g., increasing the number of staff and students of color) and *institutional* change (http://www.aacu.org/inclusive_excellence/index.cfm). For example, diversity policies (e.g., hiring guidelines) are present in most human resource materials at colleges and universities. They are often harder to find in other campus contexts (e.g., admissions materials, course handbooks, visioning and strategic planning sessions). Diversity policies need to be included and applied in all these contexts (Smith et al., 1997, pp. 43–46). Such institutional change reflects a campus climate committed to equity as a central mission of an inclusive excellence agenda. Thus, the responsibility for creating a campus free from race, class, and gender oppression rests on the shoulders of senior administrators. Presidents, vice presidents, chancellors, provosts, and deans have the power and funding to set an inclusive campus climate agenda (Hale, 2004). For black women undergraduates, a campus agenda that facilitates inclusive excellence in policy, practice, and programming means many of the institutional practices that challenge their day to day lives and that question the validity of their campus membership would be changed. What follows is a discussion of the ways institutions can realize this agenda.

Staff Training

As discussed, there are few opportunities for faculty to engage in training about inclusive campus policy and practice once they enter a college or university, and the same is true for support staff. Many members of campus support staff have no opportunity for professional development on or off of campus. The reasons presented for this exclusion range from ideas about the connection of content to their specific work to the difficulties presented for departments when they leave their posts where they answer phones, deliver mail, serve food, clean the campus, and offer other services. As shown in this text, campus staff have significant contact with students, making their understanding of their role on an inclusive campus critical.

Including residential education staff, secretaries, administrative assistants, counselors, safety officers, food services personnel, and bookstore employees (like the woman Malikah came into contact with) will have an impact on how black women undergraduates experience their schooling lives and campus settings as inclusive. Consistent training—situated in critical theoretical knowledge about ways to understand and negotiate differences within themselves as individuals and among themselves as campus community members and then learning how this informs their interactions with students—will help staff understand the need to value all members of the campus and limit some of the cultural clashes that black women undergraduates face. This training should be offered as part of orientation and entrance to a campus, and adherence should be monitored and augmented with consistent opportunities for ongoing training and evaluation. This training and evaluation will facilitate staff members' abilities to act as allies for black women undergraduates.

Training for Student Leaders

Consistent training and evaluation should also be extended to student leaders on campus. Many students make decisions that impact the lives of other students. They serve on campus judicial boards, run student governments, lead athletic teams, work as student trustees, set campus activities and agendas, and control student dollars. Administrators and staff must extend equity training to student groups who also bring their own understandings of race, class, and gender to these educational settings and leadership roles. Students are often expected and charged to work together with no understanding of experiences other than their own. Unchecked stereotyping and the inability to discuss difficult subjects or varying ideologies in productive ways led to reinforced oppression for the black women undergraduates in this study. For example, Teena explained the challenges student cultural groups face when white students label the groups as separatist and racist. This impacts their status on campus, rules and regulations that are set about their events, and event funding.

Faculty advisors can help student leaders understand the need for diverse representations on their boards, understand the ways their own experiences inform how they make decisions, and understand the importance of valuing all members of their campus—even when their ideologies differ. Student leaders who learn and utilize these guidelines can impact the educational journey of a magnitude of students as they interact day to day. Implementation of these guidelines will inform how they treat each other and expect to be treated. I argue that this knowledge is a form of cultural capital that all students can gain and that will support their work long after they graduate.

Alliance Building

Social justice educators have identified alliance building and ally work as crucial to the challenge of inequities in education (Ayers, Quinn, & Stovall, 2009; Kendall, 2006; McClintock, 2000; Sherover-Marcuse, 2000). The black women undergraduates in this study outlined some specific ways institutions can do this work in their talk about forming alliances. Faculty, administrators, and staff must start with the question, "What is my relationship to issues of race, class, and gender?" Each needs to abandon politically correct rhetoric and, instead, identity and adopt practices, behavior, language, and thought that allow us to access our deeply held beliefs about students and their ability and capacity to learn. Color blindness (A claim made which suggests that it is possible to view people without seeing their skin color) is such a practice. Fox (2001) encouraged us to "tell our stories about race," and I would add class, gender, and other social locations. These stories shape our views and require that we pay attention to our reactions to the students we come into contact with. They require that we think about the ways we are socialized to believe things about our students. How and where do deficit racist, sexist, and classist discussions about students take place? How do we respond? Do we even notice? Do not rely on the most automatic response, "I treat all students the same." Ask, "What are the ways I see and respond to people who are different than me?" It will do us well to answer honestly and adjust accordingly. Doing so will allow us to see that equal does not always mean the same.

Black women undergraduates feel valued when faculty and staff attend the cultural events they sponsor on campus and step out of comfort zones, specifically their offices and classrooms, to explore the student schooling experience. This effort on the part of faculty and staff will stem from a cultivated desire to know, serve, and teach the whole student.

The black undergraduate women in this study appreciated when their faculty and staff truly "saw them" and asked questions about their lives. Shonte illustrated that trust could be earned when educators were not afraid to ask questions and were consistent in how they treated students in and out of school. When asked how she identified allies on campus she explained:

> Shonte: People who understand what it's like to struggle and survive, you know; just positive people who are not about ripping people down. I look for a lot of support within my race. I can't lie. But there is one particular person in Academic Services. I don't think I would be here if it wasn't for her. She is one of those white people who are genuine, who care, who, you know, if she has a question, whether it's about my race or not, she will ask. She goes above and beyond the call of duty. I look for support from anyone who is not trying to hand me things but [who] teach[es] me how to help myself. You know, one professor, who I thought was really cool—she's a really nice person, but I saw her outside of the school setting and she was totally different, you know? Like, we had sat down and had very private talks, just her and I, but I saw her in [the grocery store], and she was just totally different, kind of like distant. That kind of threw me back a little bit. I was like, "Wait a minute. You are not this distant in school; but I come to [the grocery store], and you don't have anything to say to me. What's going on with that?" (Interview, spring 2004)

For Shonte interactions with faculty and staff must be consistent to support alliance. The professor she saw in the grocery store was not obligated to engage Shonte in this setting. She may have been in a rush or in need of personal time, and the lesson is not that faculty and staff must drop everything and attend to every student demand for support. Shonte's inclusion of this story, along with one about a staff member whom she believes was in tune with her experiences, was willing to ask questions, even about race, and "helped her help herself," shows the complexity of ally work. The lesson is that alliance is not formed through one form of interaction (e.g., office hours). It requires taking advantage of a range of opportunities to engage and of a pattern of consistent and supportive behavior that is not location specific. To Shonte, the professor she believed she had a bond with seemed to take back that show of support outside of the school setting, leaving Shonte confused about their alliance.

Diversity Practices

The black women undergraduates in this study expressed skepticism regarding the effectiveness and honesty of diversity practices at their institutions. Multicultural Weekend is an event that many institutions use to help students of color acclimate to a predominately white campus community. In general, students come to campus before a school officially begins and interact primarily with other students of color. For many of the women in this study, this project felt dishonest in that the weekend experience did not reflect the realities of the life they lived on campus. Several women expressed anger at what they read as attempts to "convince" or "trick" them into feeling that the student body was diverse and welcoming or attempts to "downplay" the need for the everyday negotiations they found necessary once the entire student body was present.

Finding time for black women undergraduates to learn to navigate campus spaces and interact with others with similar social locations is an important part of the retention process (Jones, 2001). Still, organizers of events such as Multicultural Weekend must examine this practice on their campus and identify ways that the structure fosters inclusive excellence and ways that it reinforces exclusion and segregation. Invitations to attend and programmatic descriptions of such academic extensions must include an honest explanation of the purposes and a discussion of the similarities and differences students will experience when the term begins. This level of honesty shows black women undergraduates that their college or university recognizes the cultural capital they bring that allows them to negotiate the ways racism, classism, sexism inform their schooling lives. It allows institutions to think about the ways they can support those negotiations rather than simply trying to minimize the need for them.

A useful multicultural orientation would include programming that reflects the life black women undergraduates lead on campus. It would include a critical mass of students from diverse backgrounds. Facilitating early interactions between multicultural students and white students from a range of socioeconomic statuses, geographic locations, ability levels, family situations, and schooling experiences can provide a clearer depiction for all students involved about life on campus. Living with each other daily, engaging with faculty and staff, and sharing in programming aimed at inclusive excellence will support alliance building. Achieving inclusive excellence might require that institutions devote more than one weekend to this endeavor.

Black women undergraduates are deeply impacted by administrative reactions to hate incidents that occur on campus, and it is right for institutions to express outrage at such acts. Inclusive excellence requires constant campus-wide work of not only showing outrage *in reaction* to an incident but also consistent expectations, programming, and assessment that highlight the value of all members of a campus community and that present indignation at every form of inequity. It should be clear that this stance is at the core of the institution's mission and branding. Colleges and universities can make this clear in many ways including inviting to campus speakers who do equity work, hosting and attending national conferences about institutional change, planning campus-wide events aimed at expanding our understanding of differences, forming coalitions with other colleges and universities that study and monitor equity issues in higher education, and clearly outlining and frequently revisiting institutional commitments to diversity in admissions, hiring, and retention.

To become allies to black women undergraduates, faculty, administrators, and staff need to face and address their own racism, classism, and sexism and the ways these problems play out in campus interactions and practice. Only honest and open recognition can lead to active change. This honesty and recognition will limit individual analysis about student learning, membership, and college success and move the understanding of the schooling lives of black women undergraduates into a conscious systemic analysis that allows for productive work to understand and negotiate their challenges. This conscious systemic approach moves discussions about black women undergraduates and college beyond deficit models and leads to models of inclusion and high expectations. Models of inclusion and high expectations are necessary to combat the normalized ways deficit discourses about black women undergraduates seep into our academic psyches. A few months ago, when I told a colleague that this book was about the cultural capital of black women undergraduates, she exclaimed, "They don't have any!" The intent of her comment was not clear, and perhaps I should have asked. What I do know is that the unexamined thought is connected to how we act and that, in part, is why I am writing this text. Ally work lets black undergraduate women know that from admissions to commencement, their institutions "have their backs."

Conclusions

Examinations of classroom and institutional practice and policy make clear that the work of challenging schooling inequities and oppression on college and university campuses requires understanding and action and each of these must be intentional and diversified. The ideas and behaviors expressed in classrooms overlap with those expressed in the larger institution; put another way, the climate and ethos in our schools is informed by practice and our practices are informed by climate and ethos. Change occurs when schools operate with an understanding of this simultaneity.

Black women undergraduates can be leaders in their classrooms when educators work to mitigate the consequences of raced, classed, and gendered schooling inequities. This work must be deliberate since socialized deficit models about black women undergraduates are always active in the classrooms they enter. The ideas presented for classroom practice do not call for a dumbing down of content. They represent the multiplicity of student ways of learning, skill sets, and evaluation, and invite everyone to bring what they have to the table. These practices set high expectations for students and professors and provide ways to reach these goals. Good classroom management means that the extra workload black women undergraduates carry that leads to defeat, tears, and other stressors will lessen, leaving more time to devote to learning. Recognizing that all students can and do make valuable contributions in the classroom will enhance the space for all students. This practice is good pedagogy, and it can help us as educators do our best work.

Higher education institutions are continually stumped about ways to increase the numbers and retain students, faculty, and staff of color on their campuses. I assert that the solution is as much about campus climate as it is about how and where institutions recruit. Numbers are important, and individuals will come to a campus where they can work with people who look like them and share other important social locations. They will *stay* where they are valued and supported and where they are not demoralized by deficit discourses about their membership. When black women undergraduates see others like them highlighted, promoted, and in leadership positions they are allowed to envision possibilities about their own abilities and the contributions they can make in the world. This is one of the loftiest of all the goals of higher education. This chapter is about the type of equity work that challenges race, class, and gender stigma. While black women undergraduates sit at the center of the discussion in this book, good teaching and institutional policy and practice centered in inclusive excellence will benefit all students, faculty, and staff in any educational setting. Inclusive excellence models a particular type of democratic citizenship that prepares students for life in the larger society and allows their cultural capital to be relevant in their educational endeavors. It allows faculty and staff to serve as allies to students and promotes social justice.

CHAPTER SEVEN

Cultural Capital and College Success

Black women undergraduates employ a variety of conceptual understandings, reworked discourses, and specific strategies to be successful in college. Recognizing that black undergraduate women and institutions of higher education do not exist outside of larger societal constructs and power structures, I have worked to show the multiple ways these structures inform the meaning making processes women engage when discussing academic and social success in school and to show that the connection of women's raced, classed, and gendered schooling lives to larger social structures and institutions makes necessary a process of negotiation that is dynamic and complex. This way of conceptualizing places at the center the lived experiences, perspectives, strengths, and abilities of black women undergraduates. This framework recognizes that there are black women undergraduates who are having academic and social success in college and listens to them to explain how and why.

While many of the navigational approaches discussed do not fall under traditional understandings of cultural capital, it is clear in this study that the processes the women described were crucial to their academic and social success and were part of their cultural capital. Their accounts are a direct challenge to the academy to open up the concept of cultural capital to include the schooling lives of groups often marginalized and rendered inadequate in the customary discussion.

Intersectionality and the Schooling Lives of Black Women Undergraduates

I have made the case throughout this text that black women undergraduates are raced, classed, and gendered beings, holding intersecting social locations that render them powerless in many settings and limit their power in others. As a result, black women undergraduates must engage in work *beyond* traditional academic endeavors to ensure college success. While it can be argued that all college students engage in work other than academics while trying to obtain a degree, it is clear that for black undergraduate women, this additional labor is connected to their race, class, and gender. Most often, their tasks involved resisting and navigating the oppressive material consequences that result as these social locations collide with racist, classist, and sexist societal norms. Black women undergraduates identified some of this work: challenging racism in classrooms and other spaces on campus, acknowledging and confronting discourses and perceptions regarding their academic preparation and practice, and finding and nurturing relationships with faculty and staff on campus that recognize the ways race, class, and gender inform their schooling lives. The group of black women interviewed was not homogenous. This examination has shown that there are multiple ways they take on these efforts and numerous explanations and viewpoints regarding its necessity. Some of the women felt that their efforts to combat racism and classism in college would make the path easier for black women undergraduates who came after them. Others felt that accepting this challenge worked to undo stereotyped ideas about the academic abilities of black students held by white students and teachers. Still others claimed that choosing to speak up and make their perspectives heard was a strategy that gave them the strength needed to persevere in school and be successful. The strategies black women undergraduates developed as they participated in the navigation processes are forms of cultural capital that fuel their day-to-day college lives and relationships and that pave their paths to graduation.

Reworking the Discourse of Cultural Capital

Any discussion of cultural capital and education *must* include the voices and perspectives of black women undergraduates if it is to advance educational equity. The black women undergraduates in this study brought a particular kind of cultural capital with them to college. Often they were not academically well prepared; they did not have great SAT scores, some were in developmental classes trying to obtain skills they did not get in high school, and others had no understanding of how to navigate campus grading practices such as dropping a class before failing it. What I contend is that if the academy only looks at the ways black women undergraduates are *deficient*—that is, that black women are often underprepared academically or live in social situations traditionally viewed as risk factors to college success (e.g., low socioeconomic status)—then academic analysis and, in turn, scholarship, policy, and practice will continue to operate from a deficit model in which the strengths these women bring with them and develop while in college are rendered invisible. For example, traditional measures of cultural capital (e.g., better preparations for college, access to high-culture experiences such as travel) are not the only measurements of college success, even for students who possess them. For some students, privileged social locations (e.g., whiteness) give them advantages. Black women undergraduates, who most often have little privilege, are forced to undergo analyses of their schooling lives because of racism, classism, and sexism. These analyses become part of their cultural capital even though traditional definitions of the theory would not identify them as such. These analyses, as capital, helped black women undergraduates in this study make sense of discrimination they experienced and helped them develop strategies and discourse to negotiate the consequences of bias.

To be equitable, any discussion of their cultural capital and college success *must* include the strengths black women bring with them and develop while they are students. It is important to note that for a black undergraduate woman such as RGB, the strategies that helped her navigate racial oppressions at her university are just as necessary for her academic survival and success as the trips she made to local museums and college libraries during high school.

Historically, black people, as a collective group, have utilized their cultural capital to navigate race and class oppression and, among other things, get educated. This historical legacy was vivid in the minds of the women in this study. As seen in Chapter Three, they expressed a connection to this history and presented it as a driving force that pushed them to reach their own educational goals.

The Sociological Imagination

The black women undergraduates in this study displayed a sophisticated way of thinking about their schooling lives. Their conversations revealed the complexities of the day-to-day navigations they utilized to get their work done, manage relationships, and mitigate the effects of negative ideas about who they were as students. Chapter Three illustrated the multiple ways the women employ sociological imagination, as a conceptual framework, to dissect and, at times, dismiss simplistic discourses about their lives as students (Mills, 1959, p. 5).

First, it was evident in their talk that they understood the impact of a collective black history on their current educational experiences. Specifically, RGB described the discrepancies in school achievement as a consequence of slavery, the refusal of whites to allow blacks to learn, and the continued exclusion of black men and women as contributing history makers. RGB's critique is a challenge to educational systems at all levels to expand the curriculum to include the accomplishments of blacks and others, not just as a special month or celebration but as an expansive and integral part of the curriculum.

The women also used a sociological imagination to challenge and overcome the impact of being traditionally unprepared for college. Understanding that being underprepared is connected to societal issues of race and class helped Nicole and Cheryl recognize that a lack of preparation is not synonymous with failure. Both women drew upon their sociological imaginations, specifically their understanding of their experiences and their ties to history, society, and biography to come to this conclusion. As a result, Cheryl and Nicole developed strategies to overcome a lack of knowledge about school policies and to overcome obstacles such as poor performance on standardized tests. This is an important process for educators, administrators, and policy makers to note. As mentioned, the use of deficit models and perspectives in discussions of blacks and education persists in educational research and practice. The black women undergraduates described ways of conceptualizing the discriminatory conversations about themselves as students. They turned the talk from deficient and inadequate to an expanded way of thinking that was less focused on the individual and more focused on the systemic reasons academic discrepancies existed. The women understood that these discrepancies were connected to their raced, classed, and gendered biographies and histories. They were able to overcome obstacles by developing strategies (e.g., seeking help from other black students, educating themselves about campus policies and practices, dismissing talk that revealed others' low expectations).

The black women participants recognized *white privilege* as a systemic obstacle that informed their educational experiences, yet they did not equate academic success with whiteness. Repeatedly, the women connected the gap in achievement between black and white students as a facet of history, biography, and society. Their sociological imaginations framed their perspectives. This was evident in references the women made when discussing inequities on their college campuses: enslaved blacks had no access to education; present-day academic curricula limit the inclusion of blacks and other groups in their depictions of history, and whiteness gives privileges (e.g., knowing the right people). Having this knowledge, the women decided that they needed additional strategies to offset what they saw as built-in, systemic inequities. They did not feel these obstacles would stop them from meeting their goals in college.

C. Wright Mills (1959) wrote that humans cannot overcome their troubles and understand their relationship with the world if they do not have sociological imagination (pp. 6–9). Some undergraduate students, who are privileged by social locations (e.g., whiteness, upper-middle class) have the luxury of not developing their sociological imaginations. Black women undergraduates holding less-privileged social locations embrace and engage this sophisticated conceptual framework in their analysis of educational inequity and use it to develop strategies for success (i.e., negotiating campus relationships, managing cultural clashes that occur at their schools).

Negotiating Relationships

As shown in this study, race, class, and gender oppressions force black women undergraduates to carry an extra load of work in school. The goal of this work is to navigate the obstacles placed in their path by racism, classism, and sexism. This additional work is separate from their academic responsibilities but must be carried out simultaneously. In talking with the 19 black women undergraduates in this study, I discovered that this labor takes multiple forms including developing strategies to negotiate campus relationships that scaffold success.

For black women undergraduates, finding allies who understand the complexities of their schooling lives is a challenge. Structural relationships such as the role of the high school guidance counselor are not always beneficial alliances. While the individuals in these positions can offer practical advice regarding college applications and financial help like fee waivers, without an understanding of the ways the consequences of race, class, and gender intersectionality inform the lives of their black women students, guidance counselors can, with discouraging words, reinforce stigma and stereotypes about black students' abilities to succeed in college. As Alana's example showed, the strategic work for black women students in this situation involved knowing what the counselor could provide, getting that help, and disregarding what she perceived as negative judgments about her academic ability.

In this study, black women undergraduates found alliances with black professors. These relationships also, at times, require negotiation. As Leviticus' example showed the complexity black women undergraduates face when they assume shared social locations with professors (i.e., *black* and *woman*) mean shared views on the effect of race, class, and gender oppression in educational settings. Since this is not the case, black women undergraduates must adjust their perspectives to include the wide range of ways individuals experience their social locations. Managing these relationships and locating allies, at times, means looking beyond their own ideas and recognizing blackness as a multifaceted identity. This skill is a form of cultural capital that will help black women undergraduates form alliances necessary to achieve their educational goals.

The participants described familial alliances with single mothers, parents with college educations, and parents without college degrees as crucial to their college success. This stands in contrast to popular social discourses that minimize the support single parents and those who did not attend college themselves could provide. The women described financial support, lessons about adaptations in academic settings, encouraging words, and the inculcation of a strong sense of identity as the cultural capital they received from these relationships. Negotiating these relationships was work for black women undergraduates. Many of them had dual roles as students and teachers as they explained to their parents how college systems worked. Even so, as Blue explained, for black women undergraduates, these relationships were alliances that "helped them grow" and motivated them to succeed.

The support of allies who understand their raced, classed, and gendered lives can smooth the path to graduation for black women undergraduates by providing, among other things, practical advice, financial support, motivation, a strong sense of identity, and belief that the students can succeed in college. The skills and strategies black women undergraduates acquire and practice as they seek out and then nurture these relationships are forms of cultural capital that can scaffold their achievements. These relationships can also help black undergraduate women manage cultural clashes they face as students.

Managing Cultural Clashes

The black women undergraduates in this study outlined how racist confrontations informed their lives in school and how navigating those confrontations was a risky and complex process. For example, the women described complications related to speaking out against racism and sexism such as, knowing when it is safe to speak up, resisting the label of *angry black bitch* when they do speak up, and alienating teachers and students in the class who do not want their privileged assumptions challenged. Black women undergraduates took on the work of negotiating these cultural clashes for multiple reasons including: exercising their rights to speak, showing the strength of their convictions, stopping the perpetuation of stereotypes, responding (or, as Shonte described, attacking back) when hurt by racist and classist verbal assaults, and carving out paths for students who will come after them.

Because, as Ladson-Billings (2003) explains, "racism is normal, not aberrant, in U.S. society," so much so that it looks "ordinary and natural," black undergraduate women's meaning making processes and the resulting strategic work were always informed by the need to offset racism's insidiousness (p. 11). This means that black women undergraduates have no choice but to question every encounter to see if racist, classist, and sexist ideologies are the basis for the interaction. For the women at Central University, this also included examining and critiquing campus policies and practices designed to promote multiculturalism and diversity. The processes associated with taking on this responsibility and strategically carrying it out are forms of cultural capital that black women undergraduates used to navigate cultural clashes that, left unattended, could become overwhelming as the women worked toward graduation.

Conclusions

Cultural capital is credited with providing useful tools for academic and social success in college. It is described as currency that gives those privileged with it an educational advantage, since their experiences with traditional forms of cultural capital were consistent with dominant ideals about school success. As seen, the raced, classed, and gendered schooling lives of black women undergraduates meant that they were rarely represented as having the types of cultural capital associated with college success. This discourse of cultural capital is limited and makes invisible the strengths black women bring with them and develop in college. This invisibility makes it possible for deficit models about their chances for school success to take center stage in scholarship about their schooling lives.

Institutions of higher education do not exist outside of the political, social, and historical memory of oppression that has plagued black students and placed obstacles, some insurmountable, in their way as they work to get educated. Even now, as colleges and universities attempt to address inequities in education, they often ignore the voices of those most marginalized on campus, and, as a result, the policies and practices they implement are ineffective and, at times, as the black women undergraduates in this study described, burdensome and emotionally draining. Poorly thought-out initiatives reinforced feelings of powerlessness, made black undergraduate women question their value on campus, fortified feelings of alienation, and, as Blue explained, "don't do enough to combat the ignorance" that leads to racist confrontations, which continue to afflict college and university campuses.

That being said, I emphasize again that despite these obstacles that require additional work to navigate, black women undergraduates are achieving their academic goals and getting a college education. Like their historical counterparts, they are using their cultural capital to "get themselves educated" in the face of oppressions. Black women undergraduates are finding allies from various social locations to support them in this endeavor, and they are taking advantage of the progress that has been made in their educational settings; the academy applauds their ability to be *resilient* in this way. What is more crucial than the applause is the recognition that, just because black women undergraduates *can* succeed in the face of racism, classism, and sexism, does not mean that they should *have to*. They, like students whose social locations are more in line with dominant ideals, should have the opportunity to get an education without fracturing themselves to do the constant arduous work of challenging oppressive schooling conditions, and it is the responsibility of institutions of higher education to facilitate this work and mandate this outcome.

To that end, college and university faculty, staff, students, and administrators, educational policymakers, and citizens outside of the academy must examine their own racist, sexist, and classist subscriptions about black women undergraduates (and all students) and actively work against the perpetuation of these ideals and the privileges they confer upon some; this work needs to be done both in their personal lives and in all societal institutions. They should value the educational narratives of black women undergraduates and other marginalized groups, and use these voices as they develop curricula, classroom practice, institutional policy, and programming for change. They must recognize that these voices can provide valuable insights that formal or traditional approaches and scholarship can miss (Rochlin, 1997, p. 14). Without this work, the ideal of educational equity cannot be realized!

Methods and Methodology

A Qualitative Study of Black Women Undergraduates

As an adolescent and then a young adult, family, friends, and employers often acknowledged my need to ask a lot of questions by politely telling me, "Just let it go!" with the spokesperson depending on what topic *it* represented in each discussion. A former boss once told me that because of the strength of my convictions, my ability to talk to people, and my skill at getting others to talk to me, he believed I should "run for political office," especially since I "love to analyze things to death." While I have no interest in being a politician, I do feel fortunate to have found a professional space where I can utilize my well-honed communication skills (or my communication faults as I am sure some would say) to facilitate my desire for equity and social justice. This space, the field of qualitative research, recognizes and values the fact that black women undergraduates and others are indeed experts on their own lived experiences (Delpit, 1995, p. 47). More importantly, the features of qualitative research, both its theoretical perspectives and its methods, demonstrate respect for that claim by providing a means to extricate and analyze the stories of black women undergraduates and others.

Qualitative Research

Qualitative research is not simply one thing. It has been described as an interdisciplinary, transdisciplinary, and sometimes counter disciplinary field that crosscuts the humanities with social and physical sciences (Denzin & Lincoln, 2005, p. 7). Qualitative research is sensitive to multi-method approaches, is committed to naturalistic perspectives, and draws on an interpretive understanding of human experience (Denzin & Lincoln, 2005, p. 7). Qualitative researchers use methods such as in-depth interviewing, participant observation, case studies, and document analysis to understand how the informants, in their own perspectives, make meaning of their lived experiences. Utilizing naturalistic approaches in qualitative research means using, at times, "actual settings as the direct source of data," and researchers spend considerable amounts of time immersing themselves in contexts to observe how action occurs in a specific setting (Bogdan & Biklen, 2003, p. 4). For qualitative researchers, collecting data that is descriptive and detailed often leads to the study of everyday events in a specific way; that is, nothing that informants do is "taken for granted" or trivial; it is, in fact, important data that give insight into how they live their lives (Bogdan & Biklen, 2003, p. 5).

Qualitative researchers are concerned with "naturally occurring" interactions and capturing the perspectives of informants accurately (Peräkylä, 2005). Thus in qualitative work, data collection often includes the use of sound or video recorders so as not to miss, for example, a nuance in speech during an interview. Qualitative researchers doing participant observation may choose to write down their notes in order to blend in with a setting. In each case the qualitative researcher takes notes, transcribes recordings word for word, writes memos, and spends a large amount of time organizing collected data for analysis. Because qualitative research is an "inductive practice," that is, theory emerges from the collected data and not a set hypothesis, analyses can include meticulous and extensive manipulation of data. Through constant comparisons, explorations of context, categorizations, reading and rereading data, qualitative researchers work to authentically represent the perspectives of their informants (Bogdan & Biklen, 2003, p. 6; see also Peräkylä, 2005, pp. 870–875).

This chapter focuses on how my qualitative investigation of the schooling lives of 19 black women undergraduates was designed and carried out. First, I present a discussion of the methodologies that guided my research project. This conversation will follow a feminist research tradition and include an examination of my place as the researcher in this study (Best, 2003; Collins, 2000; DeVault, 1990; Madriz, 2000; Taylor, 1998). Next, this chapter will explore the qualitative methods or techniques used to collect and analyze data and will conclude with identified methodological limitations of the study.

Methodologies

Methodologically, this is a phenomenological qualitative research study. Recognizing that the term "*phenomenology*" carries various degrees of meaning for theory and methods, I have used it in the following particular way (Bogdan & Biklen, 2003, p. 22). This study is phenomenological because it focuses on everyday meanings and experiences with a goal of explicating how people make sense of objects, interactions, and episodes in everyday life (Holstein & Gubrium, 1994, p. 264). This qualitative process allowed me to study black women undergraduates in one of their natural settings, that is, on their community college and university campuses, in an attempt to make sense of and interpret their schooling lives and the meanings they bring to them (Denzin & Lincoln, 2003, p. 4). This being the case, I was not interested in the facts of each woman's narrative or whether their interpretations of events and processes were always correct (Bogdan & Biklen, 2003, p. 23). Rather, recognizing that there are "multiple ways" of understanding lived events, my goal was to interact with the black women undergraduates in ways that allowed me entrance into their "meaning making processes" about their lives in higher education (Bogdan & Biklen, 2003, p. 23).

Often connected to phenomenology is *ethnomethodology*. By definition, this qualitative methodology focuses on the methods members of the social world as an "interpreted world, not a literal world" use to accomplish everyday life" and the researcher's place in those interpretations (Holstein & Gubrium, 1994, p. 486). Ethnomethodology does not take the "everyday life" for granted but rather recognizes that "common-sense understandings" and the resulting actions are ways individuals make sense of the world and organize and explain their place in it (Bogdan & Biklen, 2003, p. 30). Thus, when the black women undergraduates in this study described as racist events that occurred in their classrooms, I recognized that whether the event was *truly* racist was not a part of my analysis. My analysis focused on the "processes involved in making racism the social reality" for the women describing the event; these processes could include their language, their understanding of race relations on their campuses, and their interpretations of the motives of white students, staff, and professors (Holstein & Gubrium, 1994, p. 48). While contemplating and preparing to accomplish this study, I decided that I agreed with Garfinkel (1984), who views the "artful practices of everyday life" that individuals engage in as "accomplishment" and "phenomena of interest" (p. 11). This outlook guided both my data collection and analysis.

This study draws upon *symbolic interactionism*. This concept purports that the actions of humans are based on the "meanings" physical things, ideas, relationships, and other processes and engagements have for them and that these meanings have been constructed through "social interaction" (Blumer, 1969, p. 2). In other words, meaning making processes are not an intrinsic, individual phenomenon but rather the result of how people interact with each other. I have taken the stance that the black women undergraduates in this study are, through interaction, "actively engaged" in creating and interpreting their world and share perspectives based on this engagement (Bogdan & Biklen, 2003, p. 25). Even though they share perspectives, I have not assumed that their lives, engagements, or interpretations are identical.

Feminist and black feminist methodology and techniques of qualitative inquiry are also a foundation of this work. First-wave feminism (19th and 20th century) concentrated on women as objects concerned with equality who were often victims of incorrect social knowledge, while second-wave feminism (1960s and 1970s) focused on challenging constructed social knowledge and patriarchy (Humm, 1992, pp. 11–14). DeVault (1996) explains that it is out of second-wave feminism that the ideas of feminist sociology and multifaceted literature on feminist research methodology began (p. 30). Black feminists have presented a critique of first- and second-wave feminism and its focus on white women. Black women scholars have asserted that first-wave and early second-wave feminists were focused on white women and did not address the oppressions specific to black women's experiences (Collins, 1998; hooks, 1984). Black feminists introduced the idea that their experiences as women are not separate from their experiences as classed and raced beings. Humm (1992) captures the words of the Combahee River Collective (1977/1992), a black feminist group founded in 1974 "explicitly to contest the presumptive power of white feminists to speak for universal women" (p. 133) who declared:

> A political contribution which we feel we have already made is the expansion of the feminist principle that the personal is political. In our consciousness-raising sessions, for example, we have in many ways gone beyond white women's revelations because we are dealing with the implications of race and class as well as sex....We have spent a great deal of energy delving into the cultural and experiential nature of our oppression out of necessity because none of these matters has ever been looked at before. No one before has ever examined the multilayered texture of black women's lives. (p. 136)

Thus black feminists argue that techniques of qualitative inquiry and analysis must be intersectional. That is, they must account for "simultaneity of oppressions and interlocking systems of oppression" when studying the complex lives of black women (Cuádraz & Uttal, 1999, p. 158). Every aspect of identity must be recognized as always at work in the research process and in the lives of the researcher and the participants. The features of identity shape how social realities are formed and explain that the formation is never fixed. In addition, the elements of identity are never in existence outside of the larger, historical and social contexts and power structures.

Many white feminists and feminists of color utilize the lens of *intersectionality* when studying the lives of women (Anzaldúa, 1987; Bettie, 2003; Collins, 1995; Cuádraz & Pierce, 1994). Feminist qualitative inquiry is credited with encouraging "provocative and productive unpacking of taken-for-granted ideas about women in specific, material, historical, and cultural contexts" (Olesen, 2000, p. 215). A black feminist *gaze* on this form of inquiry recognizes that women's lives are multifaceted, have meaning, and have value. The methodologies and strategies of feminist qualitative research include using in-depth interviews to talk to women, making them the center of discourse, and viewing them as experts who produce knowledge about their lives (Cuádraz & Uttal, 1999, p. 159). Utilizing these features of feminist and black feminist qualitative research helped me place on center stage the dynamic and complicated schooling lives of the black women undergraduates I interviewed. It also helped me recognize my place in this research.

My Place in This Research

Recently, while I was speaking to a group of graduate students about the emerging themes in my research, one white woman graduate student asked if I believed that the reason I had such personal and descriptive data was because I was a black woman interviewing other black women. She hesitated to say the words *black* and *woman*, but I coaxed her into using the terms by jokingly stating, "You can say it. They're not bad words!" Everyone shared a laugh. I told her it definitely played a part, since some of my informants explained that they believed they could talk freely because they were talking to another black woman. I explained that the women also used language such as, "you know what I mean" and "girl, you know how it is," which I interpreted as a sign that, in their minds, our shared locations of *black* and *woman* gave us some collective understandings.

I tell that story to introduce the idea that who I am played an important part in my research. I do not believe that only black women can or should do the work of garnering educational equity for black women undergraduates. I do however recognize that my social locations, particularly those of *black* and *woman* played a crucial role in the interactions I had with my informants and in my analysis.

What does it mean to be a black woman interviewing black women? During the time of the interviews, I was both a member of marginalized groups (black, woman) and a privileged one as a doctoral student at a private university. I had to examine my positions *in relation to my subjects.* Gallagher (2000) reminded me that being an insider because I share race and gender with my participants does not mute the way other social locations can enter into the process and create misunderstandings or influence the interviews (p. 69). I was very close to this topic of educational equity as a black woman graduate student because, as mentioned earlier, most of my academic career has been spent in educational spaces that were predominately white and where, I feel, little attention *that led to action* was given to the voices of black women. For most of the journey, I had no academic language or analysis of my schooling experience. I have developed an intellectual understanding and academic language based on my learning in higher education. I have always had a clear sense that my experience was both different and similar to my peers in school, and my education allowed me the privilege of negotiating my lived experiences with my new academic and intellectual knowledge and language. I carried this with me to the interviews. As a result, I had to work *hard* to let my informants tell *their* stories. I had to recognize that I was organizing the world in a way that my informants may not with my pre-assumed theoretical perspectives (Cuádraz & Uttal, 1999, p. 165). I had to acknowledge that in the interview context, I held privileges that many of the women participants did not; I held privileges regarding the process and regarding the academic language and knowledge that act upon the lives of black women undergraduates.

For example, it was a challenge for me to listen to Jessica during her interview continually make comments such as, "Of course, I would like things to be fair, but what can you do?" and "I won't worry about learning about black history in school. If they don't see it, they don't. You really can't change them." (Interview, spring 2004) My converging social locations as a black woman, educated in a particular way about social justice, and my resulting commitment to educational equity made me want to tell her, "Yes, we can change things. We have to, and you as a black woman should be invested in doing it." I wanted to lecture her about what I interpreted as giving up and tell her all the things that can be done to right social wrongs. Of course, I did not give this lecture, but in my analysis, it was clear the ways my feelings about her responses informed my work. This is evident in one observer's comment: I wrote, "I feel like I am pulling teeth. Jessica seems resigned to the idea that inequity is 'just the way things are' in the world. Where does this come from?" (Observer's comment, spring 2004). I later realized that this observer's comment reflected *my* desire for Jessica to express *my* ideas about these issues. I *was* "pulling teeth" and probing to get her to give what I felt was a more active response based on my academic privilege. Recognizing this, during my analysis, I put my perceptions and evaluations aside during one of my initial readings of data. I worked to hear Jessica's interpretations and processes that helped her make sense of her world, including her deep religious convictions and her shy approach to conflict. It was also useful to examine Jessica's "naturally occurring talk," an integral part of ethnomethodology (Holstein & Gubrium, 1994, p. 48). One thing I learned is that Jessica often said, "It shouldn't matter." or "It shouldn't have to matter." in answer to the question "In what ways does it matter?" Because I was tuned in to what I interpreted as a disconnected attitude, I did not probe during these instances to sort out her meaning. I wrote in my notes, "I should have pushed here. Jessica said, '[It] shouldn't have to matter.' She didn't say, 'It *doesn't* matter.'" (Observer's comment, spring 2004). While I feel I lost the opportunity to get additional data from Jessica to help me make sense of her world, the reflective analysis I did afterward allowed me to learn a valuable lesson about the ways "who I am" infiltrates the work I do.

Feminist research methods have promoted the idea of *reflexivity* in research. The writings of Harding (1987) illustrate:

> The best feminist analysis ... insists that the inquirer her/himself be placed in the same critical plane as the overt subject matter, thereby recovering the entire research process for scrutiny in the results of research. That is, the class, race, culture, and gender assumptions, beliefs, and behaviors of the researcher her/himself must be placed within the frame of the picture that she/he attempts to paint.... Thus the researcher appears to us not as an invisible, anonymous voice of authority, but as a real, historical individual with concrete, specific desires and interests. (p. 9)

Reflexivity requires engaging in a process which allows one to "refer back to oneself" and to acknowledge and examine one's participation in social life, namely, in this instance, participation in data collection and interviewing (Johnson, 1995, p. 255). During this process I had to recognize when my own positions in relation to grand narratives about race and schooling came into play during my interviews and, at times, as reactions to participant responses. For example, in my earlier interviews, I would eagerly agree with informants and on two occasions finished their sentences. I think this occurred naturally due to my feelings of collectivity as a black woman listening to stories that were often similar to my own and that met my expectations. Since I noticed this early in the interviews, I was able to change that behavior. I learned to keep my facial expressions under control and my mouth shut.

Contexts

In this research I have taken the political stance that the black women participants exist as raced, classed, and gendered beings connected to a particular history, society, and biography (Mills, 1959, p. 6). The intersections of these contexts inform every interaction in the women's lives and are all connected to power structures that fuel inequities (Mills, 1959, pp. 7–9). None of the described methodologies used in this study exist outside of that context, neither do the women's interpretations of their daily lives nor my analysis of the interviews. While they may not verbalize these socially constructed forces as such, this work was designed and their understandings were analyzed in that context. I conducted this project with a *social constructivist* view. That is, I recognized that humans construct or make knowledge against a backdrop of shared understandings, practices, languages and histories (Schwandt, 2003, p. 305). This context also informed the techniques I used to carry out the study.

In studying the phenomenon of black undergraduate women's college success, I needed to learn how the women "make meaning of their lived events and interactions [in higher education] from their point of view" (Bogdan & Biklen, 2003, p. 23). In order to do so, I had to go to the women and talk to them utilizing techniques of qualitative research designed to extract and analyze their stories. Using a *social interactionist* approach, I relied on "conversation analysis and a rigorous set of qualitative techniques" including, interviewing, data recording, transcribing, memo writing, coding, and data analysis "to systematically record what happens when the women use and interpret symbols as they interact in everyday, natural systems" (Johnson, 1995, pp. 111, 158). I will now discuss the ways I collected and analyzed data. I note that even though I am discussing these facets separately, I recognize that during the data collection process analysis also occurred, and each technique simultaneously informed the other.

Collecting Data

The data for this study came from in-depth interviews with the 19 black women undergraduates enrolled at a community college and universities in New York, California, or Texas; the institutions and the informants were presented in the first chapter of this work. I chose to put their short biographies there instead of here, in this methods appendix, because I felt they deserved to be introduced early in this text. It is a symbolic representation of my gratitude to each one of them for speaking to me and of my hope that this research is indeed grounded in their lived experiences (Cuádraz & Uttal, 1999, p. 156).

I chose the feminist technique of in-depth interviewing as I believed this is the best way to gather these experiences. All the interviews were done in person. I interviewed 8 of the women twice for approximately 90 minutes; I interviewed 11 of the women once, and these interviews lasted approximately 2 hours. The number of times I interviewed each woman and the amount of time spent depended on each one's availability. I tended to interview the women in states other than New York for longer periods of time just in case I did not get to see or speak with them again. RGB, who attended Central University, and I spoke for almost 3 hours. I asked her repeatedly if I was keeping her from anything, and she consistently responded, "No, I want to talk."

As mentioned, this research is loosely connected to a larger study. Working as a qualitative research assistant on the Lumina project (see Appendix B) allowed me to travel to several states during my graduate studies. When I was first approached to work on the Lumina project, I was hesitant. I was fearful that I would not be able to accept this position and complete my degree in the time I had scheduled. After much thought and conversation with both my advisor and the principal investigator on the Lumina project, I realized this large, nationally acknowledged research project was a great opportunity for me to practice the qualitative inquiry skills I had learned and to meet with undergraduates all over the United States. Since the primary investigator agreed to let me collect data during my travels, I finally decided that the benefits of working on this project, including the chance to speak with black women undergraduates at several institutions, outweighed the cons of an additional year of graduate work. As I look back at the struggle to make this decision, I realize that this, too, was a facet of my colliding social locations. My fear of the consequences of another year of not working, stemming from a working-class background that left little room for dawdling (I needed to get this school thing done!), was at war with accepting the *privilege* of an additional educational experience that would enhance a professional position I would later fill.

Interviews

I began conducting interviews for this research in January of 2004 and continued until November of 2004. I contacted potential interviewees in several ways. As mentioned, some of my informants were connected with the Lumina research project. When black women interviewed with me for the Lumina research project, I simply explained my study and asked if they would be willing to participate in an additional discussion. Amari, Jessica, Jamie, and Cherry all agreed to converse with me. At International Community College, none of the students I interviewed for the Lumina project was a black woman, so I approached black women I saw in the hallways and lunch areas and asked them to take part. As a result, I was able to speak with Lisa and Kayla who later introduced me to Alex. The rest of the women participants attended Central University. I knew Roe, Malikah, Blue, and Alana from courses I had taught previously in which they were students. I sent an email to the women asking them to contribute to my work. During the summer of 2003, I had participated in a study-abroad program in Paris. It was there that I met Teena, Nadia, and Leviticus, who offered to interview with me when they heard about my research topic. From announcements made in African American studies classes, I met RGB. I stood in line next to Kimberly at Parking Services on campus at Central University, struck up a conversation with her, and asked her to interview. I knew Nicole and Shonte informally and used email to ask them to participate. Each woman interviewed individually except for Lisa and Kayla; they chose to speak with me at the same time. I was a stranger to them, and I had approached them in a hallway at their community college. When they asked to interview together, I agreed because I wanted them to be comfortable. I met with them two times.

Some may argue that my familiarity with some of the students is a limitation of the study. I would argue that, while the interviews were in some ways informed by my relationships with some of the informants, these relationships allowed me access to parts of the narratives they may not have shared with strangers. For example, after I thanked Teena for interviewing with me she stated: "Of course, I would interview with you. I can tell you stuff I couldn't tell someone else, and I know you will do the right thing with it." (Memo, spring, 2004) For members of disenfranchised groups (such as black undergraduate women) whose stories are often ignored, altered, or stereotyped, I believe that ensuring and nurturing trust are a researcher's responsibility and that trust is a necessary element of this type of research. Honest and open qualitative interviews yield data that are most useful in the work for educational equity. Thus, I believe that, in this research, familiarity with some informants facilitated the process of collecting data.

None of the women asked for anything in return when they agreed to participate in the interviews. Since completing the interviews, I have written letters of recommendation for two of the women, Cheryl and Kimberly; they are both applying to graduate school. I sent Kayla, Alex, and Lisa T-shirts at their request. Many of the women keep in touch by email; two of them eagerly read parts of this book in manuscript form and provided feedback on my analysis of our discussions.

A variety of paths to college, a range of years in college, a variety of academic interests, diverse family situations, different socioeconomic levels, first-generation students, students whose parents attended college (with some parents having advanced degrees), traditional-aged learners, and nontraditional-aged learners, all of these are represented in this assemblage, making this selection of black women a useful group to provide insight into the lives of black women undergraduates in higher education. Interestingly, the themes I have chosen to address in this research show collective experiences of black women undergraduates. These particular themes represent similarities in experience rather than differences related to geographic locations. Even so, upon reading my work, one cannot ignore the ways context (i.e., history, biography, society) informs the experiences of black women and their collective talk. The women shared many similar sentiments, stories, and analyses even though they did not all know each other and even though some of them lived thousands of miles apart.

Questions and Answers

As I sat down to design the questions for this research, I was a little overwhelmed. There was so much to ask about this huge space called higher education and the women's place in it; I was determined to get to *all* of it. Early in my interviews, I realized that my initial set of questions was much too long. It would take hours to address everything I had included—hours that neither I nor my informants had to spend on the interviews. Frustrated, I tackled the list again determined to create a list of questions that were open-ended and broad enough to allow space for probing *and* that would give good data. It was helpful to review the tenets of grounded theory, which reminded me that my work was inductive and that any theory or categories that came from this work needed to emerge from the data (Glaser & Strauss, 1967, p. 1).

The final list of questions started with general demographic inquires regarding each woman's age, family life, high school experiences, college choice, application process, majors in college, and socioeconomic status. In addition, I felt it was important in this study for the women to identify their own race and ethnicity and the importance of this identity marker in their lives. I had selected these undergraduates to participate based on their outward physical appearance as black, but I did not want my assumptions to guide their identification or my theoretical perspectives about this social location to determine the importance of this feature in their experiences. In answer to the question regarding race and ethnicity, the women identified themselves as black, African American, and Caribbean American. Alana also included being "half white" in her description since her mother is white, but she made it clear that "in her eyes and the eyes of society" she was black. In each instance, I asked the woman if she objected to my categorizing her as black and was consistently told no. Once I completed the demographic questions, I moved to having the women define terms we would be discussing during the interview. In this phase of the interview, I asked questions such as the following:

How do you define *culture?*
How do you define *black culture?*
How do you define *whiteness?*
What is *multiculturalism?*
What is *diversity?*
What is it like to be a black woman on this campus?
What is *acting white?*

It was important to me that I understood their definitions and that their understandings guided the talk. This proved to be an important strategy; I wrote my first data chapter outlining the sophisticated talk the women used as a form of cultural capital that illustrated their employment of sociological imagination and the ways their educational processes were informed by history, biography, and society (Mills, 1959, p. 6). I had to show that the women participated in this phenomenon even if they did not use the term *sociological imagination.* Their definitions of terms and then their use of the terms in the discussions that followed allowed this theme to emerge.

In order to understand how the women related their concepts to their schooling experience, I used open-ended inquiries that gave them space to apply such concepts. I would not categorize these as leading questions, since the women were aware from our discussions and the consent form they signed that they were chosen to participate because they were college students. Each participant knew that I wanted to hear about their schooling lives. During this phase of the interview, I encouraged the women to talk about their college experiences using the following open-ended inquiries:

Talk about your interactions with black students and black professors.
Talk about your interactions with white students and white professors.
Describe your academic life.
Describe your social life at school.
Describe your experiences with academic offices and student organizations.

When asking the women at Central University to talk about their school diversity policies, I showed them a copy of a brochure the school produced entitled *Diversity Digest* (*Diversity Digest* Committee, 2003). I asked the women to evaluate this text as part of their discussion. The results of this conversation are discussed in Chapter Four. Since this text was created by the administration at Central University, I did not show it to the black women undergraduates at the other institutions. I did inquire as to whether or not a journal like *Diversity Digest* existed at the other schools. None of the women was aware of such a document at their institutions.

At the end of the interview (or, for those who interviewed more than once, at the end of the final interview), I asked each woman what she thought of the interview process, what she wanted to tell me that I had not asked, and what her future goals and aspirations were. I was sad as each interview ended. I felt so connected to each of the women and realized that the benefits of our talks were reciprocal in multiple ways. I became conscious of how much *I* depended on *their* conversations to validate some of my own ideas, experiences, successes, and struggles as a black woman in higher education. This is a part of the process I am still working to understand.

Snags in the Interview Process

Overall, the interview process was smooth. There were a couple of incidents that I will call *snags* that did create little bumps in the process. For example, since a few of the women that interviewed with me also interviewed for the Lumina project, timing became an issue. Since I was only at each out-of-state site for a couple of days and I was conducting Lumina interviews most of that time, it was a challenge to find time to conduct interviews for this study. I wanted to be careful and not abuse the women's willingness to participate by overloading their schedules with appointments. This being the case, I often opted to interview the women who were also Lumina participants for a longer time rather than multiple times. Each time I visited the site, I would make contact, get an update on their progress in school, and chat with them about my research work. They often chose to tell me stories, which I incorporated as memos in my data. I reviewed their demographic information ahead of time and discussed it with them rather than asking them to repeat it.

The issue of overlap between my research interviews (this study) and the Lumina interviews came up in my discussion with Amari. While working on the Lumina project, I was part of a team of researchers. That being the case, I did not conduct Amari's initial Lumina interview. So when I interviewed Amari for my research, there was some overlap in the questions and her responses. At one point she exclaimed, "I already told the other lady that!" (Interview, spring 2004). At that point, I told Amari that I had not yet read the Lumina interview. I asked her to bear with me and assured her that the questions to come would be very different from the Lumina project questions. I wanted Amari to understand not only that this interview would be different but also, and more importantly, that the Lumina research team valued the things she had told us, and that I would definitely be reading the other interview later. As I mentioned, I was cautious about scheduling times for research interviews with Lumina participants. There was only one instance, with Jessica in California, when the research interview occurred right after the Lumina interview. This was the time most convenient for Jessica, and I did not want to lose her as a participant. Since Jessica interviewed more than once, I could tell the difference between the post-Lumina interview and the interview conducted on a different day. I think the short answers Jessica gave in post-Lumina interview were the result of this inadvertent bad timing.

A final snag involved Malikah and revealed one way my academic studies rendered me privileged in ways this informant was not privileged. Malikah had a very difficult time talking when the voice recorder was on. She would stare at the recorder and say things such as, "Oh, that thing is messin' me up." Since I had conducted many interviews and even participated as the interviewee in a few during the course of my studies, I tried to encourage her by saying, "Oh, you are fine. Just pretend it is not there." I realized quickly that this did not comfort Malikah. She was very self-conscious about her speech and her West Indian accent; she wanted to say everything just right. Early in the first interview, she asked me several times to stop the recording while she got her thoughts together. While this made the interview longer than anticipated, stopping the recording when she asked seemed to put Malikah at ease. By the middle of the interview, she spoke with no interruptions.

It seemed that the list of questions and the women's willingness to respond helped me quickly reach a point of "data saturation" (Bogdan and Biklen, 2003, p. 62). I realized that there were many more questions and answers to ask and explore, yet at the end of my conversations with these 19 women, I knew that I had plenty of data to address regarding the lives of black women undergraduates and began a more formal data analysis.

Data Analysis

Since all the interviews were recorded, it was necessary to engage in the valuable, yet time-consuming, process of transcribing. Since I was traveling with the Lumina project and was very short on time, I decided to hire Rebecca, an administrative assistant at Central University, to assist in the transcribing. My instructions to her were, "Get the words from the recording onto the paper, and I will do the rest." Even though I had hired Rebecca, I felt a strong need to participate in the transcription process which I believed was crucial during the early stages of data analysis. In order to get fully engrossed in the data, I listened to every recording and reviewed every transcript after I received them from Rebecca. During this process, I looked for patterns in speech and ideas, made corrections, added headings, memos, and observer comments, all of which allowed me to organize the data and start to develop preliminary coding categories. I then made three copies of every interview and bound each set of copies together separating each interview with a pink sheet of paper.

As is true for others, my technological skills are not as advanced as I would like them to be, and although I acquired NUDIST (QSR International, Melbourne, Australia), a computer software program designed to organize and analyze qualitative data, I soon realized learning to use this program would require hours of time that I felt would be better used getting my hands in the data. I have always worked well with paper and pen, and in this case, I attacked my data with pens, pencils, multicolored Post-it notes, and highlighters. My huge, colorful book of bound data soon became famous around campus since I was rarely seen without it. I read and reread the data. I coded in the margins and created a list of codes separately on the computer. As I grouped codes by subjects that were repeated and that held my interest, the codes became larger themes. I highlighted and printed out data that supported each theme and bound these into smaller books for each data chapter. I then read and reread these smaller texts, again coding with highlighters. This time I analyzed in memos the codes (such as the *angry black bitch*) in relationship to themes (such as *negotiating cultural clashes*) and in the contexts of (a)race, class, and gender, (b)the intersections of biography, society, and history, and (c) existing power structures in society and higher education. This scrutiny included looking for how the women conceptualized their categories of identity and how they located them in the context of power structures. Each of the data chapters examines these meaning making processes.

Limitations of the Study

My study was limited in that it only addressed the schooling lives and meaning making processes of 19 black women undergraduates in four particular settings. I am sure there are countless other stories, worthy of examination that time would not allow me to collect. I look forward to continuing this type of research in the future. An additional limitation comes from not being able to observe the women on their campuses, in classes, and in co-curricular settings in addition to interviewing them. I think this would have given a broader picture of their schooling lives. It would also have given me, the researcher, a way to constantly compare data gathered using multiple collection techniques as part of my investigation (Bogdan & Biklen, 2003, p. 66). The study was also limited in that there were many things I could have done with these data, but I had to pick and choose what to include.

What I wanted to accomplish most, however, was challenge the deficit model on multiple levels, and I met that goal. I also wanted to avoid the practice of balancing what I learned about black undergraduate women with discourses about whiteness. I wanted to be clear in this study that being a part of white consciousness was not necessary for a discourse related to black undergraduate women and education to have merit; for example, the topic of *acting white* may not be a familiar subject for many white students, but it is a valued topic for this study. Black women undergraduates' experiences are "worth knowing" on their own merits (Ladson-Billings, 2003, p. 10).

Finally, it is my hope that engaging the qualitative strategies of open-ended, in-depth interviews, word-for-word transcriptions, acknowledgment of my place in the research and presentation of the women's exact words in my analysis, has minimized my subjectivity in this work. I have, however, presented my subjectivity as "an entry into the data" in this discussion (Bogdan & Biklen, 2003, p. 34). That being said, during the interviews, the black undergraduate women in this study gave me much food for thought and examination. I am grateful for their participation.

The Lumina Project

The Lumina Foundation of Education awarded a $956,000 grant to support a multiyear qualitative and quantitative study of developmental learning communities throughout the United States. The research team on this research project included two principal investigators and four research assistants. I was one of three research assistants who worked on collecting and analyzing qualitative data for the Lumina project.

Five institutions were chosen for the exemplary ways they served students in their learning communities. This selection required that I travel to New York City, California, and Texas multiple times over a 2-year period following and interviewing students who participated in these programs, which taught basic skills. During this time, I was also able to collect data for this book. In the selected learning communities, students took classes as cohorts and all participated in at least one course designed to teach skills such as time management, study strategies, and organizational tips to support the student goals of academic success. One goal of the research team was to learn the ways these learning communities supported the retention of traditionally underprepared or underrepresented students in higher education. Another goal was to understand how the student participants made sense of their experiences upon entering the program, while they were in the program, and once they had completed the program. The research team is still analyzing data from this important study.

APPENDIX C

Student Demographics

STUDENT	INSTITUTION	COURSE OF STUDY	YEAR	SES
ALANA	Central University	History African American studies Education (minor)	Junior	Middle to upper class
ALEX	International Community College	General education requirements	First year	Middle class
AMARI	Sunshine State University	Child psychology Business (minor)	First year	Middle class
BLUE	Central University	Nursing, second degree; previous degree in social work	Senior, working on second bachelors degree	Lower-middle class
CHERRY	Sunshine State University	Criminal justice Sociology	First year	Ward of the court, "broke"
CHERYL	Central University	Information management and technology African American studies (minor)	Senior	"Just about poor"
JAMIE	University of Borders and Crossings	Physical therapy	First year	Upper-middle class
JESSICA	Sunshine State University	General education requirements Education	First year	Middle Class

STUDENT	INSTITUTION	COURSE OF STUDY	YEAR	SES
KAYLA	International Community College	Sociology	First year	Can't label SES, parents retired
KIMBERLY	Central University	Political science and policy studies	Senior	Upper-middle class
LEVITICUS	Central University	Business African American studies	Junior	Middle class
LISA	International Community College	Veterinary technology	First year	Working class
MALIKAH	Central University	Nursing	Senior	"Very bad"
NADIA	Central University	Psychology African American studies (minor)	Senior	Middle class
NICOLE	Central University	Education Sociology	Junior	Mother: "poor" Father: "well off"
RGB	Central University	Television, radio, and film African American studies	Senior	Low income
ROE	Central University (part-time student)	Child and family studies	Sophomore, non-traditional student by age	"Middle/ working class"
SHONTE	Central University	Education	Senior	Mother: "very poor" Father: "working class"
TEENA	Central University	Broadcast journalism African American studies	Senior	Lower-middle class

Note: Using the standard protocol for confidentiality in this type of research, both the students and the institutions are referred to using pseudonyms. SES = socioeconomic status

Notes

Chapter One

1. Don Imus has returned to talk radio. His show, *Imus in the Morning News Hour*, is broadcast by the Citadel Broadcasting Corporation and 77 WABC Radio (New York City) with which he has a 5-year, multimillion-dollar contract (http://www.msnbc.msn.com/id/2158064)
2. *Flavor of Love* was a popular dating reality show on the VH1 network. Tiffany Stevens (aka, Miss New York) was an original contestant whose antics on the show won her a reality dating television show of her own, *I Love New York* (also on VH1), in which men competed for her affections.
3. William Jonathan Drayton Jr. (aka, Flavor Flav) was a member of a politically conscious hip-hop group, Public Enemy. He gained media attention for his work as the central character in a reality television show, *Flavor of Love*, on the VH1 network.
4. MTV (Music Television), VH1 (VH1: Music First), and BET (Black Entertainment Television) are television networks.
5. There are 1,266,107 black women enrolled in higher education compared to 686,615 black men. Approximately 37 percent of black women ages 18–24 are enrolled in college compared to 27 percent of black men in this age group (JBHE, News and Views, 2006).
6. Historically, white women were also excluded from educational systems. White women have gained certain advances and advantages in education, and yet, their status as woman leaves them open to the impact of male privilege in U.S. educational systems.
7. Information describing each college and university was taken from the Pathways to College Success Project website at http://pathways.syr.edu and from the individual school websites.
8. Each profile describes the woman's status at the time of the initial interview.
9. "Fake the funk" is a slang reference to passing or pretending. Here, Cheryl uses this phrase to explain that her family is able to pass for a socioeconomic status above the level she feels they really rate.

Chapter Two

1. Mary Church Terrell was a leading founder of the National Association of Colored Women.

2. In *Sweatt v. Painter* (1950), the U.S. Supreme Court's decision was that the State of Texas was wrong to deny admission to Herman Marion Sweatt (a qualified black man) to a white law school. This and other cases preceded the landmark *Brown* cases and supported their legal success (Willie, 2003).
3. See also E. Higginbotham's "The On-going Struggle: Education and Mobility for Black Women" (a research paper presented at Memphis State University, 1987) for more on social class and educational aspirations of black women.

Chapter Three

1. *A Different World* was a weekly television sitcom (1987–1993) that focused on the lives of black college students at a fictitious historically black college called Hillman.
2. Kimberly went to New York City to teach an introductory public policy course to high school students with eight students who share her major.

Chapter Five

1. Stokely Carmichael (1941–1998) and Michael Thelwell, *Ready for Revolution: The Life and Struggles of Stokely Carmichael (Kwame Ture)* (New York: Scribner, 2003).

References

Abate, F. R., ed. (1997). *The Pocket Oxford Dictionary and Thesaurus.* New York: Oxford University Press.

Alexander-Snow, M. (1999). Two African American women graduates of historically white boarding schools and their social integration at a traditionally white university. *Journal of Negro Education,* 68(1), 106–119.

Angelo, Thomas A. and Cross, K. Patricia, 2nd edition (1993). *Classroom Assessment Techniques: A Handbook for College Teachers.* San Francisco: Jossey-Bass.

Anyon, J. (1997). *Ghetto Schooling: A Political Economy of Urban Educational Reform.* New York: Teachers College Press.

Anzaldúa, G. (1987). Borderlands/La Frontera: The New Mestiza. San Francisco: Aunt Lute.

Association of American Colleges and Universities (2009). Making excellence inclusive. Retrieved June 10, 2009, from http://aacu.org/inclusive_ excellence/index.cfm

Ayers, W., T. Quinn, and D. Stovall, eds. (2009). *Handbook of Social Justice in Education.* New York: Routledge.

Banks, C. A. (2004a). Black girls/white spaces: Managing identity thru memories of schooling. In P. J. Bettis and N. G. Adams, eds., *Geographies of Girlhood: Identities In-Between,* pp. 177–193. Mahwah, NJ: Lawrence Erlbaum.

Banks, C. A. M. (2004b). Families and teachers: Working together for school improvement. In J. A. Banks and C. A. M. Banks, eds., *Multicultural Education: Issues and Perspectives,* 5th ed. New York: Wiley.

Banks, J. A., and C. A. M. Banks, eds. (2004). *Multicultural Education: Issues and Perspectives,* 5th ed. New York: Wiley.

Baum S., J. Viens, and B. Slatin. (2005). *Multiple Intelligences in the Elementary Classroom: A Teacher's Toolkit.* New York: Teachers College Press.

Beoku-Betts, J. A. (2000). Living in a large family does something for you: Influence of family on the achievement of African and Caribbean women in science. *Journal of Women and Minorities in Science and Engineering,* 6(3), 191–206.

Berry, G. L., and J. K. Asamen, eds. (2001). *Black Students: Psychosocial Issues and Academic Achievement.* Newbury Park, CA: Sage.

Best, A. L. (2003). Doing race in the context of feminist interviewing: Constructing whiteness through talk. *Qualitative Inquiry*, 9(6), 895–914.

Bettie, J. (2003). *Women without Class: Girls, Race, and Identity*. Berkeley: University of California Press.

Blumer, H. (1969). *Symbolic Interactionism: Perspective and Method*. Englewood Cliffs, NJ: Prentice-Hall.

Boehlert, E., and J. Foser. (2007, April 4). Imus Called Women's Basketball Team "Nappy-Headed Hos." *Media Matters for America*. Retrieved February 2, 2008, from http://mediamatters.org/items/200704040011.

Bogdan, R. C., and S. K. Biklen. (2003). *Qualitative Research for Education: An Introduction to Theory and Methods*, 4th ed. New York: Pearson Education.

Bourdieu, P. (1984). *Distinction: A Social Critique of the Judgment of Taste*. Trans. R. Nice. Cambridge, MA: Harvard University Press.

Bowen, W. G., M. Kurzweil, E. M. Tobin, and S. C. Pichler. (2005). *Equity and Excellence in American Higher Education*. Charlottesville: University of Virginia Press.

Bowman, S. L., V. L. Cureton, K. M. Mellum, M. Alarcon, B. Altareb, and G. Valtinson. (1995). African American or female: How do we identify ourselves? Paper presented at the 103rd annual meeting of the American Psychological Association, New York, August 1995. (ERIC Document Reproduction Service No. ED409384).

Brazzell, J. C. (1992). Bricks without straw: Missionary-sponsored black higher education in the post-Emancipation era. *The Journal of Higher Education* 63(1), 26-49.

Brewer, R. M. (1999). Theorizing race, class, and gender: The new scholarship of black feminist intellectuals and black women's labor. *Race, Class and Gender*, 6(2), 29–47.

Butner, B., Y. Caldera, P. Herrera, F. Kennedy, M. Frame, and C. Childers. (2001). The college choice process of African American and Hispanic women: Implications for college transitions. *Journal of College Orientation and Transition*, (9)1, 24–32.

Coffey A., D. Foley, and H.S. Mirza (1998). Review symposium of *Blacked Out: Dilemmas of Race, Identity, and Success at Capital High. Race, Ethnicity and Education*, 1(1), 129–138.

Coker, A. (2003). African American female adult learners: Motivations, challenges, and coping strategies. *Journal of Black Studies*, 33(5), 654–674.

Cole, J. B. (1986). *All American Women: Lines That Divide, Ties That Bind*. New York: Free Press.

Collins, P. H. (1995). Symposium: On West and Fenstermaker's "Doing difference." *Gender and Society*, 9(4), 491–494.

Collins, P. H. (1998). *Fighting Words: Black Women and the Search for Justice*. Minneapolis: University of Minnesota Press.

Collins, P. H. (2000). *Black Feminist Thought: Knowledge, Consciousness, and the Politics of Empowerment*. New York: Routledge.

Combahee River Collective. (1977/1992). A black feminist statement. In M. Humm, ed., *Modern Feminisms: Political, Literary, Cultural*, pp. 133–136. New York: Columbia University Press. Originally published in 1977 using the same title.

Constantine, M. G., and T. M. Greer. (2003). Personal, academic, and career counseling of African American women in college settings, in special issue, Meeting the Needs of African American Women, ed. by M. F. Howard-Hamilton. *New Directions for Student Services*, 104, 41–51.

Crenshaw, K. (1995). Mapping the margins: Intersectionality, identity and violence against women of color. In K. Crenshaw, N. Gotanda, G. Peller, and K. Thomas, eds. *Critical Race Theory: The Key Writings That Formed the Movement*, pp. 357–437. New York: New Press.

Cuádraz, G. H., and J. L. Pierce. (1994). From scholarship girls to scholarship women: Surviving the contradictions of class and race in academe. *Explorations in Ethnic Studies*, 17(1), 21–44.

Cuádraz, G. H., and L. Uttal. (1999). Intersectionality and in-depth interviews: Methodological strategies for analyzing race, class, and gender. *Race, Gender and Class* 6(3), 156–186.

Cuthbert, M. V. (1942). Education and marginality: A study of the Negro woman college graduate. New York: Teacher's College.

Dahl, A. G. (2000). Piquing the interest of African American students in foreign languages: The case of Spelman College. *Association of Departments of Foreign Languages Bulletin*, 31(2), 30-35.

Delpit, L. D. (1995). *Other People's Children: Cultural Conflict in the Classroom*. New York: New Press.

Denzin, N. K., and Y. S. Lincoln, eds. (2003). *The Sage Handbook of Qualitative Research*, 2nd ed. Thousand Oaks, CA: Sage.

Denzin, N. K., and Y. S. Lincoln, eds. (2005). *The Sage Handbook of Qualitative Research*, 3rd ed. Thousand Oaks, CA: Sage.

DeVault, M. L. (1990). Talking and listening from women's standpoint: Feminist strategies for interviewing and analysis. *Social Problems*, 37(1), 96–116.

DeVault, M. L. (1996). Talking back to sociology: Distinctive contributions of feminist methodology. *Annual Review of Sociology*, 22, 29–50.

Diversity Digest Committee [of Central University]. (2003). *Diversity Digest: An Academic Affairs and Student Affairs Publication*, 1(1).

Duarte, E. M., and S. Smith. (2000). Introduction: Multicultural education—What for? In E. M. Duarte and S. Smith, eds., *Foundational Perspectives in Multicultural Education*, p.1-24. New York: Longman.

Edelman, M. W. (1999). *Lanterns: A Memoir of Mentors*. Boston: Beacon Press.

Ellsworth, E. (1992). Why doesn't this feel empowering? Working through the repressive myth of critical pedagogy. In C. Luke and J. Gore, eds. *Feminisms and Critical Pedagogy*. New York: Routledge.

Faber, J. (2007, April 12). CBS Fires Dom Imus over Racial Slur. *CBS News*. Retrieved September 14, 2007, from http://www.cbsnews.com/stories/2007/04/12/national/main2675273.shtml?source=search_story.

Falconer, J. W., and H. A. Neville. (2000). African American college women's body image: An examination of body mass, African self-consciousness, and skin color satisfaction. *Psychology of Women Quarterly*, 24(3), 236–243.

Feagin, J. R., H. Vera, and N. Imani. (1996). *The Agony of Education: Black Students at White Colleges and Universities*. New York: Routledge.

Ferguson, A. A. (2000). *Bad Boys: Public Schools in the Making of Black Masculinity*. Law, Meaning, and Violence Series. Michigan: University of Michigan Press.

Fordham, S. (1991). Racelessness in private schools: Should we deconstruct the racial and cultural identity of African-American adolescents? *Teachers College Record*, 92(3), 470–484.

Fordham, S. (1996). *Blacked Out: Dilemmas of Race, Identity and Success at Capital High*. Chicago: University of Chicago Press.

Foreman, F. E. (2003). Intimate risk: Sexual risk behavior among African American college women. *Journal of Black Studies*, 33(5), 637–653.

Fox, H. (2001). *When Race Breaks Out: Conversations about Race and Racism in College Classrooms*. New York: Peter Lang.

Franklin, V. P. (2002). Introduction: Cultural capital and African American education. *Journal of African American History*, 87(2), 175–180.

Frazier, E. F. (1939/1947). *The Negro Family in the United States, rev. ed.* Chicago: University of Chicago Press.

Freeman, K. (2005). *African Americans and College Choice: Influence of Family and School*. Albany: State University of New York Press.

Gallagher, C. A. (2000). White like me? Methods, meaning and manipulation in the field of white studies. In F. W. Twine and J. W. Warren, eds., *Racing Research, Researching Race: Methodological Dilemmas in Critical Race Studies*, pp. 67–92. New York: New York University Press.

Gallien, L. B. Jr., and M. S. Peterson. (2005). *Instructing and Mentoring the African American College Student: Strategies for Success in Higher Education*. Boston: Pearson Education.

Garfinkel, H. (1984). *Studies in Ethnomethodology*. Malden, MA: Blackwell.

Garrod, A., J. Ward, T. Robinson, and R. Kilkenny. (1999). *Souls Looking Back: Life Stories of Growing Up Black*. New York: Routledge.

Giddings, P. (1984). *When and Where I Enter: The Impact of Black Women on Race and Sex in America*. New York: W. Morrow.

Giroux, H. A., and S. Searls Giroux. (2004). *Take Back Higher Education: Race, Youth, and the Crisis of Democracy in Post-Civil Rights Era*. New York: Palgrave Macmillan.

Glaser, B. G., and A. L. Strauss. (1967). *The Discovery of Grounded Theory: Strategies for Qualitative Research*. New York: Aldine de Gruyter.

Grinter, R. (2000). Multicultural or antiracist education? The need to choose. In E. M. Duarte and S. Smith, eds., *Foundational Perspectives in Multicultural Education*. New York: Longman.

Guillaumin, C. (1995). *Racism, Sexism, Power, and Ideology*. London: Routledge.

Gurin, P., and E. Epps. (1975). *Black Consciousness, Identity, and Achievement: A Study of Students in Historically Black Colleges*. New York: Wiley.

Hale, F. W. Jr. (2004). *What Makes Racial Diversity Work in Higher Education: Academic Leaders Present Successful Policies and Strategies*. Sterling, VA: Stylus.

Harding, S. (1987). Introduction: Is there a feminist method? In S. Harding, ed., *Feminism and Methodology: Social Science Issues*, pp. 1–14. Bloomington: Indiana University Press.

Harris, Ron. (2007, July 8). A Black Journalist Examines the "Culture of Disrespect." *St. Louis Post-Dispatch*. Retrieved October 1, 2007, from ProQuest database.

Higginbotham, Elizabeth. (1987) "The On-Going Struggle: Education and Mobility for Black Women." Memphis, TN: Center for Research on Women, Memphis State University.

Higginbotham, E. (2001). *Too Much to Ask: Black Women in the Era of Integration*. Chapel Hill: University of North Carolina Press.

Hill, M. S., and J. C. Ragland. (1995). *Women as Educational Leaders: Opening Windows, Pushing Ceilings*. Thousand Oaks, CA: Corwin.

Holstein, J. A., and J. F. Gubrium. (1994). Phenomenology, ethnomethodology and interpretive practice. In N. K. Denzin and Y. S. Lincoln, eds., *Handbook of Qualitative Research*. Thousand Oaks, CA: Sage.

hooks, bell. (1984). *Feminist Theory from Margin to Center*. Cambridge, MA: South End Press.

Howard-Vital, M. R. (1989). African-American women in higher education: Struggling to gain identity. *Journal of Black Studies*, 20(2), 180–191.

Howard-Vital, M. R., and R. Morgan. (1993). African American women and mentoring. (ERIC Document Reproduction Service No. ED360425)

Hrabowski, F. A. III, K. I. Maton, M. L. Greene, and G. L. Greif. (2002). *Overcoming the Odds: Raising Academically Successful African American Young Women.* New York: Oxford University Press.

Humm, M., ed. (1992). *Modern Feminisms: Political, Literary, Culture.* New York: Columbia University Press.

Ihle, E. I., ed. (1992). *Black Women in Higher Education: An Anthology of Essays, Studies, and Documents.* New York: Garland.

Jackson, L. R. (1998). Examining both race and gender in the experiences of African American college women. Paper presented at the annual meeting of the American Educational Research Association, San Diego, CA, April 13–17, 1998. (ERIC Document Reproduction Service No. ED429487).

Jackson, S., and J. Solís Jordán. (1999). *I've Got a Story to Tell: Identity and Place in the Academy.* Counterpoints Series, vol. 65. New York: Peter Lang.

JBHE News and Views. (2006). Women dominate the honor rolls at black colleges and universities. *Journal of Blacks in Higher Education.* Retrieved September 14, 2007, from http://www.jbhe.com/news_views/54_women-honor-rolls.html.

Jensen, R. (2002). White privilege shapes the U.S. In P. S. Rothenberg, ed., *White Privilege: Essential Readings on the Other Side of Racism.* New Jersey: Worth.

Johnson, A. G. (1995). *The Blackwell Dictionary of Sociology: A User's Guide to Sociological Language,* 2nd ed. Malden, MA: Blackwell.

Jones, C., and K. Shorter-Gooden. (2003). *Shifting: The Double Lives of Black Women in America.* New York: HarperCollins.

Jones, L. (2001). *Retaining African Americans in Higher Education: Challenging Paradigms for Retaining Black Students, Faculty, and Administrators.* Sterling, VA: Stylus.

Kelefa, S. (2007, April 25). Don't Blame Hip-Hop: How Don Imus's Problem Became a Referendum on Rap. *The New York Times.* Retrieved October 1, 2007, from ProQuest database. Retrieved March 23, 2009, from http://query.nytimes.com/gst/fullpage.html?res=9D0DE6DB143EF936A15757C0A9619C8B63&sec=&spon=&emc=eta1.

Kellner, D. (1995). Cultural studies, multiculturalism, and media culture. In G. Dines and J. M. Humez, eds., *Gender, Race, and Class in Media.* Thousand Oaks, CA: Sage.

Kendall, F. E. (2006). *Understanding White Privilege: Creating Pathways to Authentic Relationships across Race.* New York: Routledge.

Ladson-Billings, G. (2003). It's your world, I'm just trying to explain it: Understanding our epistemological and methodological challenges. *Qualitative Inquiry,* 9(1), 5–12.

Ladson-Billings, G. (1994). *The Dreamkeepers: Successful Teachers of African American Children*. San Francisco: Jossey-Bass.

Lareau, A. (1987). Social class differences in family–school relationships: The importance of cultural capital. *Sociology of Education*, 60(2), 73–85.

Lareau, A. (2003). *Unequal Childhoods: Class, Race and Family Life*. Berkeley: University of California Press.

Latimer, L. (2004). *Higher Ground: A Guide for Black Parents to Chart a Successful Course for Their Children from Kindergarten to College*. Columbus, MS: Genesis.

Lawson, E. N., and M. Merrill. (1984). *The Three Sarahs: Documents of Antebellum Black College Women*. Lewiston, NY: Edwin Mellen.

Leadbeater, B. J. R., and N. Way, eds. (1996). *Urban Girls: Resisting Stereotypes, Creating Identities*. New York: New York University Press.

Madriz, E. (2000). Focus groups in feminist research. In N. K. Denzin and Y. S. Lincoln, eds., *Handbook of Qualitative Research*, pp. 835–850. Thousand Oaks, CA: Sage.

Majors, R. (2001). *Educating Our Black Children: New Directions and Radical Approaches*. New York: RoutledgeFalmer.

Marteena, C. H. (1938/ 1992). Bennett College: Another black woman's college. In E. L. Ihle, ed., *Black Women in Higher Education: An Anthology of Essays, Studies, and Documents*. New York: Garland.

Martin, R. S. (2007, April 24). Imus Might Be the Spark for Debate on Sexism. *CNN.com*. Retrieved October 1, 2007, from http://www.cnn.com/2007/US/04/13/martin.imus/index.html.

Matthews-Armstead, E. (2002). And still they rise: College enrollment of African American women from poor communities. *Journal of Black Studies*, 33(1), 44–65.

McClintock, M. (2000). How to interrupt oppressive behavior. In M. Adams, W. J. Blumenfeld, R. Castaneda, H. W. Hackman, M. L. Peters, and X. Zuniga, eds., *Readings for Diversity and Social Justice: An Anthology on Racism, Anti-Semitism, Sexism, Heterosexism, Ableism, and Classism*, pp. 483–485. New York: Routledge.

McCombs, H. G. (1989). The dynamics and impact of affirmative action processes on higher education, the curriculum, and black women. *Sex Roles: A Journal of Research*, 21(1–2), 127–144.

McLaren, P. (1998). *Life in Schools: An Introduction to Critical Pedagogy in the Foundations of Education*, 3rd ed. Reading, MA: Addison Wesley Longman.

Mills, C. W. (1959). *The Sociological Imagination*. Oxford, United Kingdom: Oxford University Press.

Minh-ha, T. T. (1989). *Woman, Native, Other: Writing Postcoloniality and Feminism*. Indianapolis: Indiana University Press.

Morgan, R. M., D. T. Mwegelo, and L. N. Turner. (2002). Black women in the African diaspora seeing their cultural heritage through studying abroad. *NASPA Journal*, 39(4), 333–353.

Mullen, A. L. (2001). Gender, race, and the college science track: Analyzing field concentrations and institutional selectivity. *Journal of Women and Minorities in Science and Engineering*, 7(4), 285–300.

Noble, J. L. (1956/1987). The Negro woman's college education. In B. M. Solomon, ed., *Educated Women: Higher Education, Culture, and Professionalism 1850–1890*. Garland Series. New York: Garland. Originally published in 1956 using the same title.

O'Connor, C. (2002). Black women beating the odds from one generation to the next: How the changing dynamics of constraint and opportunity affect the process of educational resilience. *American Educational Research Journal*, 39(4), 855–903.

Olesen, V. L. (2000). Feminisms and qualitative research at and into the millennium. In N. K. Denzin and Y. S. Lincoln, eds., *Handbook of Qualitative Research*, pp. 215–255. Thousand Oaks, CA: Sage.

Peräkylä, A. (2005). Analyzing talk and text. In N. K. Denzin and Y. S. Lincoln, eds., *The Sage Handbook of Qualitative Research*, 3rd ed., pp. 869–886. Thousand Oaks, CA: Sage.

Perry, T. (2003). Competing theories of group achievement. In T. Perry, C. Steele, and A. G. Hilliard III, eds., *Young, Gifted and Black: Promoting High Achievement among African-American Students*, pp. 52–86. Boston: Beacon Press.

Perry, T., C. Steele, and A. Hilliard. (2003). *Young, Gifted and Black: Promoting High Achievement among African-American Students*. Boston: Beacon Press.

Ponec, D. (1997). African-American females: A theory of educational aspiration. presented at symposium of African-Americans and Their Great Plains Experiences. (ERIC Document Reproduction Service No.ED.415 457).

Randolph, A.W. (2002). Building upon cultural capital: Thomas Jefferson Ferguson and the Albany Enterprise Academy in the southeast Ohio, 1863-1886. *The Journal of African American History*, 87, 182-195.

Read, F. M. (1937/1992). The place of women's college in the pattern of Negro education. In E. I. Ihle, ed., *Black Women in Higher Education: An Anthology of Essays, Studies, and Documents*. New York: Garland. Originally published in 1937 in *Opportunity* using the same title.

Rhoden, W. C. (2007, April 9). The Unpleasant Reality for Women in Sports. *The New York Times*. Retrieved March 22, 2009 from http://www.neuro.uoregon.edu/~tublitz/COIA/News of interest/The Unpleasant Reality for Women in Sports/ NY Times 9 Apr 2007.pdf

Robinson, E. (2007, April 13). Why Imus had to go. *The Washington Post.* Retrieved September 14, 2007, from http://www.washingtonpost.com/wp-dyn/content/article/2007/04/12/AR2007041201825.html.

Rochlin, J. M. (1997). *Race and Class on Campus: Conversations with Ricardo's Daughter.* Tucson: University of Arizona Press.

Rockquemore, K. A. (1999). Rethinking race as a "metalanguage": The intersections race and gender in locating black women's voices. *Race, Gender and Class,* 6(2), 48–72.

Rodriguez, S. (2001). *Giants among Us: First-Generation College Graduates Who Lead Activist Lives.* Nashville, TN: Vanderbilt University Press.

Roebuck, J. B., and K. S. Murty. (1993). *Historically Black Colleges and Universities: Their Place in American Higher Education.* Westport, CT: Praeger.

Rosenbloom, S. R., and N. Way. (2004). Experiences of discrimination among African American, Asian American, and Latino adolescents in an urban high school. *Youth and Society,* 35(4), 420–451.

Rosenwald, G. C., and R. L. Ochberg, eds. (1992). *Storied Lives: The Cultural Politics of Self-Understanding.* New Haven, CT: Yale University Press.

Rothenberg, P. S., ed. (2002). *White Privilege: Essential Readings on the Other Side of Racism.* New York: Worth.

Sanders, M. G. (1997). Overcoming obstacles: Academic achievement as a response to racism and discrimination. *Journal of Negro Education,* 66(1), 83–93.

Schwandt, T. A. (2003). Three epistemological stances for qualitative inquiry: Interpretivism, hermeneutics, and social constructionism. In N. K. Denzin and Y. S. Lincoln, eds., *The Landscape of Qualitative Research: Theories and Issues,* pp. 292–331. Thousand Oaks, CA: Sage.

Schwartz, R. A., and B. L. Bower. (1997). "Ain't I a woman too?" Tracing the experiences of African American women in graduate programs in education. Paper presented at the annual meeting of the American Educational Research Association, Chicago, IL, March 1997. (ERIC Document Reproduction Service No. ED414773).

Schwartz, R. A., B. L. Bower, D. C. Rice, and C. M. Washington. (2003). "Ain't I a woman too?" Tracing the experiences of African American women in graduate school. *Journal of Negro Education,* 72(3), 252–268. (ERIC Document Reproduction Service No. EJ680114).

Schwartz, R. A., and C. M. Washington. (1999). Predicting academic success and retention for African American women in college. *Journal of College Student Retention,* 1(2), 177–191.

Sherover-Marcuse, R. (2000). Working assumptions and guidelines for alliance building. In M. Adams, W. J. Blumenfeld, R. Castaneda, H. W. Hackman, M. L. Peters, and X. Zuniga, eds., *Readings for Diversity and Social Justice:*

An Anthology on Racism, Anti-Semitism, Sexism, Heterosexism, Ableism, and Classism, pp. 486–487 . New York: Routledge.

Shock jock Don Imus returns to radio Dec. 3. Retrieved June 2009 from (http://www.msnbc.msn.com/id/2158064)

Shorter-Gooden, K., and N. C. Washington. (1996). Young, black, and female: The challenge of weaving an identity. *Journal of Adolescence*, 19(5), 465–475.

Sleeter, C. E. (2000). Multicultural education, social positionality, and white-ness. In E. M. Duarte and S. Smith, eds., *Foundational Perspectives in Multicultural Education*, pp. 118–143. New York: Longman.

Smith, D. G., G. L. Gerbick, M. A. Figueroa, G. H. Watkins, T. Levitan, L. C. Moore, P. A. Merchant, H. D. Beliak, and B. Figueroa. (1997). *Diversity Works: The Emerging Picture of How Students Benefit*. Washington, DC: Association of American Colleges and Universities.

Span, C. M. (2002). "I must learn now or not at all": Social and cultural capital in the educational initiatives of formerly enslaved African Americans in Mississippi, 1862–1869. *Journal of African American History*, 87(2), 196–202.

Spradlin, L. K., and R. D. Parsons. (2008). *Diversity Matters: Understanding Diversity in Schools*. Belmont, CA: Thompson Wadsworth.

Stewart, P. (2002). Responding to the voice of black women: Black women's unique style of leadership enables them to meet the challenges of academe, scholars say [special report]. *Black Issues in Higher Education*, 19(3), 24–26. Retrieved March 23, 2009, from http://findarticles.com/p/articles/mi_m0DXK/is_3_19/ai_85461883?tag=content;col1.

Tatum, B. D. (1996). Talking about race, learning about racism: The application of racial identity development theory in the classroom. In C. S. V. Turner, M. Garcia, A. Nora, and L. I. Rendon, eds., *Racial and Ethnic Diversity in Higher Education*, Chapter 12. Needham Heights, MA: Simon & Schuster Custom.

Tatum, B. D. (1997). *Why Are All the Black Kids Sitting Together in the Cafeteria? and Other Conversations about Race: A Psychologist Explains the Development of Racial Identity*. New York: Basic Books.

Taylor, V. (1998). Feminist methodology in social movements research. *Qualitative Sociology*, 21(4), 357–379.

Terenzini, P. T., L. I. Rendón, M. L. Upcraft, S. B. Millar, K. W. Allison, P. L. Gregg and R. Jalomo. (1994). The transition to college: Diverse students, diverse stories. *Research in Higher Education*, 35(1), 57–73.

Terrell, M. C. (1901/1992). Defense of black women's college education. In E. L. Ihle, ed., *Black Women in Higher Education: An Anthology of Essays, Studies, and Documents*. New York: Garland. Originally published in 1901 using the same title.

Thomas, V. G. (2001). Educational experiences and transitions of reentry college women: Special considerations for African American female students. *Journal of Negro Education*, 70(3), 139–155.

Thomas, W. H. (1901) *The American Negro*. New York: Macmillan.

Tinto, V. (1993). *Leaving College: Rethinking the Causes and Cures of Student Attrition*, 2nd ed. Chicago: University of Chicago Press.

U.S. Department of Labor. Office of Policy Planning and Research. (1965). *The Negro Family: The Case for National Action* [also known as the Moynihan Report]. Washington, DC: U.S. Government Printing Office. Retrieved (in part) March 23, 2009, from http://www.dol.gov/oasam/programs/history/webid-meynihan.htm or http://www.blackpast.org/?q=primary/moynihan-report-1965.

Villegas, A. M., and T. Lucas. (2007). The culturally responsive teacher. *Educational Leadership*, 64(6), 28–33.

Watson, Terrell, Wright and Associates (2002). *How Minority Students Experience College: Implications for Planning and Policy*. Virginia: Stylus Publishing

Wentworth, P., and B. Peterson. (2001). Crossing the line: Case studies of identity development in first-generation college women. *Journal of Adult Development*, 8(1), 9–21.

White, H. (1980). The value of narrativity in the representation of reality. *Critical Inquiry*, 7(1), 5–27.

White, M. A. (2002). Paradise lost? Teachers' perspectives on the use of cultural capital in the segregated schools of New Orleans, Louisiana. *Journal of African American History*, 87(2), 269–280.

Wildman, S. M., and A. D. Davis. (2002). Making systems of privilege visible. In P. S. Rothenberg, ed., *White Privilege: Essential Readings on the Other Side of Racism*. New York: Worth.

Willie, C. V., and A. S. McCord. (1972). *Black Students at White Colleges*. New York: Praeger.

Willie, S. S. (2003). *Acting Black: College, Identity and the Performance of Race*. New York: Routledge.

Wolf-Wendell, L. E. (1998). Models of excellence: The baccalaureate origins of successful European American women, African American women, and Latinas. *Journal of Higher Education*, 69(2), 141–186.

Yoo, G. J. (1999). Racial inequality, welfare reform, and black families: The 1996 Personal Responsibility and Work Reconciliation Act. In R. Staples, ed., *The Black Family: Essays and Studies*, 6th ed., pp. 357–366. New York: Wadsworth.

Zerai, A., and Banks, R. (2002). *Dehumanizing Discourse, Anti-Drug Law, and Policy in America: A "Crack Mother's" Nightmare*. Burlington, VT: Ashgate.

Index

advice from, 128
black professors, 116–20, 145
faculty advisors, 136
family
  as motivation, 112, 114–16
  support from, 104–16
  See also mothers
Feagin, J. R., 38
fee waivers, 97
feminism, black, 10–14, 152
feminism, early, 10, 151–52
feminist qualitative inquiry, 152
feminist research methods, 152, 154
Fine Arts class, RGB's experience in, 67–68
first-generation students, 110–13
Foley, D., 5, 6
Fordham, Signithia, 5–6
Fox, H., 136
Franklin, V. P., 25, 26
free writes, 126

Gallagher, C. A., 153
Garfinkel, H., 151
gaze, upon black women undergraduates, 49
gender, 11, 61–63
gender typing, 127–28
Giroux, H. A., 8
"giving attitude," 90
grading rubric, 128, 129
grounded theory, 158
group work, 129–31
guidance counselors
  advice of, link with race and class, 98–104
  benefits, 96
  classed talk by, 97
  as gatekeepers, 98–104
  need to challenge stereotypes, 104
  negotiating relationships with, 145
  and obtaining information, 97
  placement of obstacles by, 98–99

Harding, S., 154–55
hate incidents. *See* racism
Higginbotham, E., 31–32, 37
Higher Education Act of 1965, 30

high school
  black women's negotiations in, 32–34
  counselors in (*See* guidance counselors)
  discrimination during, 33
  See also preparation, academic
history
  collective, impact of, 143
  curriculum, Alana's experience with, 70–71
  Eurocentric views of, 55
  intersection with biography and society, 41–43 (*See also* sociological imagination)
Hobart and William Smith Colleges, 129
Hrabowski, F. A. III, 35
Humm, M., 152

identity
  complexity of, 12
  defining in face of stereotypes, 37–38
  and intersectionality, 10–11
  issues for black women undergraduates, 34–35
  multifaceted, blackness as, 120
identity work, support for, 125
Ihle, E. I., 27
Imani, N., 38
Imus, Don, 1–2, 11
inclusive excellence, 134–35, 138, 140
inequity
  analysis of and strategies for success, 144
  combated by education, 5
  considered burden of marginalized groups, 132
  fueled by education, 5
informants. *See* participants in study
input, from students, 129
institutional practice
  administrative reaction to hate incidents, 138
  alliance building, 136–37
  impact on educational equity, 134
  need for honesty in diversity practices, 137–38

Questions about the
Purpose(s) of Colleges
and Universities

Norm Denzin,
Shirley R. Steinberg
General Editors

What are the purposes of higher education? When undergraduates "declare their majors," they agree to enter into a world defined by the parameters of a particular academic discourse—a discipline. But who decides those parameters? How do they come about? What are the discussions and proposed outcomes of disciplined inquiry? What should an undergraduate know to be considered educated in a discipline? How does the disciplinary knowledge base inform its pedagogy? Why are there different disciplines? When has a discipline "run its course"? Where do new disciplines come from? Where do old ones go? How does a discipline produce its knowledge? What are the meanings and purposes of disciplinary research and teaching? What are the key questions of disciplined inquiry? What questions are taboo within a discipline? What can the disciplines learn from one another? What might they not want to learn and why?

Once we begin asking these kinds of questions, positionality becomes a key issue. One reason why there aren't many books on the meaning and purpose of higher education is that once such questions are opened for discussion, one's subjectivity becomes an issue with respect to the presumed objective stances of Western higher education. Academics don't have positions because positions are "biased," "subjective," "slanted," and therefore somehow invalid. So the first thing to do is to provide a sense—however broad and general—of what kinds of positionalities will inform the books and chapters on the above questions. Certainly the questions themselves, and any others we might ask, are already suggesting a particular "bent," but as the series takes shape, the authors we engage will no doubt have positions on these questions.

From the stance of interdisciplinary, multidisciplinary, or transdisciplinary practitioners, will the chapters and books we solicit solidify disciplinary discourses, or liquefy them? Depending on who is asked, interdisciplinary inquiry is either a polite collaboration among scholars firmly situated in their own particular discourses, or it is a blurring of the restrictive parameters that define the very notion of disciplinary discourse. So will the series have a stance on the meaning and purpose of interdisciplinary inquiry and teaching? This can possibly be finessed by attracting thinkers from disciplines that are already multidisciplinary, for example, the various kinds of "studies" programs (women's, Islamic, American, cultural, etc.), or the hybrid disciplines like ethnomusicology (musicology, folklore, anthropology). But by including people from these fields (areas? disciplines?) in our series, we are already taking a stand on disciplined inquiry. A question on the comprehensive exam for the Columbia University Ethnomusicology Program was to defend ethnomusicology as a "field" or a "discipline." One's answer determined one's future, at least to the extent that the gatekeepers had a say in such matters. So, in the end, what we are proposing will no doubt involve political struggles.

For additional information about this series or for the submission of manuscripts, please contact Shirley R. Steinberg, msgramsci@gmail.com. To order other books in this series, please contact our Customer Service Department at: (800) 770-LANG (within the U.S.), (212) 647-7706 (outside the U.S.), (212) 647-7707 FAX, or browse online by series at: www.peterlang.com.